David Freeland

University Press of Mississippi
Jackson

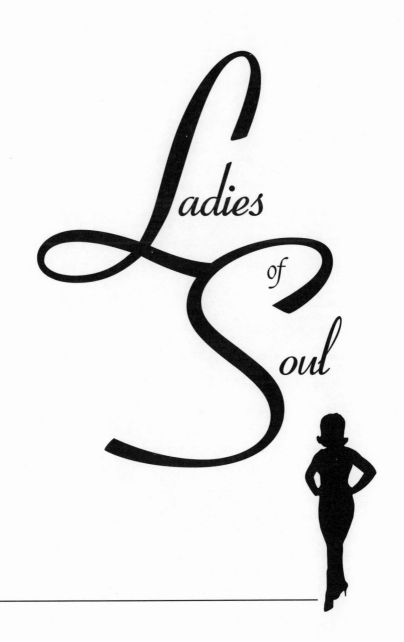

www.upress.state.ms.us

Library of Congress Cataloging-in-Publication Data

Freeland, David.
    Ladies of soul / David Freeland.
      p. cm.—(American made music series)
    Includes bibliographical references (p.) and index.
    ISBN 1-57806-330-2 (cloth : alk. paper)—
    ISBN 1-57806-331-0 (paper : alk. paper)
     1. Women singers—United States—Biography.   2.
Soul musicians—United States—Biography.   I.
Title. II. Series.

    ML400.F634   2001
    782.421644'092'273—dc21
    [B]   00-061450

British Library Cataloging-in-Publication Data available

Contents

Preface

I have wanted to write a book on soul music ever since falling in love with soul and rhythm & blues as a teenager growing up in the Washington, D.C., area. At about age sixteen, frustrated with the limited choices and heavy formatting of FM Top 40 stations, I let my fingers explore more obscure and (at least for me) uncharted areas of the radio dial. Stopping just shy of the far right end of the AM band, I found something that would challenge and ultimately change my perception of what makes great music: WOL—by the mid-'80s one of the last AM stations in Washington to resist the tide of talk radio by holding on to its music format. At the time, WOL still had a handful of old-time disc jockeys, DJs who played what they wanted, made numerous pitches for local businesses ranging from thrift stores to cafeterias, and strove to entertain their listeners as much through their distinctive personalities as through the music they played. These disc jockeys, with catchy names like "The More Better Man" and "The Moon Man," were treasure troves of musical styles long since passed—post-war jump blues, '50s rhythm & blues, classic pop à la Johnny Mathis and Nat "King" Cole, southern soul. You could never be entirely sure what they were going to play next, but one thing was certain: listen long enough and you would get a musical education.

To me, the music on WOL sounded like some heroic remnant of a vivid, exciting world otherwise lost to the recesses of time. I knew that I had to become a part of it. To this end, I made repeated excursions to the station to visit its DJs, essentially becoming a WOL groupie. In particular, the More Better Man (whose real name was eventually revealed to be Raymond Woods) always took time to talk with me, even if a two-and-a-half-minute record was rapidly spinning towards its conclusion in the control room. The More Better Man's generosity with his time was no small gift. Unlike most contemporary stations, where the DJ simply presses a button to activate a pre-selected sequence of tracks, at WOL the disc jockeys had to do *everything*, including selecting and cueing each record and making sure that the next one was always primed and ready to follow.

At the same time that I was hounding the More Better Man (it got to the point where the WOL receptionist would announce bemusedly, "More Better Man, your little friend is here"), I amassed all the information on '60s soul music that I could find and became an avid collector of old soul 45s, records that had been released more than twenty years earlier, soon forgotten, and only blessed with re-exposure when played by sympathetic DJs like those on WOL. It took little time to find an inexpensive supply center: New Wax Unlimited Records, a WOL hangout that contained an entire basement full of decades-old 45s priced at $2 each. It was through the DJs at WOL and the staff at New Wax Unlimited that I first got to know the work of many of the women whose stories appear in this book: copies of Barbara Mason's "Bed and Board" were always displayed prominently on New Wax's racks, while the owner once told me that he felt Bettye LaVette was the finest blues singer he had ever heard.

In college I had the chance to expose others to the scratchy charms of my New Wax records as part of a soul radio show that I hosted. At first, the show could hardly qualify as a success. I co-hosted with a fellow student who wore bright lime-green blazers and played nothing but Beatles records (the partnership came to an abrupt end after he insulted Esther Phillips's version of "And I Love Him" on the air). By my senior year, however, the program had attracted a large number of followers, many of whom begged to know where I had found the music I was so enthusiastically promoting. Around the same time (the early '90s), something surprising was happening in the public musical consciousness: soul music was becoming popular again—or, to be more exact, was achieving a popularity and critical respect greater than what it had known when originally released in the '60s. It seemed that both critics and music fans were beginning to take '60s soul seriously: long-out-of-print albums suddenly became available on CD, snippets of classic soul grooves found a new, transmogrified existence in the mixes of countless rap artists, performers like James Brown were being universally recognized as innovators, and articles and books on soul were appearing so quickly that it was hard to keep track of them. Clearly, soul was now hip in a way that I, as a teenaged disciple of a lost art form, could never have anticipated back in the '80s.

As the '90s progressed and the public and critical appreciation of soul grew, I found myself asking the question that eventually germinated into the inspiration for this project: how was soul's surprise early '90s comeback benefiting its female practitioners? I couldn't help but conclude that, aside from Aretha Franklin and a few select others, women were largely being ignored as creators and shapers of the soul sound. For all of the critical ink that was (justifiably) being spilled over artists like Marvin Gaye, James Brown, and Al Green, path-breaking female performers such as Esther Phillips, Millie Jackson, and Irma Thomas were virtually absent from the printed media. Any trip to the local record store proved equally dispiriting. As an example, while Gaye's work (both greater and lesser) was being remastered and repackaged many times over, Phillips's best music was practically unavailable in the U.S. until 1997, when a comprehensive CD collection of her work was finally released. In the same way that the presence and vitality of the blues woman had been obfuscated by the journalistic veneration of the "blues man" during the blues revival of the '60s, was the soul woman destined to remain hidden in the soul man's shadows?

To me, this situation was highly paradoxical, since some of the most powerful soul records in my collection had been recorded by women. I felt that the lack of attention given to female performers within the popular and scholarly literature on soul could partially, if simplistically, be explained by male critical bias: as men, most pop critics tend to write about other men. More importantly, it seemed to me that female soul singers were in less of a position to be examined by critics because of the journalistic emphasis on artistic totality. Rock and pop critics rarely write about singers; they write about *musicians*. Often, female artists in search of critical respect must not only sing but compose their material and play it themselves (it's not surprising that women were first taken seriously as rock artists in the '70s, when critics began to extol the rise of the "singer-songwriter," and that the '90s critical emphasis on female rock performers was directed almost exclusively towards women who write their own songs). Aretha Franklin fits perfectly into this critical mold: a great musical force, her role as the *auteur* of her work is never in doubt. While the most remarkable element of Franklin's performances has always been her voice, she is also a fine pianist and composer, each of her most famous records stamped with her unique, highly personal musical vision. On the other hand, many of her female soul contemporaries—women who in the tradition of the classic pop singers find their primary form of artistic expression through vocal interpretation—are overlooked or devalued as "journeywoman" performers.[1]

My initial impulse in choosing to focus specifically on *women* in soul music was therefore one of rectification: I wanted to bring exposure to female singers who, in my opinion, had not received the recognition their talents deserve. With the body of written work on soul music steadily increasing, I felt that the time was ripe for a book devoted exclusively to women. Equally important was my belief that these women would have fascinating stories to tell, for in a certain way they represent a world that doesn't exist anymore. Since the time of their entry into the music business in the early '60s, entire social movements have sprung up and changed the way we as a society think about issues of race and sex. Through their choice of profession, female soul vocalists were forced to become businesswomen in a largely white, male-dominated industry, as the civil rights movement was only brewing and the women's movement was still largely unformed. How did these women handle themselves in the music industry (an industry not known for its sensitivity or compassion) during this heady social period? Did they feel that their status as women had a bearing upon their degree of success? I felt that the answer—or, at least, an exploration of the question—could provide a story every bit as interesting as that told by the music itself. Although the interests of fans would have to be considered, I didn't want to merely chronicle the women's recordings. Rather, I hoped to attempt some understanding of how they viewed their world.

Since it was my desire to present the stories of female soul singers in their own words (to allow their real-life "voices" to come through), I conceived the project as a series of narrative oral histories, structured and assembled through first-person interviews. My initial research, performed under the auspices of Columbia University's anthropology department, involved tracking down and contacting the women I hoped to include. Each was a performer whose music I loved and knew comprehensively (I was first and foremost a longtime fan). It was not my intention to pursue superstars; rather, I wanted to learn about the experiences of singers who had not succeeded on the grand scale of Aretha Franklin, Gladys Knight, Patti LaBelle, or Tina Turner.[2] As much as I admired and loved the work of these famous women, I suspected that discussions with the "lesser lights" (in a commercial, if not necessarily an artistic sense) could potentially tell more about the desires and frustrations, hopes and disappointments of African-American women trying to carve out successful music careers during the '60s. I strongly believed that these women were just as talented as many who had gained more widespread recognition. What forces, both in their own lives and the larger community, prevented them from achieving greater fame?

The seven women profiled in this book differ in terms of background and experience but share the common thread of having been soul performers during the '60s: Denise LaSalle, who started out as a songwriter and record label owner, then went on to enjoy a second life as a bluesy singer with a humorous, sassy persona; Ruby Johnson, a little-known performer who made a handful of great records for the legendary Stax label in Memphis; Carla Thomas, Stax's biggest female star and one of the most distinctive voices in all of soul; Bettye LaVette, a Detroit-based singer who has never quite hit the big time, despite a scintillating stage presence, an ardent European following, and fine singles on well over a dozen labels since 1962; Barbara Mason, a pioneer of Philadelphia soul and one of the few female soul artists to have written nearly all of her hits; Maxine Brown, who moved into soul music after a career in gospel in the '50s and whose hits "All in My Mind" and "Funny" go back to the dawn of the soul era; and Timi Yuro, a "blue-eyed" soul singer whose gutsy performances and gigantic voice earned her the praise of luminaries like Dinah Washington and Frank Sinatra.

Taken together, the women represent a wide range of musical approaches and performance styles. The diversity of their music points to the multiple variations soul developed as it became a national force in popular music. In a sense, the story of soul is one of regional sounds: cities such as Memphis, Philadelphia, and New York, with their unique social and musical perspectives, each had something special to offer to soul's production. As with any attempt at categorization, the lines between these regional sounds were often blurred, and the book's classificatory scheme (with the chapters arranged according to the geographical regions with which the singers are associated) is intended as a historical guideline rather than a conclusive summation. It is worth noting, for example, that Barbara Mason, most closely identified with Philly soul, has also recorded in Memphis and New York, while Denise LaSalle started her career by making records in Chicago, experienced her greatest commercial success cutting records in Memphis, and has since recorded in cities as diverse as Detroit; Jackson, Mississippi; and Muscle Shoals, Alabama.[3]

It is important to emphasize that *Ladies of Soul* is not conceived as a *history* of soul music. There are already a number of fine studies dealing with the development of soul as a social and musical force.[4] Rather, the book uses the women's words, experiences, and impressions to offer varying perspectives on the music and the era of which it was a part. While the emphasis is always upon the women themselves, my own commentary is included as connective tissue and as a means of underscoring certain sections of the narratives. This commentary, along with the Introduction, will help give readers enough information to place the interviews in context.

If there is one overriding concept informing my philosophy of soul music, it is that soul represents a state of mind—a way of looking at the art of singing—that emphasizes *emotion* above all other technical or musical considerations. Timi Yuro attests that she gave her audiences "the truth of me": soul singing is about taking what is real and true about oneself and, without judgment or hesitation, putting it into a performance. "If I can't feel it, I won't sing it," a sentiment that has been voiced by many soul singers, is a perfect summation of this philosophy. When a soul singer is "phoning in" a performance, going through the motions without truly feeling it, the lack of sincerity is all too apparent. Like any other musical style, soul has its own set of rote mannerisms and tricks for singers to fall back on. But when the singer truly experiences the song and imbues it with a degree of personal truth, the effect is exhilarating—matched in intensity only by great gospel music. At its best, soul music cuts through all posturing and attitude to deliver something honest and real about the human experience. *Ladies of Soul* attempts to capture that same honesty in the form of the spoken word. It is my hope that even readers without an extensive knowledge of soul music will find in the experiences of these women something to which they can connect and relate.

Since I began work on this project in 1997, numerous individuals have provided invaluable assistance. Most importantly, I would like to thank the seven women I have profiled for allowing me to come into their lives and for giving me such a warm welcome. Maxine Brown, a person as kind as she is talented, deserves special thanks for sharing important contact information early in the project, information which helped get the ball rolling. I would also like to thank all who have taken the time to answer questions, give advice, or assist in my efforts to promote soul music. In the process, they have provided many insights: Roger Armstrong at Ace Records, Bill Belmont at Fantasy Records, Ahmet Ertegun and Vicky Germaise at Atlantic Records, David Hinckley at the *Daily News*, Harold Lipsius of Jamie/Guyden Distributing Company, George Steel and the staff of the Miller Theatre, Elder Locke of Temple Beth-El, Isabel Barber, Dottie Blount, Rob Bowman, Ruth Brown, Chuck Citrin, David Cole, Herb Cox, Irane de Costa, Michelle DuVal, Karen Gravelle, Brian Greene, Marci Haun, Robert Hodge, Raul Morales, Rebecca Murphy, Juggy Murray, Rudy Robinson, Lisa Timmell, Billy Vera, B.C. Vermeersch, Dale Wilson,

James Wolfe, Bari Wood, Anthony Yuro, and the Staff at the Institute of Jazz Studies at Rutgers University in Newark.

Furthermore, there are a number of people who have helped to an extraordinary degree: David Evans, the general editor of this series, who has offered encouragement, helpful ideas, insightful suggestions, and support ever since I first suggested the idea for the book on an otherwise unrelated trip to the University of Memphis back in 1997; Craig Gill at the University Press of Mississippi, whose guidance, patience, and friendly manner have been a constant pleasure; David Koester, my thesis advisor at Columbia, who introduced me to life-history method and inspired the early stages of this project; Ellen Marakowitz at Columbia, for reading and offering comments upon several early versions of the manuscript; Murray Nossel, for taking an interest and inviting me to speak to his class at the Columbia University School for Social Work; Tony Luciano, who, in addition to being a true friend, made the interview with Timi Yuro possible; Ralph McKnight, who helped get everything started; Rita and Sutton, for having me on their show and offering great advice; Arlene Gallup, a wonderful human being who has done enough fascinating things to fill two lifetimes; Paul Williams, who put me in touch with Bettye LaVette and has helped in countless ways; my parents and family for their constant support (my mother, Ann Freeland, even helped me find Ruby Johnson), and, finally, Mino.

Introduction

Soul Music

In today's age of catch-all mass marketing, when it seems as if the music of every hot young discovery is being touted as "a mixture of pop, gospel, and rhythm & blues," *soul* as a descriptive term can be confusing. In its most general sense, soul refers to African-American popular music and is thus indistinguishable from contemporary rhythm & blues or hip-hop. In the early '60s, however, *soul* as a musical category was quite distinct and new. *Ladies of Soul* is based upon an understanding of soul in a historical sense, that is, as a musical development that germinated during the mid- to late-'50s and achieved its commercial and artistic flowering by the end of the next decade. While traditional soul music has continued to be recorded (and has most recently become understood as another variant of "roots music"), its days as a force on the Top 40 charts were largely over by the time disco gained prominence in the mid '70s.

Chronologically, soul was the next major African-American popular musical development following the evolution of rhythm & blues ("R&B") during the late '40s and '50s. While R&B had always borne a distinct gospel influence, the new soul music—exemplified by the pioneering work of performers such as Ray Charles and Little Willie John—made the church connection even more prominent, drawing upon rich and distinctive gospel techniques such as melisma (the bending of a single syllable over several notes), sermonizing (the insertion of spoken passages into songs), call-and-response patterns, and exhortatory tactics such as shouting and testifying. Like the R&B singers who preceded them, many (though, contrary to popular conception, by no means all) soul vocalists received their early training in church, and the religious background of certain soul performers no doubt accounts for the churchy feel of their records. The church influence was further evident in soul's instrumentation. For example, one of the most salient features of the Memphis brand of soul was the Hammond B-3, an organ associated with gospel's "golden era" during the 1950s. The awe-inspiring sound of the Hammond B-3—rich, plaintive, and extremely sensitive to the slightest variation in touch—delivered an emotional punch that perfectly matched the soul singer in intensity.

As with any related musical forms, the line between gospel and soul was not always distinct. Many performers—Little Richard, Al Green, and Laura Lee among them—vacillated between the two genres, with the choice of one frequently precluding the simultaneous performance of the other. The perceived conflict between secular music and the divine "higher good" associated with gospel was the source of great turmoil for a number of soul singers. For instance, Maxine Brown, the singer in this book with perhaps the most extensive gospel background, almost never sings gospel music in a public setting, admitting that the soul/gospel dichotomy is "still a debate in my own mind." This conflict and the personal ambivalence that both informs and results from it is also evident in the chapter on Denise LaSalle. LaSalle, a singer who got her start in gospel but whose soul records are marked by a patently salacious flavor, makes it clear that she eventually wants to return to religious music. She is, however, careful to leave her future open: "I probably won't cut any more blues records, maybe . . . I'm gonna say right now I have plans to do gospel, and if this gospel turn out to be what I hope it will be, then I can go on from there and don't have to cut any more blues."[1] LaSalle's ambivalence is understandable: working as a professional gospel singer often means years of performing under the most difficult conditions for very little pay. Bad food, poor lodging, unscrupulous promoters, cramped traveling conditions, and long, arduous drives in buses and vans are just a few of the hardships endemic to the gospel circuit. These challenges can take a toll, both mentally and physically. As a fellow gospel singer said at the funeral of Ruth "Baby Sis" Davis, the leader of the Davis Sisters and one of the most powerful voices (with a physical presence to match) in all of gospel, "If Baby Sis, strong as she was, couldn't stand it, I know this life will kill me; I'm staying home."[2] It's true that soul and R&B performers didn't always have it much easier (Maxine Brown's tales of her years as a touring performer give a good indication of the rigors of life on the road), but, unlike gospel, the secular field at least carried the potential for financial success. With rare exceptions, such as the Edwin Hawkins Singers' 1969 hit "Oh Happy Day" and the more recent work of Kirk Franklin, gospel records sell only a limited number of copies. When soul suddenly turned into a hit-making force during the mid to late '60s, with records by Aretha Franklin and Wilson Pickett (both former gospel singers) hitting the top of the pop charts, the temptation for gospel performers to "cross over" became especially acute.

Soul's crossover success (starting around 1965 and peaking in 1967, when Franklin's "Respect" became a #1 pop hit) was significant: for the first time, the music of African Americans was gaining acceptance *on its own terms* by middle America, without being watered down for quotidian tastes. Given its new-found mainstream prominence, some performers and fans began to view soul music as an opportunity to advance the causes of the civil rights movement (a movement that, like soul, was heavily influenced by the African-American church). Soul's unique sound was certainly up to the task; moodier, darker, and painted with higher, sharper contrasts than the R&B of a decade earlier, soul was an especially powerful channel for the conflicted impulses and desires of the era. "The Love You Save (May Be Your Own)," a 1966 hit by the late Joe Tex, perfectly illustrates soul's extraordinary ability to address social issues in a serious, even angry way while remaining firmly within the "safe" confines of a '60s love song. The song's superficial theme is found in the chorus:

> *You better stop, find out what's wrong*
> *Get it right, or please leave love alone*
> *Because the love you save today, may very well be your own.*

But Tex's real message comes through in the second verse:

> *I've been pushed around, I've been lost and found*
> *I've been given 'til sundown to get out of town*
> *I've been taken outside, and I've been brutalized*
> *And I had to always be the one to smile, and apologize*
> *But I ain't never in my life before, seen so many love affairs go wrong as I do today. . . ."*

The clever way in which Tex frames this trenchant piece of social commentary within a highly conventional structure (a tactic that insured the record airplay) indicates just how much African-American popular music had changed in the years since the R&B era.

But if a number of soul performers—James Brown, Curtis Mayfield, Sam Cooke (in his epochal, posthumously-released "A Change Is Gonna Come"), Syl Johnson, and a handful of others—seemed especially interested in chronicling the era's social unrest through song, the majority of soul music remained relatively apolitical (significantly, with the exception of Barbara Mason's discussion of her 1974 *Transition* album, none of the women profiled in this book identify their music *itself* as a vehicle for socio-political commentary). As the title of the chapter on Denise LaSalle ("True-to-Life Stuff") suggests, soul music is most often concerned with everyday experience, a quality that emphasizes soul's blues roots as well as its close ties with country. Despite the presence of steel guitars on a few soul recordings (LaSalle's version of Tom T. Hall's "Harper Valley PTA" comes to mind), the soul-country connection can best be described as one of *sensibility* rather than sound. Country and soul's frequently recurring themes—hardship, loneliness, infidelity, and the ever-present love triangle—reflect an acceptance of things as they *are*. Even in cases where this acceptance is couched in ambivalence, a struggle for change is rarely considered as an option (Charlie Rich's masterpiece "Life Has Its Little Ups and Downs," is as moving an example of this philosophy as can be found). Life, by definition, is full of disappointment and sadness but also moments of intense joy. Like gospel and blues music, soul and country give voice to the entire spectrum of human emotions.

Soul's commercial influence gradually declined during the early '70s as newer styles such as funk and disco began to dominate the airwaves. More significantly, soul was becoming a casualty of larger shifts within the infrastructure of the music industry. Since the end of the Second World War, African-American popular music had largely been the province of independent record labels. This pattern continued into the 1960s, with small but important companies such as Atlantic, Stax/Volt, Fame, Chess, Dial, Sue, and Scepter/Wand making innumerable contributions to soul's commercial and artistic development. By the '70s, these labels were either going out of business or, to an increasing degree, coming under the control of major corporations. By 1973, Atlantic—arguably the most influential label in the history of R&B and soul music—was one of the only major independents left in New York, and it too was sold that same year to Warner Communications. In this aggressively corporate climate, small companies like Sue and Scepter found it difficult to survive.

This shift in the nature of record label ownership had dire consequences for the future production of soul music. Whereas a company like Atlantic had achieved success through a skillful balance of commercial and artistic considerations, the emphasis now became fixed upon product, with the more eccentric and individualized voices in African-American popular music being quelled.[3] With the exceptions of Denise LaSalle, who retained her success by producing her own records and shifting to a more blues-oriented approach, and Bettye LaVette, who found work in the Broadway musical *Bubbling Brown Sugar*, the careers of each of the women in this book were in a depressed state by the late '70s. The labels for which they had recorded their finest work—for Maxine Brown, Scepter/Wand; for Carla Thomas and Ruby Johnson, Stax/Volt; for Timi Yuro, Liberty; for Barbara Mason, Arctic and Buddah—were either out of business or operating in name only. Unfortunately, very few new record companies were stepping up to take their place. That factor, combined with the overall decline of soul music as a commercial force, led many soul singers into the darkest periods of their careers.

Female Voices

In a sense, the decline of soul music, and the female soul singer in particular represented the end of a dream that had originated in the 1940s and 1950s when unprecedented numbers of African-American women began to find mainstream stardom within their own country (in sharp contrast to earlier entertainers such as Josephine Baker and Florence Mills, both of whom had acheived their greatest fame overseas). As they came of age in the '50s, future soul women were influenced by commercially successful singers like Della Reese, whose tart, biting vocal quality made her one of the finest vocalists of the '50s and '60s and a popular performer in nightclubs and on television; Joyce Bryant, whose operatic range and bold fashion sense (she was famous for her startling crop of platinum blond hair and tight, fishtail gowns) endeared her to supper club audiences from New York to Vegas; Ruth Brown, perhaps the finest exemplar of swaggering, uptempo '50s R&B, whose record sales virtually transformed small Atlantic Records into a major musical force; Etta James, who first hit at the age of seventeen with "Roll With Me, Henry" (1955) and gradually evolved into one of the most moving vocalists of the R&B and soul eras; and LaVern Baker, whose chart success with novelty records ("Jim Dandy," "Tweedlee Dee") belied her skills as an interpretive balladeer. In addition to their R&B success, these women also became known for their intense and personal treatments of popular standards, a quality that links them to their pop and jazz vocal contemporaries—singers such as Sarah Vaughan, Billie Holiday, Lena Horne, Ella Fitzgerald, and Nina Simone. Like the great pop/jazz singers, female R&B performers cultivated images that were sophisticated, glamorous, and worldly—attributes that were passed down to the female soul singers of the '6os, many of whom recorded standards alongside their more contemporary material.

But the one singer who has undoubtedly exerted the greatest influence upon the women in this book is the legendary "Queen of the Blues," Dinah Washington. In fact, *Ladies of Soul* could easily have been subtitled "Daughters of Dinah," for virtually every singer I interviewed cited her as a formative influence. To describe Washington as purely an R&B singer would be a vast understatement. Broadway tunes, tough blues, jazz—she sang it all with astonishing command of form. Relegated to relative obscurity following her death in 1963 at the age of thirty-nine, Washington's contribution to soul music and the entire corpus of contemporary vocalizing is only now being fully appreciated. The renown of Washington's voice, with its three-octave register, flawless diction, distinctive vibrato, and intense dramatic capability, was matched only by her reputation for capriciousness and volatility.

Like many of her later disciples, Washington (born Ruth Jones in Tuscaloosa, Alabama, in 1924) got her start in gospel music, originally performing as lead vocalist for the Sallie Martin Singers. Washington eventually became fed up with the gospel circuit and with Martin, who was famous for not tolerating any fractiousness (speaking to gospel historian Anthony Heilbut around 1970, Martin said of Washington, "She could really sing but, shoot, she'd catch the eye of some man and she'd be out the church before the minister finished off the doxology").[4] After leaving gospel, Washington never went back, refusing all requests to perform religious material. She became a consistent hit-maker on the R&B charts during the '40s and '50s, first performing with the great vibraphonist and bandleader Lionel Hampton, then breaking out on her own for a long series of remarkable recordings for the Chicago-based Mercury label.

After sixteen years of success in the R&B field, Washington finally crossed over into the pop market in 1959 with her version of the Tin Pan Alley standard "What a Diff'rence a Day Makes," still the song with which she is most closely identified. Suddenly, Dinah Washington was a bona fide star, breaking down racial barriers by performing on the Ed Sullivan show and appearing in Vegas's swankiest clubs. Artistically, however, the hit was the beginning of her decline, as Mercury began to saddle her with increasingly bathetic arrangements and material, an encumbrance in which she was most likely complicit. Having struggled so many years for mainstream acceptance, she wasn't about to give it all away by repudiating the approach that got her there. These years also marked the sudden decline of her voice, a loss brought on by carelessness (Washington never stopped performing long enough to give her vocal chords a rest) and her increasing reliance on alcohol and prescription drugs, a combination that eventually led to her demise. Many of her new fans in 1959 did not realize that, just a few years earlier, Washington had possessed one of the most breathtaking upper registers in all of pop music. On her finest records, however, Washington fused the vocal bravura of the great gospel singers, the interpretive ability of Bessie Smith and Billie Holiday, and the dramatic power of Ethel Merman and Judy Garland into a style that was completely her own. Even today, despite being the subject of a hit off-Broadway show and the focus of praise by countless great singers (truly, she epitomized the often overused term "singer's singer"), Washington has yet to receive her rightful respect as an innovator— one of the first female performers to break down pop's rigid conventions by infusing them with the passion of gospel.

The women profiled in this book are without doubt Washington's spiritual heirs, carrying her performance style to a new generation of listeners. But the most direct link between Washington and the soul-music era was provided by Washington's greatest disciple, Little Esther, or, as she was later called, Esther Phillips. The extraordinary career of Little Esther (born in 1935 in Galveston, Texas) would eventually encompass thirty-five years' worth of African-American musical idioms, from hard-core blues to disco. But in many ways her biggest commercial success would always remain her first: in 1950, at the age of fourteen, she became an overnight star in the R&B world through her recording of "Double Crossing Blues" for the Savoy label. The record hit the top of the R&B charts and stayed there for twenty-two weeks, an astounding achievement for such a young performer. Sadly, Little Esther's success was almost immediately curbed by a crippling drug addiction—one that would hamper her career throughout the '60s.

During the early part of her career, Little Esther's singing style so closely resembled Washington's that many criticized her work as imitative. As she matured into an adult, however, Phillips (she reportedly took the surname from a gas station sign) developed her own highly personal style, one more in keeping with the qualities of the new soul music. While Phillips had Washington's distinctive phrasing, affecting vibrato and sardonic sense of humor, her sensibility was profoundly country in orientation (in fact, some of her greatest performances were big-hearted country ballads, like her version of the Curly Putnam composition "Set Me Free"). Both were skilled at projecting a certain *hauteur*, a tough attitude formed by years of hard living and disappointments, but Phillips was in a sense the more courageous singer. Although she didn't possess Washington's vocal range, Phillips took risks in her performances in ways that Washington never would have considered. Often pushing the limits of the top end of her range—just listen to her heartbreaking delivery on Carolyn Franklin's "Too Many Roads"—Phillips brought to her music a go-for-broke emotionalism offered without pretense or embarrassment. Like Washington, Phillips was destined to die young, passing away in 1984 at the age of forty-nine. Her body, ravaged by years of heroin and alcohol abuse, simply gave out. Rarely discussed by critics, Esther Phillips will hopefully be appreciated one day as a truly influential force—a performer who endowed R&B with the spirit of what would become known as soul.[5]

Another great '50s R&B singer who influenced '60s soul women was Mabel Louise Smith, better known as Big Maybelle. A shouter in the big-voiced Bessie Smith vocal tradition, Big Maybelle was equally skilled at interpreting tender, delicately shaded pop ballads. Way ahead of her time, she would have fit perfectly into the soul era had drug addiction and poor health not hindered her career throughout the '60s. Born some time between 1920 and 1924 in Jackson, Tennessee (the exact year of her birth has never been determined), Smith was a child gospel prodigy at the Rock Temple Church of God in Christ. Discovered singing at one of her church's services by legendary talent scout/promoter Dave Clark, she achieved immediate local success in 1935 by winning a contest at the Cotton Makers Jubilee (an African-American version of the all-white Cotton Carnival) in nearby Memphis. In the '40s, she became a featured vocalist with several well-known big bands, including the Christine Chatman Orchestra and the International Sweethearts of Rhythm.

Although she issued a handful of recordings—as Mabel Smith—in the '40s, it was her '50s work for the Okeh and Savoy labels that made her an R&B star. Changing her name to Big Maybelle to capitalize on her size (merely plump in the '40s, she eventually came to weigh 300 pounds), manager Fred Mendelsohn produced her on a series of major R&B hits, including "My Country Man," "One Monkey Don't Stop No Show," and the one for which she is best remembered, "Candy," recorded in 1956. Big Maybelle's music combined the fervor of the sanctified gospel church, the emotional depth and power of the blues, and the showmanship and technique of pop (a true entertainer in the vaudevillian sense, she did leg splits, told raunchy jokes, and performed certain songs in Yiddish). Most of all, Maybelle brought to her performances a profound sense of world-weariness that seemed to speak volumes about her own personal condition. As drugs came to rule her life to an increasingly debilitating degree, she faded out of the business, eventually dying in 1972 while living with her mother in Cleveland. Because of the freedom through which she allowed her emotions full expression in her performances, Big Maybelle was a soul singer long before the term found its way into the argot of popular music.

Beyond their influential singing and salient commercial presence, each of these women brought to the music world a fierce independent spirit. In particular, Washington, Phillips, and Della Reese had reputations for determination, toughness, and unflinching honesty in their relations with the men of the music industry. This assertion of autonomy can be traced not only to the drive fostered in performers who are thrust into highly competitive situations but also to the unique position in which women were situated in the gospel music world (and significantly, all three of the abovementioned women started out in gospel). In the 1950s, gospel was one of the only musical fields where women were permitted (and expected) to act as *leaders*. In striking contrast to the "girl singer" tradition inherent in '40s and '50s pop music, the frequent structuring of gospel groups along gendered lines allowed female performers to do things *their* way. Female group leaders commanded a striking degree of respect and control that no doubt influenced the attitudes of many future soul singers, some of whom (like Denise LaSalle) had worked in all-female gospel ensembles. Women like Sallie Martin, Dorothy Love Coates (whose raspy, heartfelt singing is one of soul's great unheralded influences), Earnestine Rundless (adoptive mother of Laura Lee), and Albertina Walker not only founded their own groups but arranged the vocal parts, wrote much of the music, rehearsed the performers, made business decisions, oversaw group discipline, and handled bookings and promotion. In short, the great women of gospel fostered a boldness that would manifest itself in the lives and careers of the female soul singers who followed them.

The Interviews

The bold, independent outlook (and, in some cases, sharp tongues) of the female R&B and gospel stars of the '50s is very much evident in the words of the women in this book. At times, I was surprised at the forthright quality of much of the material I was getting during the interviews, but upon further reflection I began to understand how the women could feel so comfortable with their candor. In soul music, as in gospel and country, honesty and sincerity of emotion is the one quality prized above all others. As an art form, soul is profoundly *un*self-conscious— performers pride themselves in their ability to convey something true about their lives and experiences through their music. In this context, it makes sense that the singers would imbue their spoken words with the same degree of honesty that they bring to their songs.

Barbara Mason was the first person I interviewed, in the fall of 1997. Although I was nervous to be interviewing a performer whose work I had admired for many years, Mason's kind, open personality and obvious enthusiasm put me at ease. My personal guidelines for each successive interview remained the same: anything the women wanted to say could potentially be interesting because it would shed light on how they viewed themselves and the community of which they were a part. I always kept a memorized list of issues I wanted to address but never approached an interview with a predetermined plan of how it should turn out. While I wanted to discover as much about the women's careers as possible, I found that other observations—even those completely unrelated to music or the record industry—could be equally enlightening. For this reason, I have included Denise LaSalle's critique of the Jackson, Tennessee, school system and the state of African-American economic initiatives. Similarly, I found Ruby Johnson's description of her activities since ending her music career especially interesting in showing how her years as a performer have fit into the larger arc of her life. There were many other instances in which the women's personal experiences influenced their careers in very specific ways. Maxine Brown's frustration with the men in her life, for example, gave her the impetus to write the song that became her first hit; Timi Yuro recorded "Hurt," her first big record, as a way of avenging the boyfriend who had cheated on her. In short, I wanted to show how the women's personal philosophies affected their perceptions of their environments.

Although in some cases I sensed that the singers had given serious thought to what they were going to say beforehand (Barbara Mason even began her interview with, "I'll just start from the beginning"), the interviews as a whole were marked by a surprising degree of looseness. The first part of each session was often less about the spoken words than the dynamics of becoming comfortable with one another, while the second part tended to be more relaxed and conversational. The most interesting material almost always surfaced in these later sections, after an hour or so of my listening, taking in what each singer was saying while maintaining an awareness of where the interview was headed. The length of the interviews (ranging from ninety minutes to several hours) had little to do with the quality or depth of the material evinced but was instead a reflection of each singer's style of narration. Some of the women (such as Maxine Brown and Denise LaSalle) are natural storytellers who can hold a listener rapt for hours at a time, while others (like Ruby Johnson and Carla Thomas) convey the main idea of their observations using fewer words (a distinction that, especially in the cases of LaSalle and Johnson, mirrors their performance styles). The narrative techniques discernible in the interviews are varied and highly personal, and I have tried to preserve each singer's unique way of speaking—in other words, I hope I've captured some sense of how the women really talk.

It's important for readers to remember that the narratives are based upon individual perception and understanding, not necessarily upon events in a literal sense. Any observations made from a vantage point of thirty or more years later will naturally reflect the contemporary emotional, physical, and spiritual experience of the speaker; the recounting of a past event will undoubtedly be colored by the way the speaker perceives herself now. This understanding—that each narrative's depiction of reality is highly subjective—does not detract from an appreciation of the larger truths inherent in the stories the women tell; namely, each story is true as a *story*, as an indicator of how the speaker views her world. For example, when Barbara Mason describes her decision to make her first record, she also claims that she got permission from her parents to drop out of school. On a literal level, her assertion is hard to understand: how would making one record (a record that carried no guarantee of success) require her to leave school? But the important part of the story is what it tells us about the value Mason attaches to this period of her life: her pairing of the two events represents her prioritization of music over other pursuits, one of her narrative's recurring themes. In Mason's internalized time line, refiltered through the perspective of age and experience, leaving school is the moment when she realized that music would define her life.

Time and again during the interviews, I found myself impressed with the women's strength and resilience. These qualities were evinced through a number of similar themes and situations, one of the most prominent of which was the dependent and often contentious relationships the women shared with their male managers. While they were undoubtedly aided by a manager's promotional support and his connections to the record labels and disc jockeys, the women often came to resent his bids for control over their careers. This resentment was intensified in cases in which the manager was also a husband or domestic partner.[6] Impressively, the women found ways to extract themselves from these situations and apply what they learned to their new lives. Denise LaSalle, for example, took a bad experience with her one-time manager and turned it around for her benefit: she started her own record company and found the success that had eluded her while her career had been under her manager's control. Similarly, after years of dissatisfaction with Jimmy Bishop, her former manager and producer, Barbara Mason learned to take an extremely active role in the copyright enforcement of the many songs she has written.

Nearly all of the women attested to the presence of gender-based prejudices within the music industry, during the '60s as well as today. Maxine Brown voiced her frustration at being paid less than men who shared the same bill, Denise LaSalle expressed regret at being denied the chance to produce an album on a male artist, and Barbara Mason recounted the derision she and her current manager have met in their attempts to form a publishing company. With many independent '60s record companies there seemed to be an unwritten understanding that no more than one female performer could be heavily promoted at the same time, a grievance described by Gerri Hirshey in her section on former Motown star Mary Wells in *Nowhere to Run: The Story of Soul Music:* "She signed with the Atlantic subsidiary Atco in 1966 . . . and left voluntarily when she was told she'd have to wait a year, until after the initial promotional push for Aretha Franklin, before Atlantic producers could get to Mary Wells."[7] As a further example, while the Stax label had many successful male artists on its roster—Otis Redding, Sam and Dave, Eddie Floyd—its sole major female performer was Carla Thomas. During our interview, Ruby Johnson confessed that she often felt ignored and overlooked during her tenure with the company, suggesting that Stax did not have the energy or inclination to support *two* female stars.

The sexism female soul singers frequently endured was compounded by the racism that was an ingrained part of American life during the years just prior to the civil rights era. Nowhere was racial prejudice more immediate and threatening for performers than on the road tours that formed such a vital element of the '60s soul industry. As legendary producer and Sue Records founder Juggy Murray attests, there was always an element of danger associated with the tours, especially those that took performers through southern states: "[The performers] used to get killed. They'd run 'em off the road. A lot of them had car wrecks. They caught hell down South. They were riding in big Cadillacs—them crackers didn't like that shit . . . You always knew something could happen, but there was nothing you could do about it. [The artists] wanted the gig—that's what it's all about." As one of the first performers in the book to begin touring (1961, the year of her first record), Maxine Brown provided in her interview sharp recollections of the challenges traveling soul performers often experienced.

The problems female soul singers faced during the '60s—sexism, racism, poor working conditions, unsatisfactory managers and record companies—may be less prevalent today, but there is another, just as severe, problem: the scarcity of jobs and viable outlets for their talents. Most of the women in this book have weathered soul's loss of popularity with the American public by finding work overseas, where

'60s soul has long been venerated by European fans. English record companies such as Ace, Sequel, and West Side have catered to European soul lovers through their intelligently programmed, packaged, and annotated releases by performers whose music often remains out of print in the U.S. As Barbara Mason, most of whose work is available only through European imports, says of her overseas fans, "They know *everything* . . . they cherish us." The paradox, especially detectable in Maxine Brown's fame in England and Timi Yuro's in Holland, is that the women have achieved a kind of sustained stardom in Europe while rarely reaching beyond a cult audience in their own country.

This difficulty in finding opportunities to perform and record is responsible in part for the palpable sense of anxiety lurking beneath the surface of the women's words. Many are still searching for another big break—a revived stardom—almost forty years after entering the business; their fear is that they will run out of time. This fear is noticeable in Bettye LaVette's struggle to find a company that will record her: "I'm hoping that I can get something out in the streets, if I can only get one in before the deadline." The anxiety is very real and justified: American culture is fanatically obsessed with the new, and there's no way to insure that the next job will be forthcoming. For soul performers, the transitory nature of success is summed up in the oft-repeated observation, "You're only as hot as your last record," a thought that appears in one form or another in virtually all of the chapters. During the '60s, a soul singer lacking the proverbial "hot record" was in danger of imminent obscurity. Even when it came to the output of artistically noble labels such as Stax, the first consideration was by necessity commercial. With competition coming from the dozens of small record labels specializing in soul, companies couldn't take a chance on releasing something they didn't think was going to sell. Sixties soul was still a *business,* a fact evident in the response of Stax writer/producer David Porter when questioned about his productions with Ruby Johnson: "Ask me about 'Soul Man.' Don't ask me about songs that didn't make it."[8]

As the women described their struggles to find consistent work and their frustration at lost or missed opportunities, I began to understand just how much they had been forced to sacrifice in their pursuit of stardom. Although I had always known, at least on an abstract level, that being a soul performer was difficult work, I was unprepared for just how competitive it could be. The competition between female performers was especially intense: any assumptions I held of sisterly unity were quickly displaced by statements such as the one Bettye LaVette made early in our interview: "I think that there's something in me that's always known that women and I weren't going to be the best of buddies." I began to view these sentiments as a response to the very real problem discussed above—the scarcity of work for female soul performers, during the '60s and now. The fierceness of the competition also helps to explain the women's frequent attempts to assert their uniqueness (as Barbara Mason says, "There's not another female that I know in the industry that I sound like or that sounds like me"). Even Timi Yuro's efforts to compare herself favorably to country singer Wynonna Judd ("there *is* one chick who possibly *could* go where I was . . . Only she don't, she's shuckin' and jivin' ") can be seen as a reflection of this need to have an edge over other female performers.

Stardom as a notion and ideal must be viewed as independent from actual commercial success. Each of the singers in this book is affected, to one degree or another, by stardom's pressures and expectations, pressures that remain painfully intense even for a performer who hasn't had a hit in decades. Timi Yuro, for example, became an overnight star when her first record, "Hurt," leapt to number four on the pop charts in 1961. Although she had a few more hits, nothing else matched the success of that magical first recording. Yet in many ways Yuro, who has resided in Las Vegas for the past thirty years, still conducts her periodic contacts with the public as a star. A brief anecdote will illustrate this point. During our first phone conversation, Yuro seemed extremely excited and pleased to be asked for an interview, but as the months wore on it became difficult to pin down a date or time. I sensed that the idea of being part of the project very much appealed to her, but that the actual nuts and bolts of the interview process—planning, negotiating the details of time and place— were too complicated to consider.

At the time I ascribed Yuro's reluctance to her recurrent illness—she has been battling cancer on and off since the mid '80s. It wasn't until over a year later, when, as a last-ditch effort I made a trip to Las Vegas without a definite "yes" from her, that I finally got the interview and, simultaneously, understood the reason for her reticence. Yuro was definitely pleased during that early phone conversation, but not because she was looking forward to doing an interview—the actual interview was irrelevant and perhaps not even a consideration. Rather, Yuro was happy because for those few minutes someone had made her feel like a star. Over the phone the illusion of stardom was easy to maintain, separated by thousands of miles and entire realms of experience from the sickness and hardships that have characterized so many of her recent years. In the succeeding months, when I had begun to push for the interview, Yuro had been caught off guard, the prospect of actually being seen and questioned by a member of the public after so many years perhaps a bit frightening.

The interview with Yuro turned out to be relaxed and enjoyable, but the days I spent in Las Vegas attempting to reach Yuro and wondering if the interview would take place or not gave me an insight into the tenacity of the behavior patterns associated with stardom. This tenacity is evident throughout the interviews, but most importantly in the women's determination to keep on going, to constantly work towards the next big opportunity. It's a struggle that informs the lives of all of the singers in this book, except for possibly Ruby Johnson, who seems largely at peace with her past accomplishments: "when I think about how close I've come sometimes—never quite close enough to reach that level—I'm almost convinced that that may not have been what God intended for me to do . . . I never reached that level of international prestige, I've never really earned the money that I probably would have earned had I reached that level, but certainly I have not wanted for one thing that I desired . . . That achievement helps me to . . . maybe to realize that I'm not missing anything."

In this sense, Johnson is an anomaly. Most of the women in *Ladies of Soul* definitely feel as if they have missed out on *something*, be it a record deal, a lost performance opportunity, a song that should have been a hit but wasn't, or royalty rights that were carelessly signed away. As I return to the subject of the original question I posed in the preface—the factors that prevented these women from attaining greater success—I see an answer even more complicated than I had realized, and I can't escape the conclusion that in some cases the women themselves have been at least partially responsible. The predicaments in which they found themselves during the early part of their careers were often the result of naiveté, of not understanding the way the record industry works. A good case in point is Bettye LaVette's walking out on her first Atlantic Records contract (there would be two more for the company) in 1963. Atlantic was her first label, and she simply didn't realize the importance of where she was. But it would be disingenuous to ignore the role of outside forces: an industry that shows little respect for female performers, a culture that tragically underappreciates African-American artists, a public that latches on to hot musical trends only to toss them aside after losing interest. Acknowledging their mistakes but ever hopeful that the future will present the chance to rectify them once and for all, these women have survived through an adept mix of perseverance, hubris, sheer talent, and most important of all, by being as honest in their own lives as they are in their music.

Part One

The South

Peter Guralnick has written that "Soul music is Southern by definition if not by actual geography."[1] While the soul sound eventually spread to points as distant and diverse as Philadelphia, New York, and Chicago, its historical and emotional core always lay in its heady admixture of three southern musical forms: blues, gospel, and country. But equally important is the notion that soul music—its sparse elegance and richness of imagery, the pain and feeling evident in its grooves—is somehow representative of something distinctly *southern*. Soul embodies the complexity and contradiction of southern life: adversity, joy, hardship, determination, and loss. The South is a place where things of great artistic worth seem forever in danger of slipping away, where fine singers like Ruby Johnson burst upon the scene to release a handful of classic records and then just as quickly fade out of sight, never to be heard from again. A desire to comprehend the sadness and mystery behind this evanescence, accompanied by the longing to keep such great voices from disappearing forever, insures that one will always return to the South to grasp an understanding of soul's true heart.

The Memphis Sound

It can be argued that no city has played a more important role in the development of American popular music than Memphis. Strategically located north of New Orleans on the banks of the Mississippi River, this unique city has contributed to the evolution of gospel, blues, rock & roll, jazz, and soul in ways that are still being analyzed and understood. A trip to Memphis provides a fascinating glimpse into the country's musical past, although, like so much that is worthy in American culture, the beauty of Memphis's art has not always been appreciated, even by those who live there (I'll never forget a visit when I made numerous attempts to ask Memphians about Rufus Thomas, one of their most legendary fellow residents, and received nothing but blank stares). A rich musical scene has always thrived in Memphis, however, and by the end of the 1950s the city was developing a wave of talent that would eventually change the face of modern American music.

The most famous Memphis soul label, and the one with the most relevance for this book, is Stax. Founded in 1959 as Satellite Records by Jim Stewart and Estelle Axton, a white, middle-aged brother-and-sister team with virtually no knowledge of the record industry, Stax in a few short years blossomed into one of the most innovative and influential record companies of the rock era. Almost by accident, Stax created a sound that would essentially define the southern brand of soul music: heavy percussion with strong backbeat, sparse but majestic guitar accompaniment, emotive playing on the Hammond B-3, and expressive, almost conversational horn lines. Key to Stax's success was its reliance on "head arrangements," arrangements that, rather than being worked out ahead of time, were created through collective musical input at the session itself. By the middle of the '60s, Stax had cultivated a roster of artists that included many of the great soul performers of the era: Otis Redding, Eddie Floyd, Sam and Dave, and Rufus and Carla Thomas. Thanks to the presence of the studio's ace house band, Booker T. and the MG's (Booker T. Jones on organ, Al Jackson on drums, Donald "Duck" Dunn on bass, and Steve Cropper on guitar), Stax's sound was remarkably uniform and cohesive through the end of the decade.

By the early '70s, another Memphis label had started to give Stax serious competition. Surprisingly, Hi Records was founded first (in 1958) but had spent most of the '60s recording instrumentals, records that sold moderately well but were unable to give Hi the trademark sound it needed for serious recognition. That recognition started to arrive around 1969, when Willie Mitchell, a producer, trumpeter, and arranger who himself had achieved a hit instrumental on Hi in 1968 with "Soul Serenade," began to take an active role in the management of the company. Under Mitchell's expert guidance, Hi produced an astonishing array of hits with its core stable of artists: Al Green, Ann Peebles, Otis Clay, Syl Johnson, and O.V. Wright.

The deep, distinctive Hi sound was also featured on the records of non-Hi artists (such as Denise LaSalle) who leased Mitchell's Royal Recording Studio and musicians for one-off sessions.

Numerous smaller labels abounded in Memphis during the '60s and early '70s, such as Goldwax (home to soul cult-hero James Carr and underrated artists like the Ovations and Spencer Wiggins); AGP (American Group Productions), which scored a Top-30 R&B hit with the Masqueraders' "I'm Just an Average Guy" in 1969; Sounds of Memphis, Home of the Blues, and XL. In addition, the American Recording Studio (led by producer/writer Chips Moman) produced a steady stream of hits on a wide variety of artists throughout the late '60s: Elvis Presley, Dusty Springfield, Neil Diamond, and Dionne Warwick all recorded albums there. By the latter half of the '70s, however, the recording scene in Memphis declined as the increasingly consolidated, corporate nature of the music industry made it difficult for small labels—the lifeblood of the Memphis R&B and soul industry—to stay afloat. One of the only studios in Memphis to continue producing hit records during the late '70s was Ardent, a high-tech recording facility frequented by artists such as ZZ Top, Isaac Hayes, and (during her tenure with ABC Records) Denise LaSalle. Things didn't really start to turn around for the city until the early '90s, when a number of excellent releases such as Ann Peebles's 1992 *Part Time Love* (on Rounder, one of the contemporary labels most devoted to the continuing development of soul music), Charlie Rich's *Pictures and Paintings* of the same year, and B.B. King's acclaimed *Blues Summit* in 1993—proved that Memphis soul was as vital as ever and here to stay.

The Muscle Shoals Sound

While Stax Records in Memphis was developing into a national force in African-American popular music, another soul sound was brewing not far away in northern Alabama. Unlike Memphis, the four towns collectively known to soul fans as "Muscle Shoals" (Florence, Sheffield, Tuscumbia, and Muscle Shoals itself) did not bear a rich musical heritage, although both W. C. Handy and Sun-founder Sam Phillips were originally from Florence. An active country publishing scene developed in the area during the '50s, however, attracting a large number of songwriters, performers, and industry hopefuls.

One of these hopefuls was Alabama native Rick Hall, who (along with future countrypolitan producer Billy Sherrill and local song publisher Tom Stafford) founded the Fame (Florence Alabama Music Enterprises) studio in 1959. Achieving its first big R&B hit in 1962 with Arthur Alexander's "Anna (Go To Him)," Fame by the middle of the decade had developed into a nationally-recognized soul hotspot. With its crack house rhythm section (drummer Roger Hawkins, keyboardist Spooner Oldham, bassist David Hood, and guitarist Jimmy Johnson) providing a hot, danceable sound, Fame's recordings were every bit as unique and influential as those of Stax. By the end of the '60s, singers such as Wilson Pickett, Aretha Franklin, Etta James, Laura Lee, and Arthur Conley had all benefited from the studio's expert guidance.

Key to the success of both Fame and Stax was Atlantic Records, the legendary New York R&B label, which not only sent many of its artists to Memphis and Muscle Shoals to record but also entered into distribution agreements with both labels. This arrangement was part of Atlantic's larger commitment to the promotion of southern soul, having recognized its commercial potential as early as Carla Thomas's "Gee Whiz" on Satellite in late 1960. Atlantic also released all of Percy Sledge's biggest hits (which had been recorded at another Muscle Shoals-area studio, Quinvy) and continued to work with the Fame rhythm section after it defected in 1969 to form its own studio, Muscle Shoals Sound. Muscle Shoals Sound was an immediate success: by the early '70s, it had become even more active than Fame, with artists as diverse as Willie Nelson, Cher, and Millie Jackson making trips there to capture some of that Muscle Shoals magic. Both studios have continued to operate over the years, although Rick Hall now focuses primarily on country music. Muscle Shoals Sound, currently owned by Malaco Records of Jackson, Mississippi, was particularly active during the '80s and '90s. Virtually all of Malaco's artists, among them Denise LaSalle, Johnnie Taylor, Little Milton, Dorothy Moore, and Bobby Bland, have recorded there, and in 1992 legendary Atlantic producer Jerry Wexler selected the studio for his second collaboration with Etta James, *The Right Time.*

Although stylistically more diffuse than the Memphis Sound, the soul music produced in Muscle Shoals shares the same gospelized flavor. On ballads, the church connection is particularly evident, the frequent use of the Hammond B-3 and the call-and-response stylings of backup singers lending the slow numbers a heart-tugging sense of drama. It could hardly be argued that the latter-day Muscle Shoals recordings on Malaco are imaginative (a complaint voiced by Denise LaSalle), but few soul records during the late '80s and '90s were more poignant than Dorothy Moore's "It's Rainin' On My Side of the Bed" (1992) and Johnnie Taylor's "Without You" (1989). If Malaco sticks to what it does best, it's clear that Muscle Shoals will continue to be a vibrant force in the soul music of the twenty-first century.

Denise LaSalle
True-to-Life Stuff

Denise LaSalle, circa 1975

*I*n a remarkable career that has encompassed publishing, label ownership, songwriting, production, and, finally, soul stardom, Denise LaSalle has proven her talent for longevity through adroitly balancing an understanding of new trends with a respect for the idioms of the past. While frequently capable of creating great music, she never pretends to be so enveloped in her art that she can't see its hitmaking potential. In fact, LaSalle's music gives credence to the notion that some of the best art is created with commercial considerations in mind.

That said, LaSalle has produced a fascinating body of work, the best of which ranks alongside that of her long-time idol Aretha Franklin in terms of heartfelt communi-cation and soulfulness. Those who only know her through her 1971 breakthrough hit on Westbound Records, "Trapped By a Thing Called Love," or her latter-day work as a soul-cum-blues belter on Malaco are missing out on hearing some of soul's great unheralded performances. Take, for instance, "Don't Nobody Live Here (by the Name of Fool)," an early '70s track that may well be the finest thing she has ever done (sadly, along with much of her best work, it is out of print in the U.S.). Part of what makes the record so great is the sound itself: a tight Memphis band (the Hi Rhythm Section) provides all of the requisite peaks and valleys, with horns, drums, guitar, strings, and backup vocalists

(Memphis stalwarts Rhodes, Chalmers, and Rhodes) all coming together on the chorus, then separating on each verse. Like so many great Memphis records, the band pushes even harder near the end, so that the song fades out at the peak moment of intensity. But it is LaSalle who commands the greatest attention. She simply outdoes herself, matching one of her finest compositions with a vocal that is worthy of Aretha herself—all the more impressive because LaSalle (as she will be the first to tell you) doesn't possess anything near Franklin's vocal range or power. Alternately plaintive and declamatory, she wrings especial poignancy out of lines like "It looks like you overrated the powers of your charm/when you tried your game on me today/But you underestimated the vengeance of a woman's scorn/I've been scorned, and now you're gonna pay." But most of all, the performance features a solid emotional commitment to the moment that just can't be faked. As LaSalle says of another great self-composition, "Trying to Forget About You" (recorded around the same time), "It sounds like I'm hurting."

LaSalle was born Denise Allen in rural Leflore County, Mississippi, on July 16, 1941.[1] As a child she picked cotton in Humphreys County, where her family had moved when she was seven. After moving to Chicago in the mid '50s, she sang gospel with the Sacred Five (a local all-female ensemble) and worked a variety of jobs before even thinking about breaking into the record business (as we shall see, it was her love of writing that led to her eventual entry into professional music). Even then, stardom was not overnight. She released records for several years, both for herself and others (under the auspices of Crajon Productions, a record and publishing company she owned with her then-husband, Bill Jones) before the success of "Trapped by a Thing Called Love" escorted her into the big time.

Since 1977, LaSalle has lived in Jackson, Tennessee, with her current husband, disc jockey-turned-radio entrepreneur James Wolfe (together the couple owns three local radio stations) and their teenage son. Jackson, a city of 53,000 about seventy-five miles east of Memphis, was at one time known as a musicians' town. The clubs of Shannon Street used to attract John Lee Williamson (the first "Sonny Boy") and the young Big Maybelle, while Carl Perkins resided in Jackson for many years until his death in 1998. Wolfe and LaSalle live a few miles outside of town on a small, twisting road in the midst of farmland and cotton fields (despite the bucolic surroundings, LaSalle says she is afraid the area is being overdeveloped). The first thing one sees upon entering the house is a life-size painting of LaSalle, based upon a photo that graces the cover of The Bitch is Bad album, a late-'70s release on ABC. On the album cover, a svelte LaSalle dressed in a black negligee (like Aretha, LaSalle slimmed down in the '70s) is standing atop a tiger skin at the edge of a swimming pool. At the bottom of the photograph, a muscular male swimmer can be seen reaching out for her leg. The painting in LaSalle's house differs from the original album photo in one respect: the tiger skin has been replaced with an image of a live tiger. The painting—juxtaposed with the country roads and cotton fields that surround *the house—is an apt metaphor for a woman who manages to be both larger than life and down home at the same time.*

I grew up a reader, an avid reader, from comic books to *True Confessions* and all these magazines, love stories. And I daydreamed and I fantasized all my young life. This is all I wanted to do and something I always could see myself doing: singing or being a movie star or being *something*. All these daydreams would come to me and I'd say, "I'm going to write some stories. I'm going to write my life." I'd think about what I'm going to do and I'd write it, you know. Finally one day I got it into my head that I could write a story and send it in to a magazine. So I sent one to *True Confessions* and one to *Tan* magazine, and I had both of them published in the issues. I couldn't miss them because I bought every one. And you know, they didn't pay me, they didn't contact me or tell me I was being paid or nothing, they just put them in a magazine. And I read this and said, "This is my story!" And I contacted them and got paid. They paid me—nothing—but they paid me, though.

After that I said, "Oh, I can do it, I can do it!" So I went after it. I left Mississippi, went to Chicago. In Chicago I decided to get a typewriter. I'd sit up and I'd "hunt-and-peck" type, 'cause I couldn't type real good—I'd just hunt and peck. Finally I'd do up all of these stories. I'd just send them in, send them in, send them in. And one day I came home from work and I had eight manuscripts returned, 'cause after the first time, I would write to them and I'd tell them how much I wanted for my stories! All these manuscripts was laying at my front door! And that just discouraged me. "Oh! How many hours I put into this." But my head was just filled with things, so I started writing poems, and as I would write poems, for some reason they would come to me as a song. I could do all this rhyme and stuff, but then I could hear the lyric in my head, with the melody. There was people like Jerry Butler and Aretha Franklin who were big stars at the time, and I'd say, "Oh, this sounds like a Jerry Butler song, this sounds like it could fit Aretha Franklin, this would sound good for Gladys Knight." You know, I'd just go down the line. And so the songs would just lay there. I would just write them. I didn't know how to get them to anybody, but every time the Regal Theatre in Chicago opened its doors, I was always sitting watching some Motown Revue or somebody. You name it, I was there. James Brown, Sam Cooke, Dinah Washington, anybody. Whoever was there, I was there looking. I didn't miss nothing. And sometimes two or three times a week I would go. The Chicago Theatre also had big shows. Josephine Baker—I was always there. Steve Lawrence and Eydie Gorme—I was there, I would be right there.[2]

But anyway, I didn't know anything to do with my songs. And finally I became a barmaid in 1963—the year that President Kennedy was killed. I was a barmaid at a bar there in Chicago. And this guy, Billy "The Kid" Emerson, had this record out called "If You Make the Trip, I'll Pop the Whip." He had that record, a local Chicago hit record. He was one of the guys that came into the bar.[3] I'd never met him before, and someone kept hearing me around the bar. I would sing all the time, and I'm always writing something. In between customers, I'd write down something. "What are you doing?"

—"I'm writing a song."

And so one of the guys said, "Hey Denise, I want you to meet this guy. This is the Whip (they called him "the Whip") that sings 'You Make the Trip, I'll Pop the Whip.' Maybe he can look at your songs." I'm sure they didn't think anything would come of it. You know how you mess with people who say, "I'm a writer." You say, "Oh, she's a writer there." Nothing's gonna come of this, you know. But hey, "this guy might look at your songs." So I went up and asked him, "Would you?" He said, "Yeah. Can you sing them?" I said, "Sure." He said, "Well, I'm a musician. Would you like to sing the song and let me play it, so you can put some music to it and put it on tape? Maybe, if it's any good, I'll let Chess listen to it." And I said, "Yeah." So he picked me up that afternoon, and we went to his place and we taped it. He took it down to Chess Records, and they fell in love with my voice. They said, "Oh, we like the song, but we want to know—who's the girl?" He said, "Oh, she doesn't sing." He [the man at Chess] said, "Well she's doing okay with that one. Can you bring her down here? I'd like to talk to her." We went to Chess, they were interested, and they said, "Tell you what you do. This is one song. Why don't you come back and we're going to cut some things on you."

In 1963, Chess Records was on the cusp of a second round of glory. At the forefront of Chicago blues, R&B, and doo-wop in the '50s with artists such as Chuck Berry, Muddy Waters, Howlin' Wolf, and the Moonglows, Chess in the '60s was (along with Vee Jay, which folded in 1966) the primary purveyor of Chicago soul, home to Billy Stewart, Etta James, Little Milton, Fontella Bass, and many others. Chess, with its superb in-house production and songwriting staff (the underrated Billy Davis was responsible for much of the distinctive "Chess sound" in the '60s), would have been the perfect home for the young Denise Allen (in 1963, she still had not taken on her present name). As it turned out, however, it would still be a number of years before she would find her niche as a performer.

So Little Miss Cornshucks was one of their artists, and they lowered her voice and let me sing on about three of her tracks.[4] I did "Try a Little Tenderness" and something else I've forgotten, and they signed me to a contract. I was scared to sign it. I said, "I have no experience." But as a gospel singer, I'd been singing in church all my life. They said, "Well, if you're willing to take a chance on us, we'll take a chance on you." And so they talked to Billy and asked him if he would help me out. He said, "Yeah, I'd be glad to." So Billy was going to be my manager and all of this stuff. We went home and we rehearsed, and he gave me pointers on what to do and how to be onstage and tried to get me into this thing. He started taking me around to nightclubs, entering me in talent shows. And all of a sudden I started winning, coming in first place. And I got job offers and started working in some of the clubs.

Chess never recorded me. They would send for me, and I would go and Billy would go with me. I would never go without Billy. And I'd go down there and they would just talk. Then finally one day one of the guys [at Chess] asked me, "Why do you bring him with you all the time?" I said, "Well, because I don't know what to say or do, and he's supposed to be my manager." "Have you signed with him?" I said, "No. I haven't signed anything." And they said, "Well, why don't you come down here and leave him at home?" And I couldn't understand why. I kept saying, "I'm not gonna do that." I just knew better than to do that, because I just felt like they were getting ready to take advantage of me in some way, one way or the other. I was a young girl, pretty and sexy and all that stuff, and I didn't want to be taken advantage of. I said, "If they want me as a singer, then I'm going to sing. I'm not gonna be a couch potato for them." I wasn't going to do that. I was raised different from that. I would not do it, and a whole year went by—they never recorded me. 'Cause every time they sent for me, Billy was right there. I couldn't say that they really wanted to take advantage of me. All I know is that they didn't do anything with me. And that was enough for me. So when the year was up, I wrote a letter asking for a release. "Oh, we'll have your record cut in three weeks! I promise you, three weeks!" I said, "No way. I've been with you one year and you didn't cut it, so now I just want a written release." I only had signed for a year, so the contract was really up, but it did say there were options that could be picked up, and I just let them know that I didn't want no options and I wanted out. So that's the end of Chess Records, except for when Billy finally cut a single on me. He had sold numerous copies of it on his own label, Tarpon Records, and when Chess heard it, they purchased the master from him.

The record bought (and then distributed) by Chess, "A Love Reputation" (cut in 1967, almost four years after Allen's initial Chess experience) did not chart but was nonetheless a fine example of hard-driving, bluesy soul. In addition to producing this first single, Emerson changed the stage name of the singer to Denise LaSalle.

So from there, Billy's and my relationship kind of soured when I had an opportunity to be on a Jackie Wilson show at the Regal Theatre. A disc jockey named E. Rodney Jones from WVON had booked the show, and they were giving me a play on it. They told Billy they wanted me on there. Well, the Red Saunders band was going to play for all the acts, but Billy insisted that *his* band play behind me. So as it turned out, I was dropped from the show, because Billy insisted on being a part of it, and they said no. I didn't understand why I was canceled from the show, and I kept inquiring and never knew. So finally one day one of the disc jockeys from WVON told me that I was dropped from the show because Billy's band insisted on playing, and Red Saunders was the overall band. 'Cause, see, a lot of acts like Jackie Wilson would come and they would only bring their immediate rhythm section, and the big band—Red Saunders' band—would back everybody. They would bring a music director for themselves, and Red Saunders's band did the rest. And Billy wouldn't have that. That's what went down, and when I got the news, we just had a big blowup. I goes, "Now how do you create me and want me to be a star, you're trying to push me out here, then when an opportunity comes along, you kill that opportunity out of selfishness." I said, "Well, we have not signed anything as a manager, so right now I'm eliminating your control over me. I appreciate everything you've done for me, but right now, you can't control my bookings no more." So from then on I started working for myself. So we had this big falling out, and I don't want to get into details about how bad it was, but it was really bad. It was really bad. The tide was totally severed between us from that point on. And I give him due respect, because he taught me an awful lot that I even adhere to today. I remember the things he taught me on stage today and they've been a part of what helped me to become Denise LaSalle. Helping me get a publishing company, watching him, how he did it—he had his own publishing company—and how he ran his record label, little stuff. I learned a lot of that from him.

The break from Emerson signaled the beginning of LaSalle's career as a businesswoman.

In later years I went on to organize and do my own thing. I just said, "Well OK, I'm a good songwriter." I knew I had that talent, so I went ahead and got my own publishing company and started writing and doing songs on my own. Because one time I wrote songs with Billy and never even got credit. I would just help write them, he'd put them in his publishing company, and the credit was gone. Now I got credit on *some* of them, but some of them I didn't.

In 1969 LaSalle married Bill Jones and opened Crajon Productions in their Chicago home (the first three letters of "Crajon" came from Craig, a surname that LaSalle had used briefly during the '60s after a short-lived first marriage). In addition to the publishing side of the business, Crajon incorporated three labels: Gold Star, Parka, and Crajon itself. The couple was the company's driving artistic force, writing and producing most of the material recorded for the labels.

Crajon's biggest artists were LaSalle herself, Bill Coday, and the Sequins. Coday was a rugged-sounding soul singer who hit #14 on the R&B charts with "Get Your Lie Straight," while the Sequins were a teenage "girl group" whose first session for Crajon produced a #34 R&B hit, "Hey Romeo." Despite being a Chicago record company, Crajon recorded most of its releases at Willie Mitchell's Royal Recording Studio in Memphis, which would go on to play an integral role in LaSalle's career in the '70s.

So I met Bill Jones in 1967, and we got married, 1969. The "Love Reputation" song had kept me working from '67, when that was recorded, through '69, when I married Bill. We started accumulating some money together, setting up, trying to get our money together, and decided to go to Memphis and record with Willie Mitchell, whom I had heard so much about through a disc jockey friend of mine, Al Perkins. Al Perkins could not stay in key when he sang, but Willie Mitchell cut records on him and kept him in key. And I said, "If he can do that much for Al Perkins, he can do it for me." 'Cause I had tried to cut several songs after Billy had done the "Love Reputation" song. I tried to cut some tunes on myself in Chicago, with local Chicago musicians, and I didn't get anywhere with them. Totally nothing. They just didn't make it. And I said, "I'm going to Memphis. This man made Al Perkins sound good." 'Cause I used to go to Al Perkins's live shows, and he couldn't sing in key. And this man made him sound like a professional.[5]

The first record I cut with Willie Mitchell, I think, was "I Believe I'm on the Right Track." The old Billy Butler song. That was my first effort with Willie Mitchell, and it was a groove, it was great. I loved it. It didn't become a hit because we just didn't get it out there. We didn't have no money, didn't know nothing about distribution, and it was the first thing we'd done. But with Bill Coday we did a song called "You're Gonna Want Me Back" the same time I did "the Right Track." It went the local thing right there [in Chicago], and then we cut "Hey Romeo" and we hired a guy named Fred Richter to distribute it nationally on our label [Gold Star]. And then we came back with "Get Your Lie Straight" on Bill Coday, 1969.

Now 1970 was when I cut my second Willie Mitchell record, the up-tempo "Hung Up and Strung Out." And it made so much noise around Detroit, Michigan, till Armen Boladian of Westbound Records talked to Al Perkins about it. He said, "Oh man, that's a bad record. I like that record." 'Cause we had got Armen Boladian's distributing company to distribute it for us in Detroit. He talked to Al about it: "I understand you and Denise LaSalle good friends. See can you get her to talk to me. I want at least a master to that record." And so he purchased that master, "Hung Up and Strung Out." It did pretty well for him, but it wasn't a big deal. He got all he could get out of it, you know. But then all of a sudden he says, "Denise, we need to go back in the studio and cut another one. That one did good, but it's not the one. It's not the big one." He said, "Can you go back and do another record?" I said, "Yeah." He sent me the money, and I went down there and cut "Trapped By a Thing Called Love." It was 1971.

"Trapped By a Thing Called Love," with its swaggering, Gene "Bowlegs" Miller-arranged horn line and LaSalle's relaxed but forceful delivery, was a #1 R&B hit and a million-seller for Westbound Records. It is without doubt one of the great soul records of the '70s, practically defining a new "Memphis Sound"—one that was as distinctive in its own way as the Stax sound had been in the previous decade. The entire recording has an organic, languid feel—everything seems as if it has simply fallen into place without effort. Thirty years later, it still sounds remarkably fresh and soulful. The success of the record made the thirty-year-old LaSalle an overnight soul star and enabled her to finally quit her day job.

As a matter of fact, I was working as a cashier in a supermarket called Dell Farms supermarket in Chicago, and they used to tease me 'cause my record, "Hung Up and Strung Out," was played on the radio. And folk would walk by me ringing up groceries, and they'd say, "How does it feel to have your record playing on the air and you standing up in a grocery store bagging groceries?" I said, "Well, I tell you, it feels good because I know that I can have some money in my pocket when I go home, because the record's on the air but it's not paying me any money." [Laughs.] You know, I feel okay. I'm not ashamed of the fact that I'm here. So when they sent me the money to go cut this, I took a leave of absence. I was going to be gone more than a week or so, so I told them I need to get about a month's leave of absence, 'cause we had to cut the record, then we had to mix it, put background vocals and all, and I didn't know how long I was going to need.

So I took about a month off, goes down there and cut the record. Everything was head arrangement then, nobody write down nothin,' you know. It's Teenie

Hodges, Leroy [Hodges], Howard Grimes, and Charles Hodges.[6] We're sitting there and Willie Mitchell's working the thing, so I'm standing out on the floor singing. And Willie says, "Denise, get on the microphone, let me hear what you sound like today. Ooh, you're in good voice today. You're in *good* voice today." And so we went down and got to the end of the song. Willie said, "Hey, come on in here and listen." I said, "Willie, I want to do that again. Let me do one more take on it. I missed something." He said, "Nuh-uh. Come in here and listen to this. You ain't gonna mess this up." We went up there and listened, and I said, "Willie, I wanted to go up in this spot, I wanted to just. . . ." He said, "Look. I'm not cutting it over again." One take. He said, "We're not going to touch it. Forget it now, you got a smash." Just like that. And he would not touch it. He said, "I'm not ruining this tape. This is it."

And so we went on to cut some more songs. We just went on to the other songs, you know. So when we took the tape up to Westbound, everybody freaked out. Everybody just called it, Willie Mitchell called it from the very first day. "You made a million-seller, you got a smash right here." And we got up to Al Perkins, and he went, "Um, um, that's it." That was the beginning. I was very pleased. But from the day that I cut that tune, I never went back. I told you about the supermarket, so I could tell you—*I* knew from the time I left the studio that that was the beginning, and I never went back. I would not. When my leave of absence was up, I was gone. I just went on from there. "You're not coming back?" I said, "No. Thank you, no."

LaSalle loved cutting records in Memphis, using the city as her recording base for the remainder of the '70s. In particular, she found the Memphis musicians' "take-it-as-it comes" attitude towards recording more conducive to her own level of musical ability.

I'm not a musician. Know absolutely nothing about music, in spite of my two years as a child piano lessons. [Laughs.] So these guys in Memphis are good accomplished musicians, read and do everything. They can do all this, but that's not the way that they do records usually. They normally do head arrangements, go in the studio, create, and make it up as they go along. And this is what I liked about them. In Chicago, I never could ever get anywhere with the musicians because everything that you go to do— "Write it down. What do you want here?" "I don't know what I want there. I'm gonna sing this song for you, and I'm gonna tell you this is the sound I want right here." I may do it with my mouth. I may say, I want to [sings a horn line] "dah dah dah dah." Now I'll tell you that. I can't tell you what notes these are, and I cannot tell you what key this is in, I can't tell you nothin' about it.

I just know this is the sound I want right here. This is all I can tell you, you know? I do it with my mouth, and every musician in Memphis is on top of it. This is what I liked about Memphis. I didn't have to go in there trying to talk musician language to them. It's really kind of dumb that you don't know, and I didn't know, but they understood.

Within a year of the success of "Trapped by a Thing Called Love," the Royal had become one of the hottest recording centers in the South, producing hits like "Let's Stay Together" for Al Green, "Trying to Live My Life Without You" for Otis Clay, and "Breaking Up Somebody's Home" for Ann Peebles. A key ingredient in the success of Mitchell's productions was the distinctive sound he created: full, rich, and bottom-heavy, with the impeccable drumming of Howard Grimes (and on some sessions the late great former Stax drummer Al Jackson, Jr.) and the soulful backup vocals of Rhodes, Chalmers, and Rhodes providing easily-identifiable trademarks. Like nearby Stax, the studio was located in a former movie house (eponymously named the Royal). Many have attributed the beauty of the sound in the studios to the strong acoustics and sloping floors that had been a part of both theatres.

I often wonder is that old eight-track studio still in that building, 'cause that was the best sound I ever heard in my life. I know they built upstairs with a thirty-two-track, but that little bitty eight-track was the one that I did my recordings on. I often wonder what happened to those machines. Are they still there? Because I would love to just own that eight-track.

After a couple hit records out of Memphis, I moved on to another studio, 'cause Willie had Ann Peebles, then Al Green and O.V. Wright. He was pretty busy, and if I wanted the studio, sometimes I couldn't get it. So what we did was just moved on to another studio. I think it was Mark IV at the time, which is the studio that Isaac Hayes finally bought. We moved over there with Gene "Bowlegs" Miller doing the arrangements and used all the same musicians mostly. Unless Willie was using his musicians, I could use Teenie, Charles, anybody. We used them several times. Then I got [keyboardist and brother of Carla] Marvell Thomas and [guitarist] Michael Toles. That's where they came in. When we couldn't get Hi Rhythm, we would move on and get Marvell and Michael. So we didn't seem to lose anything. We lost maybe that Hi sound, but we still had a good sound. That was important. 'Cause at one point in time almost everything that was coming out of Hi sounded the same. You know, when the introduction hit off—it's kind of like Malaco—when they hit off, you just know Hi Records. Not saying that that was bad, 'cause Hi Records was what was happening. You know, Willie said, "If it's not broke, don't fix it. I'm not changing horses in the middle of the stream. I'm gonna ride this one till it fall dead." And I admired him for that, 'cause he stuck to his gun. I don't care how much sameness they said it was, he rode it until it fell dead.

For a short period following the success of "Trapped By a Thing Called Love," LaSalle effectively maintained a dual career: joint owner of Crajon Enterprises and a star soul performer. By 1974, however, she had split with Bill Jones, given up the company, and had left Chicago altogether.

My husband [was] a very nice man, but I think my career overshadowed him. He was lost. After I got hit records out, he got lost. You know, how can I be Denise LaSalle's husband? He felt like he was nobody, I guess. He was just a lost soul. You know, he was a chef by trade. He refused to work as a chef because he said, "Denise LaSalle's husband shouldn't be a chef." But now, what can you do? You gotta work somewhere; you gotta do something. And consequently he didn't know, so he started drinking. And so we just separated after that. He just went off into a state of alcohol, and we separated. Good man, nice person, and I'm sorry that happened to him. Only that could have driven me away from him, 'cause I loved him dearly. We got into that stage where there was no growth from him and he refused to grow, and I just moved. I just moved out of the house, car, everything. I just moved to Memphis. And just relocated, started all over again with nothing, rented me some furniture, put it in my apartment and everything. And finally he gave up the house and moved out. You know, everything worked out. We're good friends right now.

But anyway, that's that part. But then when I finally met [James] Wolfe—him being a disc jockey and all this stuff, we had a big long talk before we got married, and I told him I don't want my career to overshadow you like it did my ex. It's not important who makes the most money, to me. What's important is that we care about each other and we love each other. And you do what you do, and I do what I do. You can't be what you're not. You can't be a record producer just to prove that you got a part in my life, 'cause you don't know nothing about this, which is what my ex tried to do. He wanted to become all these things, and he couldn't do them, so just drinking, drinking, drinking. So that was over. But anyway, Wolfe and I talked about this, and he said, "Well, you know, I'm like this,"—he's a college graduate—"I've taught school before; now I'm a disc jockey, and I have my own little thing going, and that's what I intend to do. I don't intend to sit down on nobody." And so we talked about it. "Well, we could go ahead, we could get married if it's not going to interfere with you and now you can't interfere with me, because I got to do what I do. 'Cause this is all I know to do too, and I'm gonna do this."

So our careers complemented each other. So he's been right there for me, and I've been there for him.

The mid '70s brought other changes: LaSalle's contract with Westbound expired in 1975, and she decided not to renew, citing the label's distribution problems as the reason. The next year she signed with the much larger ABC label (then home to performers such as Isaac Hayes, Bobby Bland, and Rufus featuring Chaka Khan) and recorded the first of four albums (she would remain with the label once it was acquired by MCA in 1980 and release three more albums). As for letting go of Crajon Productions, LaSalle says that she got out just around the time it was getting harder for the small independent record label owner to survive.

You can't run a small company like that anymore. At that time, almost anybody that had the money could have their own label and produce their own records, and, if you were lucky, you could strike up on a distribution deal. After the demise of Motown in Detroit, it seemed that some big conglomerates had made up their mind that no African American would probably ever get that big again. I think somebody made that decision. High up. And they decided to prove that point.

I can tell you that when a young black person would develop a label and get a little momentum going, some big major company would come to you and make you an offer you can't refuse. 'Cause you have your record out there, and what you're doing is working it market by market. You basically would start in Mississippi, Alabama, Georgia, little bitty states at a time. You could never get it moved all around the country at one time 'cause you didn't have the money and you didn't have the manpower to move it around. No matter how you ship it out there, it was not going to get played because payola used to be very visible in those days, and you didn't have to do payola in the South. These guys were so glad to get your record they just played it. So anybody stopped by and paid attention to those poor little guys down in Alabama and Mississippi— they were just glad to shake your hand, glad you came by. In Nashville, Tennessee, John R.[7] You could go up there to Nashville, I could take John R. a record, and he'd just jump right up and play it while I'm sitting there. And I could drive down the highway and turn on the radio— he'd be playing it again. They was just like that, in those days. You could get those people in those small markets to do this for you.

So we would work it market by market. You'd just take whatever you could get. And these big conglomerates came up, and they'd say, "I like your product. I heard this record, I want to buy it. Who is that?" You got your record, they want to buy. Sometimes they'll make you a great big offer. They gonna tie you up, they want to tie your artists up: "For three years, we're gonna do this." I got bought up by Fantasy Records. Fantasy/Galaxy on Bill Coday. Fantasy/Galaxy on the Sequins.[8] Now I didn't have that problem with [her own releases on] Westbound 'cause they were a small company. So that's how *I* survived, okay? Fantasy/Galaxy didn't do no more for Coday and the Sequins than I had done. I got more records out of Coday's "Get Your Lie Straight." When I turned it over to Fantasy/Galaxy, that was the end of it. Came out with another one—end of it. I mean, they just throw it out there, no push, no nothin.' They didn't do nothin' for your artists, they didn't do nothin' for you—you got nothin.' So that's how they kill you. You're tied up now for the next—how many years? However long you signed that contract. You're tied up and you can't go nowhere, and you can't do nothin.' You haven't a leg to stand on. Oh, you want to cut another record? They'll fulfill their obligation, cut you another album. But the album ain't goin' nowhere, so why cut it? You end up bogged down, you owe them everything, you got no royalty coming, you can't go nowhere. So the little ten thousand, fifteen thousand dollars you got from them doesn't mean a hill of beans anymore. So you just got nothin.'

LaSalle's frustrations certainly have a base in reality. A company like the California-based Fantasy didn't have the understanding of the southern R&B market that was crucial to the success of artists like Bill Coday.

That's how we ended up in a bog with the Sequins and Coday. I got Coday back from Fantasy Records. I didn't realize that it was a conspiracy-type thing almost. I got Coday back, and I signed him with another label. I can't think of the name of it now—it was a CBS label, but it was a subsidiary. It was a song called "I'm Back to Collect."[9] I put that out on Coday, and Coday blew that himself. I didn't even get a chance to know what they would do for him. Because when I put that record out on him with them, it had jumped up on the R&B charts—number forty-something I think. And Coday had married a girl down in Macon, Georgia, who insisted that he not sign this piece of paper. You know, when you release an artist to a company, you have to have the artist's consent to do it. So [CBS] took our word for it that everything was cool, 'cause we had never had no problems with Coday, and everything *was* cool. Coday wouldn't never sign the paper that give us permission, so we lost the money because they were waiting on this paper to arrive before they would pay us the money for the lease of the record. But they went ahead and put the record on out. They pulled the record off the air and sent us the masters back, and we never got any money. That's the way it went down. Coday wouldn't sign it, and we lost the deal with him. We had him under contract, but we couldn't make him sign the thing, so it was nothing we could do. And we lost all that. It taught me a lesson: never do anything backwards. If you want this record out, you sign this thing—*then* we'll let the company have it. You learn. You live and you learn.

But running a company at that time, like I say, it was easier to run it if you run it yourself like we were doing. We may not have made a bunch of money, but we made our money even if it was city by city, little by little. All the sales came back to us. That was better than putting out to somebody else and you don't get nothin' back. But today, *today*, I don't think I would want a record label of my own. If I had one and had me on it, maybe we could get some airplay, but if you released somebody else, an unknown on your label like that, I think you'd catch hell. I don't think you'd get nowhere. Because I don't think it's any room out there.

In the days of the indie soul label, it was still possible for a two-person operation like Crajon to place records on the charts. LaSalle's work with Crajon gave her the kind of experience that would prove valuable during the mid to late '70s when she produced her own albums in Memphis for ABC.

You know, a lot of people have problems realizing, getting to the fact that I did it all—you know, write, produce, publish, and sing, and all that stuff. A lot of people had a real problem with that. As a matter of fact, I was asked one time to—I don't want to call names, but I was asked by ABC Records to produce a record on one of their male stars, and at that time we had quite a few on that label. We had Lenny Williams, Bobby Bland, B.B. King—just numerous people were on the label. A whole bunch of us were on there. But one of their male artists, they asked me if I would produce a record on him 'cause they liked what I was doing in Memphis. I was coming out of Memphis with some great stuff for them. And they said, "Would you do this and see what you could do for this person, and come up with some good songs for him and produce it yourself? Go ahead and do it." They were giving me $75,000 an album to produce my own album, and they gave me a budget like that to produce [the album on the male artist]. And this person said, "I don't want no woman producing me." So I never got a chance to show I could do it. They knew I could, 'cause they'd heard the work I'd done for Coday and stuff like that, and they knew I could work with other people singing. So I didn't get a chance to do it.

As her own producer, LaSalle recorded a steady stream of R&B hits during the first part of the '70s, most of which she wrote herself. "Now Run and Tell That," "A Man Sized Job" (both 1972),

"Trying to Forget About You" (1975), and "Married, But Not to Each Other" (1976) rank among the best R&B records of the decade. Many of her songs had a pronounced country feel, an association that LaSalle says is a product of the music she heard while growing up in Mississippi.[10] Country has always been an important element of LaSalle's songwriting. In 1992 she told Living Blues *magazine, "I write heavy, strong lyrics because that's what country music is, and I think I got that from them. . . . I feel country music more than I do any music there has ever been."*

As a child I listened to more country music than I did anything else. I'm greatly influenced by country singers. When I write songs, I have a very hard time sometimes trying to take the country out of my songs, because I would sit up and write them and I'd sing them and they'd sound country. Everybody said, "Well what are you doing country?" And then I kept on with it till I tried to make it sound more rhythm and blues-ish. I have a real hard time trying to get away from that. And it still comes out; it comes out in many songs that I write. My brother picks 'em out all the time. You've probably heard of him—Na Allen? He had records out once a long time ago. He had several records out, but they were never really big. Have you ever heard of Vee Allen? She had a record out called "Can I?" It was a very big record.[11] She was Al Perkins's sister. That was my brother that married her. They both could sing so beautiful. But they both were educators, and they did it more or less for a hobby. She has a Ph.D., cut that song, and it went all the way—she wouldn't even do any engagements. It was a smash, but she wouldn't tour, she wouldn't make pictures, she didn't want any problems. All she wanted to do was teach school or do whatever she was doing in the school system. And my brother was virtually the same way. If you want to go whole-heartedly, you have to give it all to one of those careers. I'm not sure that you can have success in your teaching career or anything like that fooling with entertainment, because I don't think it works. But anybody want to try it, I say go ahead and try it if you can handle it. But see now, she had the problem because she wouldn't entertain, so therefore her name was just wiped right out of the pages of history. Most people don't even remember who Vee Allen is, because she wouldn't be known. Now if you go and pick up some educational literature, she's got all kinds of writings and all kinds of stuff, as far as that is concerned. She made her mark in that world. As for me, I just wanted to be a little ole blues singer!

And I wanted to do country music. I didn't really have the voice to do real hard country, but on every album that I cut, there's usually a song that's country. I even went as far as to put steel guitar on a couple of tunes. I did "Harper Valley PTA" on my [*On the Loose*] album, and then I did "Two Empty Arms" on one of my ABC albums. And that's when I stopped trying to go completely country with a song. I decided to let a country flavor come in there, but I'm gonna still keep it R&B. Because when I did the [ABC] album, one critic wrote that the album was great, Denise did her best on all the tunes, but it sounds real funny to come off a total R&B album and climax with a country song. It was a big letdown, and he thought that I should have stuck to one of the two. He didn't appreciate it, I don't think. He was one of my critics, and so I said, "Well, I may not agree with him, but I have to respect his opinion." And I imagine it did sound funny. Anyway, I decided that I'm going to do my songs, and if some country influence come in there, let it be, but I'm not gonna try to do just a straight hard country album or country song no more, in the middle of an R&B album. If I'm going to do a country song, then just do the whole album country. I imagine that did sound funny, 'cause even a lot of black people said the same thing. They didn't like it either. "Why'd you put that on there?" I have a beautiful song on one of my last albums—I think it's the *Still Bad* album. You know that little song about, [sings] "She was 16 and on her own. . . ."

LaSalle is referring to "Child of the Ghetto" (1994), a moving composition about a single parent trying to provide a decent living for herself and her son.

Now is that country or not? To me, it's country. To me, I feel country. I don't know what you thought about it, but if you put a steel guitar on there, you would have a country song. When I sang it, you know who I could see singing that song? Every song I write, I almost can see somebody else singing it. Kathy Mattea. I betcha she could do the heck out of the song. Every time I hear it I think of her. I think of her when I sing that song.

In addition to the styles and themes of country music, LaSalle was also heavily influenced by Aretha Franklin, even though they are roughly the same age.

The people that I grew up with were like Dinah Washington, and I hate to say I grew up with Aretha—I didn't grow up with Aretha. 'Cause Aretha's probably as young as I am, or younger, I don't know. We're in there somewhere together. But I put it this way: Aretha had been singing—she was a big-time singer as a gospel singer with her dad. I wasn't even dreaming of singing then. You know, I was just working in Chicago. I was just singing in church, that's all. So when I started singing rhythm & blues, I was in my '20s. I didn't start as a kid with R&B. When Aretha's R&B record came out, I was still working at a dry cleaners. And I only was singing in church. And so I consider her a great influence on my career, because the voice I have now, I only have it because I've tried all my life to sound like Aretha, and I can't [laughs]. But every effort in me strives for Aretha. I mean, every song I sing I'd be pressing trying to curl my voice and do what Aretha does, and it won't come out that way. My voice decides to do what *it* wants to do! I want to go there, my voice says, "No, I'm going over *here.* This is where I can go, so this is as far as I'm going with you." Now I actually did develop my own style because I was *trying* to sound like Aretha.

Surprisingly, Aretha Franklin also inspired the spoken passages, or "raps," that LaSalle often incorporates into her songs.

Aretha Franklin is the reason [for the raps] and I've never heard her talk on a song. But she's the reason. Let me tell you how. I love to tell this story, it's funny—I get tickled myself when I think about it. In trying to go after Aretha, I would do all I could do with a song. And you know how on the end of most people's song in person, they ad-lib? They call it "souling." So on the end of songs Aretha goes through this high-powered ad-lib, but she does it in tune with a melody. She'd do all this with her voice, you know: [sings] "I love you baby, and I really do love you, and da, da, da" [imitates Aretha ad-libbing]. But I can't do that. I would try to do it, and my voice would just fail me. People would be looking at me, and it seemed as though they would be saying, "Why don't she just quit 'cause she ain't sounding good. Why don't she quit?" This is the way I would feel, because I would not get a rise out of my audience when I would try to do that on the end of my songs. So I said, "Well, I have more I want to say." I want to talk about this man, I want to tell him how much I love him, I want to tell him what he did to me or how I don't like what he did to me or something. Instead of me trying to do it in tune, [claps hands] I'd break the band down and start telling him, talking. [Laughs.] I'd get to talking that stuff, and I'd get to saying everything that I wanted to say in regards to what the song say he did to me. I want to tell him off and tell him about himself or whatever, and that would get the people hollering, "Yeah! Right on!" When that happened for me, I realized, "Hey, I got something here. This is it. I can't sing it, but I can talk it." I'd get my point over that way. Sometimes a song didn't have a lot of ending that I could do that rap on, I couldn't think of too much to do. So I would do a rap in front of the song. I would just talk about it, lead into it—in other words, explain to you *why* I'm singing this song. I'll tell you what this man did to me and what I'm not gonna want to take from him and why I'm singing this song, so this is what I want to tell him today, and then I started singing.

As LaSalle suggests, her raps (which have been more prominent on her records since her late '70s work on ABC) often focus on the dynamics of male-female relations. Also key to the popularity of her raps is her occasional insertion of a mildly raunchy bit of dialogue. For example, in "Workin' Overtime" (from Under the Influence, *1978), one of her best songs, she breaks off in the middle of her performance to announce, "I want to have a little talk with all of the ladies out there. I want to ask you just one question: how many times did your man call you up lately to tell you that he had to work overtime?" She then begins to explain her own situation: "Well you see, my man used to call me up every day with the same old shit. But it's a funny thing about him workin' overtime, because his paycheck seemed to be gettin' smaller instead of gettin' bigger."*

It started working for me. I'd been doing it on stage all the time, but I started incorporating it on records. At first I was real clean with it. I would just say it, and I would never do anything dirty with it because society didn't allow that dirty stuff on the record then. Then I was on a show with—now I'm not gonna say that Millie [Jackson] got this talking from me, I would not say that. But I had worked shows with her, and she wasn't talking. And I was, 'cause that's all I could do [laughs]. And then I'd notice that she was talking. I had only done a couple shows with her, and she was really singing and I didn't hear her talk. I don't know who started, but I know I was talking ever since I started singing, 'cause I couldn't do what other people would do, and I would just talk. And that's been since the beginning of my career before I ever cut a record. I was always onstage talking.

And then people have had a problem distinguishing me and Betty Wright or me and Millie Jackson, but that's because of the talking. It's not because of the singing, 'cause when Betty Wright starts singing, you know that's not me. When Millie Jackson starts singing, you know *that's* not me. But when they hear all this controversial talk we do, you know, they'll have a problem trying to distinguish whether or not it's the two of us.

As LaSalle attests, it is the subject matter of the raps that invites comparison to Millie Jackson. Too often, however, writers have tended to overstate the similarity. Unlike Jackson, LaSalle prefers innuendo to explicitness (LaSalle has never even come close to the likes of Jackson's pornographic tour de force "Lovers and Girlfriends," for example). Also, LaSalle's persona is more good-natured in general. One sometimes suspects that Jackson is contemptuous of her audience, confronting it with bald antagonism. LaSalle, on the other hand, is a warm, wry humorist whose work evinces a real talent for detailed observation of the ins and outs of romantic relationships. For example, in her own composition, "Learning How to Cheat on You" (1986), she makes it clear that she is out for equality and respect, not revenge: "You told me that a woman's place was in the home/I don't mind staying home, but I sure don't have to be alone/You said there was so much that I still had to learn/Well, I think I learned my lesson, and now it's gonna be my turn." The core motivation for LaSalle's character to cheat on her husband is not so much a "tit-for-tat" ethic, but the frustration that results from the age-old belief system that grants the husband his freedom while pressuring the wife to remain at home.

Since so many of LaSalle's protagonists are strong women who refuse to stand for social or sexual subjection, it is interesting to consider how her songwriting reflects elements of feminist thought. LaSalle's own personal take on the feminist movement is, however, somewhat different from the attitudes of the characters in her songs.

A lot of feminists have the idea that they want to do everything a man does, but I don't think that it should mean that you got to carry a mill sack to prove that I'm good as a man. I don't know how to put this . . . I believe in being a woman. I don't want to be a man. I don't want to do a man's job, I want to do a woman's job. I like cooking, I like fixing my man's meal, I like bringing it to the bed. I *like* that. Now you may have took it that I meant the feminist movement like these women have, talking about carrying mill sacks and driving Greyhound buses and doing this and doing that. I believe in equal pay for equal work, but if a woman work on a job that she can't handle this job—she got to call a man to help her lift this sack—then she has no right to get the same pay he's getting, if he's got to help her lift this sack, you know what I'm saying? But if she can lift this sack as good as he can, and she can throw as many sacks up there on the dock as he can, then she should get paid the same thing he gets paid. But I don't believe in women going to fighting in no wars—I don't believe in that kind of stuff. Now if they go to service, I think they should do a lady-like job. I don't know if I'm contradicting what I say in my songs. I feel like if a man has a right to cheat and not be called a whore, then I think a woman has a right to cheat and not be called a whore. Now, that's the way I am about that. Like they'll say, "Oh, he's a playboy." But she's not a playgirl—she's gonna be a ho'. And I think that's a double-standard right there. I don't think that's right. I think it's right for *both* to be true to each other. That's the way I feel about that part of it.

Now in my songs, I say, "If you do this to me, I'll do that to you. You want to mess around on me, I'll play around on you." I'll say that because I believe that. I believe *in* that [laughs]. But I also tell women on my shows a lot of times, "Look. A lot of this stuff that I'll be talking up here on stage will mess around and get your butt kicked. So y'all be careful what you go home and say to your man, do to your man. Make sure you can back up what you say, 'cause I don't talk to my man like this. This is just a show I'm doing." And I'll do that a lot of times, because a lot of times I'll say some things, and people will say, "I did this, I did this." I say, "Well honey, you better be careful what you do, 'cause I don't talk to my man like that. 'Cause actually, I'm just doing a show now. This is all about a show. This is not the way I treat him." Now I will be honest with people about that, because I believe in being a feminine female. I don't want to be a masculine female. When I was talking about cheating and going on like that—of course people cheat, but I don't tell people, "Just because he's cheating on you, cheat on him." I say it in songs, but I don't really mean that. Not from my heart, I don't mean it, because I don't think you have a right to just do wrong because somebody else is doing wrong. In my heart, this is the way I am. But my song might say different because I'm really just saying what I know people want to hear [laughs]. When I write these songs, I know what make people buy your record, and I write the songs that make people buy your records, not because this is what I'm gonna do.

LaSalle, who probably counts more women than men among her fans, has often been unaware of how much influence she conveys through her records.

People actually believe what Denise LaSalle says. I have people come to me and tell me I straightened out their life, that I was the cause of them being able to get their lives together, and so people believe what I say. And I'm sorry that they do all the time, because it's not always meant to be that way. It's more or less like a movie. You make a movie and you don't intend to influence the world with it. You make it a form of entertainment. That's the reason I try to be careful what I sing now. I *have* kind of toned my stuff down a little bit to try to be careful what I say. I realized how influential some of my stuff was. If you notice on my last album [1997's *Smokin' in Bed*], there may be a little change in the way I talk. I try not to be so controversial, 'cause you realize you're leading so many people, and there's so many young people out here already going in the wrong direction, so I'm trying to change the way I'm talking and doing things. A little more on the positive side, instead of being so negative.

I just keep telling stories about what happens to other people, not necessarily to me.

When people meet me, they're really surprised at me. Somebody says to me one day, "So look at her, she's shy." And I said, "I'm not really shy, but it's just that people expect me to be, 'Aw tell that m-f so and so. Come on in here you son of a so-and-so!' " They expect this from me because I might say something like that on a record. And they'll sit down and talk to me, and a curse word never come out of my mouth, and they're shocked. And then they find out I'm a very religious person, and that shocks them too. You know, they go, "Well how do you do . . . ?" I say, because on stage, I'm performing. I'm doing a job. And I say, "If I was picking and chopping cotton out in a field somewhere, that's not serving God. That's working to make a living." So I can do that and still feel that I'm safe to do this. So I feel very comfortable with where I am and, hey, my husband's a minister now, and he's not against my career at all. A lot of people say, "Well, what are you going to do now? You gonna quit singing the blues?" I say, "Of course, I'm gonna quit singing the blues one day. Whenever the time is right and I feel it's right, I'm gonna quit singing the blues."

I'm getting ready to cut a gospel album, by the way. But I'm still doing performances and so on. My husband—there's no pressure on me from him. He is my number-one fan, and he's with me whatever I choose to do. He stands behind me one hundred percent. But he understands where I'm coming from, 'cause he's always known me to be what I am. I grew up in a church family, very religious—two ministers in my family and all of us sang in church choirs and groups, and I sang with a gospel quartet in Chicago, so, hey, I've been there all the time. Just like Aretha. I was listening to a bio on TV last night—they had the black history month legends. I was listening to her, and I said, "Oh, that sounds just like me." You know, the way she was talking about where she's been in her life and where her roots are and how she feels inside and where she's coming from. And I can relate very much to that, because that's exactly the way I feel about life. And I'm gonna do my first gospel album.

I probably won't cut any more blues records, maybe. I may not. My plan is to finish my concerts, and if I get any concert offers, I'll do them, but I may not cut any more blues records. I'm not sure of that. I don't want to say that that's definite, because I don't like to lie. I'm a very funny person about lying. I don't like to lie. I don't want to say never, but I'm gonna say right now I have plans to do gospel, and if this gospel turn out to be what I hope it will be, then I can go on from there and don't have to cut any more blues. I hope that the name Denise LaSalle would mean enough to my fans that I can carry them one way or the other. 'Cause the first thing I believe, and I know for a fact, that the same people that go to blues concerts are the same people that go to gospel concerts. Now there are some people that don't go to blues concerts that go to gospel concerts, and I feel like I can keep my blues fans in gospel and then gain some gospel fans that don't go to blues concerts, so I feel that my audience should grow. And I don't feel that my fans should feel that I've let them down. I think they should probably feel that I've elevated them up, because I don't feel that gospel is a down. And this has always been my destination. I've always known that one day I would come back to gospel. It's always been there. I always knew, no matter where I go and what I do, one day I was going to sing gospel again.

And you know, with me not having that shouting voice, that Aretha-style, Shirley Caesar-style voice, I always doubted myself as a gospel singer for some reason. I always wanted that kind of voice, and I always said, "I'll never make it as a gospel singer with this voice I have." I don't know why I thought I could probably make it as an R&B singer with this voice. I guess it's because I heard a lot of simple R&B singers. I heard a lot of singers that didn't have the powerful voice that made it on little soft hit records. And maybe that's why I had the belief in making it in this field. A lot of soft singers have made it in this field—Barbara Mason, for instance. But most gospel singers that make it big have power. I always felt that God was molding me for gospel. I've said this before to several people. I said, "Oh, one day I know I'll go back to gospel." I think God will let me know when that time is right to go and I think he's fixing me so I can hold my own in the gospel field. And I feel that now with the name I have, the recognition that I have as being who I am, I feel if I cut a gospel record, then I think I could make an impact somehow, because I now know how to tell a story. I don't have to be a powerhouse with a voice, but I can tell a story. God has given me that talent to be able to be one of those storytellers, and I can do that. And I might as well tell it about Him, as to tell it about anybody else.

It's unlikely that the proposed gospel album will be recorded for Malaco, her record company of fifteen years (even though Malaco has a successful gospel division). Although LaSalle's recent album, Smokin' in Bed, *has sold well, she emphasizes that her contract with Malaco is up and that she probably won't re-sign. In particular, she is frustrated by what she feels is the company's unimaginative marketing strategy.*

You listened to *Smokin' in Bed,* I know you heard it all. I don't think there's a tune on there that's short-stepping. Not one. Any tune that they pulled off and decided to play could have made my album just as popular as the others. For instance, the two hip-hop tunes. My husband—to prove my point—that's all he would play in Jackson [on his radio station]. That's all that was heard here. And that album sold like hotcakes in this area. I mean, people were running over each other trying to get a copy of it, as a result of "If I Don't Holler" and "Never Been Touched." My husband did it to prove a point to Malaco. If you put these records out as a single—either one of these records—you would pull in a whole different audience. I said to Malaco, "I already have the R&B people in my hand. They're in the palm of my hand. They're there for me, I don't care what album I come out with. But now, if you want to ever get a big record on me, you've got to tap another market." I haven't had a super-big hit since "Don't Mess With My Tu-Tu" [1985]. Because "My Tu-Tu" reached over into the young market, the pop market and everything. It generated a bigger, broader audience. Because see, Malaco don't do nothin' for nobody. Malaco just sends the record out there. They're not into trying to give the DJs anything.

So anyway, I haven't captured that young market again since. I had it with this album [sings] "Never been touched like this. . . ." That song, and [sings] "If I don't holler. . . ." Boy, kids was standing up there. Malaco didn't even believe me. They thought I was hyping the record: "Y'all are probably playing it every thirty minutes." I said, "Look, you know the problem with you all is can't nobody tell you nothin.' We put the record out on the air before there were ever records anywhere." We went down to Malaco and picked up some copies and brought it here and put it on the air [Kix96, the R&B station in Jackson she and Wolfe own]. And then we didn't have any to sell, so I had to make [another] trip down to Malaco to get some copies that they had—the DJ copies. I sold 'em [laughs]. They're supposed to be sending them out—I had to sell them. People were breaking our door down. There are only two major record shops here, Cat's Music and Camelot, and they were trying to get them, and nobody had them. I went to Malaco and got 'em myself, brought 'em here, and sold 'em. We put them on for sale at the radio station. I guess we sold about a thousand out the radio station before Cat's even got theirs in.

But we've had to tell Malaco—my husband and I would be *embarrassed* to put my songs on the air that much. Because we've got to live here in Jackson. And we wouldn't want people saying we're pushing Denise LaSalle down their throats. We wouldn't do that. We put the record in regular rotation. It didn't get played no more than anybody's else's record. There was no advertisement promoting the album or nothing. Just this: when you play that record the phone would just light up. "Where can I get it? Where can I get it?" But you couldn't tell Malaco nothin.' When they came out with the record, they wouldn't even release a single. We told them, "If you just release the single, send it to the radio stations as a single, make every DJ play one of these tunes only, then all the momentum would be on that tune. Then when the album comes out, they'll buy the album. And then that'll give us some other tunes to work later as a single." 'Cause you know if you send the album to the DJs they're gonna play the bluesy stuff. That's what they're gonna play. 'Cause if the first track was the hip-hop, they wasn't gonna play it. They going to definitely play blues, and they went "Smokin' in Bed," "Going Through Changes," "Why Am I Missing You," "Blues Party Tonight," and they played all over the album. And see that hurts. That hurts. What can you come back with as another release now for them to play? They've played 'em all! 'Cause you've sent 'em the whole album!

LaSalle can't help but compare Smokin' In Bed *to Johnnie Taylor's* Good Love! *album, which was released in 1996 and has gone on to become a big seller for Malaco.*

When Malaco did Johnnie Taylor's album, they sent out his "Good Love!" [single] only. They wouldn't release the album to the radio stations. Then they came back with a slow one to the radio stations, then they came back with that blues thing. They did Johnnie Taylor like they should have done me. They sent my album to the DJs; they sent Johnnie Taylor's single to the DJs. They don't have enough confidence in me. 'Cause Malaco told me my whole album was a dud. They told me I didn't have nothin.' Malaco listened to my whole album, they didn't like but one tune on my album—"Smokin' in Bed." They said, "That's the only hit you got on there." I said, "I heard that." They said, "Well, you come down here. We want you to cut some more tunes." I went down there, and I cut five. I listened to the five that I cut. I said, "You know what, 'Blues Party Tonight,' 'Juke Joint Woman,' and that Rich Cason tune, these are the only three I like. If you put any of them on my album, then I'm gonna pick the ones that I would let go off the album, because I don't want you to touch nothin' else, 'cause I know they're all right." But they told me I didn't have nothin.' And the most-played tunes on the album are the ones I had already. Those are the tunes that everybody comes to the stores to buy.

LaSalle's insights into the ways of disc jockeys and radio stations are based on solid experience— Kix96 is one of the most successful stations in Jackson. The couple now owns two other stations (all three are housed in the same building), one devoted to "soft rock" and the other to gospel. The decision to buy the first station came after a period in which Wolfe, a disc jockey by trade, had left the field.

We owned a nightclub at one time, but then we got out of the nightclub business and [Wolfe] was right back to all the radio stations, begging for a position on everybody's station. All of the stations were country in this area—country and rock—and they would only give him 10:00 [p.m.] to 2:00 a.m. That's the only hours they would ever give him on a radio station. And he would fight and he tried to force them into a 6:00 [p.m.] drive time. You can't force these people into giving you spots on their station. This is their station. Why don't you try to get your own station? 'Cause his ambition had always been to own a radio station, but not knowing how to get one. And he kept saying, "I'd like to own a station one day, I'd like to own a station one day." But talking, this is lip service. Let's put some action behind this talk. Stop worrying these people about their station and try to get your own. I said, "Ain't no such thing as we can't do it—we *can* do it."

He started searching, trying to find out how to do it. It took us five years to find out how to get a radio station, and we finally, through a lot of efforts and prayers, got the station, which he didn't want—he wanted it to be a total black station. I said, "Look, let me tell you something. If you can't get in the door one way, you can get in another. So step back and let somebody else help you get in that door. Once you get in there, then you do your thing." So we had three partners, all white. We did not own fifty-one percent of the company. We had to take a back seat to get in it. No, we never stopped trying. They outvoted us every time on everything that they wanted to do. Then one of the guys got kind of sick and had skin cancer and wanted to kind of lay back and get out of it. We said, "How much do you want for your share?" And he quoted a figure that he didn't think we could probably make, I guess. I put it down on the desk for him. He says to me, "I want more money than that." I said, "No, no, no, no, a deal is a deal. You told me you wanted x amount of dollars for your share. Here's the x amount of dollars for your share. Now this is a deal we made. You're gonna be one of those kind? You're gonna go back on the deal?" He don't want that. He reluctantly went on and let us have it.

So we got it, got his part. That put us in the driver's seat. So we bought everybody out. We got one white guy still in there, he owns twelve percent. That's the first station, the 1984 station. Since then my husband and I have purchased WZDQ, which is the white rock station, and the gospel station. That's ours totally. My husband's doing a magnificent job at the station. We come in number one in the Arbitron rating every year, every time. We're the highest-rated station here.

LaSalle and Wolfe maintain a high profile within the community. As Wolfe and I were standing outside after a post-interview tour of the Kix96 offices, our discussion was interrupted several times as he responded to the numerous honks of recognition from cars passing by in the street. Wolfe, a friendly and soft-spoken man, responded with a nod and a smile to every one. LaSalle says that she and Wolfe are committed to creating work opportunities within the Jackson community.

We've done more, I think, with so little, than most people have done with so much, because you won't find Mercedes Benzes and Rolls Royces and things around this house, and all kinds of diamonds and furs and stuff. You'll find what an average person would buy. And this is the way we choose to live. My husband and I have this thing about trying to promote job opportunities for other people, instead of just, "I got this and I'm gonna live this way." We've always tried to make jobs, create jobs, because we have in our heads that black people can do better if everybody would try to create a place to help somebody else. And you've got so many selfish people in the world that are so selfish with what they do, and that hurts. And everybody's scared that somebody's gonna take something. Well, we can't run everything. We know that we've got this station—we can't run it and all these things. We got to let somebody else be in charge of some things, but so many people are so scared somebody's gonna take stuff from them that they got to be the whole show or nothing at all. And that's bad, when you're that way. We eat more food than anybody in the world—we black folk, we eat more food than anybody, I would say. How do we not own a chain of supermarkets? I look at that kind of stuff.

And Bill Cosby and all these people. God knows he's a very generous man. Donates, donates, donates. *Donates.* Donating is not creating jobs. Donating is helping people do without a lot of things. Okay, I can sit here and I can donate food to a bunch of folk over there that's in need. They come and get this food and they eat it, but they still don't have no job. I get so upset because I want to say this to somebody, and I don't have anybody to say it to. I don't know Bill Cosby, I don't know Oprah Winfrey, I don't know Michael Jackson. I don't know these people. You've got all of this money. Now Bill Cosby does great things. Spelman College, a million dollars a year. That's great for education. You're saying, "Educate these people." You educate these people, they're coming out of school with all this education and no place to work. People don't have no place to work, okay? We wear clothes. Why aren't there big manufacturing companies? Michael Jordan got his own line. Who's manufacturing it? Why is there not a black manufacturing company manufacturing his stuff? It could happen. Somebody could do it. They got the money to do it. And these people got enough money that people couldn't run over them, you know what I'm saying? They could run over me—I ain't got nothin.' But how could you run over Oprah Winfrey, with all the money she's got? You've got to reckon with her. She's got some money. I mean, she's making jobs for those people right there in Chicago. That's fine, but as a national thing, if Bill Cosby, Oprah Winfrey, Michael Jackson, and a whole bunch of other black folk that's got millions of dollars, if they came together and said, "We're gonna have a grocery chain like Kroger," you couldn't beat it. If they really wanted to.

I feel like they're scared somebody's gonna rip 'em off. You got a bunch of folk out there gonna go sour with their money and not gonna run the stores right, but I think you could find qualified people. They got qualified managers out here everywhere, running Kroger stores and all the other stores. You could find them. I'm not gonna say that they won't take a little bit from you, 'cause most people get their hand in money find a way to get some of it anyway. Most people find a way. If they get their hands on some money, they'll find a way to get some of it from you. But that goes for white, black, anybody. There's gonna be some embezzlement in the world but, you know, you can find some honest people. There are some honest people in the world. And everybody's not gonna do that to you, so why be so negative? I don't understand it. I guess you could find that, deep down inside, I hurt a lot. I hurt for my people. I hurt. Because I see so much that could be done, if only I knew how to do it. If I could do it, if I had any say-so or any power.

In another attempt to promote the city's economy, LaSalle operated Denise LaSalle's Wigs and Souvenir Shop for many years in downtown Jackson.

My husband and I, right now, we try to make a difference where we can. I believe in one step at a time. I believe you help where you can help. I kept my wig store open for all those years—and I really didn't want to let go—trying to create jobs, and I realized it was just going in the hole. I was just losing money, and I just said, "Well, it's not worth it if I just keep losing money like this." I kept thinking I could probably bail it out. I catered to the chemotherapy people, you know, discounts—thirty percent off on wigs and stuff like that. I did a lot of stuff to try to help with things like that. It's Blake shoe store down there in my building now. We have a building down there that I had been in. We rented it all out. My husband and I own the building the station is in; we own the building next to it. We've got a job-training program in the building next door—JTPA. They train people how to be interviewed. You know people that don't know how to interview and fill out application stuff—that's what's over there.

And then my husband has this church. West Jackson Baptist Church moved, and they have this huge church over on Deaderick Street that my husband is in the process of getting now. And it has a school on the back where West Baptist had a day-care center and a kindergarten on it. So my husband and I are using the school. We're planning to have day care center a part of it, and the rest of it is going to be a school for the kids. We have a problem here that I'm totally in disagreement with. When a child does something in school, they suspend them from school and kick them out on the streets with nothing to do. And these kids are out here up and down the street with nothing to do but watch television and get into stuff. And I disagree with that. So my husband and I decided that in a part of this school, if the kids get suspended [from regular school], their alternative is going to be they have to come there. And we'll have qualified teachers to see to it that these kids are taught with a strenuous curriculum over there. We don't want to make it easy for them over there; we want them to want to stay in regular school. 'Cause I feel that the school board is missing the point, because I feel the school board should say, "Okay. So you've done this. Now here's a part of the regular school set aside to kids that's been suspended." And you have a program over here, you put more work on them than you put on them over there. And no matter what they say or do, they can't leave; they've got to do this work. This is what I think would make kids do better in school. What child wouldn't most-time be glad to get out and walk the street? No supervision, Mom and Dad at work. They come home and do anything they want to do.

To my surprise, this is the exact moment that LaSalle's seventeen-year-old son and his schoolmate walk in the front door. LaSalle's reaction to their entrance is ebullient and gracious: "Well, hello! Hi, boys! Come on in and meet. . . ." She gives her son a hug and kiss and then good-naturedly chides his friend for not offering to do the same: "You too!" she says, laughing (he complies).

After the teenagers leave to do some work in the family's basement recording studio, LaSalle and I get back to talking about her music. We soon touch upon a contentious subject. Since the early '80s, LaSalle and other soul artists of the '60s and '70s have found themselves in a strange situation: their music—the same style of music they have performed since the '60s—has become subsumed under the category of "blues," while most hard-core blues fans view their music as a diluted, inferior mutation of traditional blues. This paradox (one that LaSalle and most of her labelmates at Malaco are forced to deal with every time they try to book a gig or attend an awards ceremony) has evolved through changes in marketing trends. As southern soul ceased to be at the vanguard of popular music, it began to be lumped into a category with other types of "roots music" (a term used to connote older, more venerable musical styles) such as blues. Although she does not consider herself solely a blues artist, LaSalle's albums (along with those by the likes of Tyrone Davis, Shirley Brown, and Johnnie Taylor) can usually be found only in the "blues" sections of record stores. At the same time, the few disc jockeys who play blues (mostly for college or public radio stations) tend to be purists who avoid what LaSalle terms "soul-blues."

I'm sure different from most artists, you know. A lot of artists may say the same thing I'm saying, I don't know. 'Cause I don't talk to them, I haven't got deep with them, you know. We see each other in passing and that's it, but my feeling is that I resent being put in a category that really isn't a category. I'm in a place where there is no category. I'm forced into it. All my life, during my Westbound career, ABC, MCA, I was considered an R&B singer. And all of a sudden disco came in and everybody got crazy. And Malaco said, "Well, hey, can you sing the blues?" I said, "I don't know. I've never done blues." They said, "Well, you might could sing blues." Malaco is—they are smart people in some ways and not so smart in others. They are smart enough to only want an artist that has made a name for themselves. They want to pick up a has-been, somebody who's on the down. They know you got fans, and anything they put out on you is gonna sell. They can't lose with you. They're not gonna spend but so much money on your album anyway, so if they get anything else out of it it's gravy. Therefore, they don't push it 'cause they make their money back and always make a little bit on the side. That's why they do that. But if they were just a little bit smarter, I would think they would make so much more. I think they could.

But I was pushed into the blues category because I signed with Malaco. And all of a sudden, you're no longer an R&B singer. You're a blues singer now. Like my first album on Malaco, *Lady in the Street* (1983)—I cut "Please Don't Mess With my Man" and "Down Home Blues" just to prove to Malaco that I could do a blues. The only two blues on the whole album. Everything else is what I've been doing all the time. That Frank Johnson tune, "Lay Me Down," that's the same kind of stuff as "We're Married But Not to Each Other." That's just soul music. And from that point on I couldn't get played on no major radio stations, because now I'm a blues singer, and Malaco don't get played on here because we don't play Malaco Records 'cause they ain't got nothin' but blues artists. So I got pushed over here, okay? And then you got stations like the station in Little Rock [a traditional blues station] that don't play nothing but blues, and when they play the blues, they'll play T-Bone Walker, and then they'll always give you history on the people; they talk and tell you about them. Real serious blues. You think they'll play a Denise LaSalle record? No! 'Cause she's not blues.

And then when you go to the Grammys, who they put in a blues category is going to be KoKo Taylor, Etta James, and people I ain't never heard of before. People that never seen a record on a major radio station in their life. And they're in the Grammys. And then they'll put a white girl up that ain't nobody ever heard of but white folk. And KoKo Taylor performs mainly to white audiences. They'll pull these people and put them together and they'll ignore me over here. Then they go to the soul music; I'm *ignored* there. Then we'll go to the pop music; I'm ignored there. You go to R&B, I'm ignored there. So what am I? I'm nowhere. So I say, "Well okay, so I'm not a blues singer, y'all say." But the R&B people say, "You're a blues singer." And then the blues singers say, "You're not a blues singer, you're R&B." So I'm here in this middle of nowhere. And I say, "OK. I'm a soul-blues singer." I'm a soul-blues singer. Why can't I get someone to see that? And every time I'm interviewed I say, "I am a soul-blues singer." I cannot get people to recognize that terminology. Give me a category. I deserve it. They pushed Tyrone Davis out. He's in the same category I'm in. They pushed Johnnie Taylor, they pushed Shirley Brown out, we're all out here, and we have no category. They call us blues singers. Blues folk don't want us! They don't want us. I can hardly get a gig in a white club. They don't want me. I don't [imitates KoKo Taylor's growl] and yell like KoKo. I don't know. Somebody can sit down and take an old guitar, pat their feet, and have a harmonica player playing over his shoulder and get more recognition than I'll get any day.

I was nominated for a Handy Award last year. My husband went one year; I didn't win nothing. My husband said, "Denise, they got to give it to you this year. You've got the best album you've had in I don't know when. They've *got* to give you an award." I go to the Handy Awards. I sit there to watch my name come up three times: Album of the Year, Entertainer of the Year, and Best Record of the Year. And I lost every category. Had a little white girl—can't think of her name. She sits down in the chair and plays the guitar and sings and put her legs up like this. That's what she's doin,' and they call it blues. And Pinetop Perkins and these people like this and these old folk that's about to fall down. I guess age doesn't matter, but I just don't understand. Some of these people haven't had a record played since when. That's who they think is called blues singers. That's what they want, and that's what they think. For instance, I bet you right now [Alligator Records owner] Bruce Iglauer wouldn't even want me as an artist. I guarantee it. I bet he wouldn't want me as an artist. I wouldn't be in his category, 'cause he's not into the kind of blues I sing. I would have to change altogether to be that kind of blues singer.

I did a show for KoKo's daughter in Chicago recently in her club, and I asked [KoKo] to come back and give me a return visit, so she played for Kix96's anniversary, which was just on the seventh of February. I brought KoKo in—the first time she ever played for anybody black in ten or fifteen years. And she says, "Girlfriend,

I'm gonna do this for you, but you know, most black folks don't want me, so therefore I don't play for them. They don't want me, and I don't care. I'm gonna make my money over there where the people appreciate me." And I said, "Well, hey, I want you. 'Cause I think it's time for our people to stop ignoring their heritage." This is where blues started; it doesn't mean that it can't advance and move on to something else, but I want to show people where we come from. This is one style of blues, and I do another style, so we were all on one show. The Dramatics was on this show, KoKo Taylor, and me. And ahead of us was a rap group, and my son performed with the rap group. We had all this going for us that night, so we had something for everybody. It was a night to remember. It was great, it was great. We gave the people all segments of music that they could really identify with. We had young people there, old people there, and everything. I just think we should just accept music as music.

In spite of her frustrations, LaSalle says she is deeply thankful for the success she has enjoyed over the years. Chiefly, she credits her faith for getting her through the rough periods in her life.

I feel so proud of how people have stuck by me through the years. I'm very pleased, and I'm just grateful that I've had this success. I don't know, sometimes you say nowhere else but in the United States could you have this kind of success. I don't know whether other countries could do it or not, but I just feel privileged just being here, in this country. I've done so much with so little, I feel. I feel like I've done a lot with so little. 'Cause I really feel I have a little talent, but I feel that God has manifested. God has blessed me to be able to do what I can do with it. And the money I've made in my lifetime has been very minor compared to other artists, and I just think God is behind every fiber of my being. I believe that from the bottom of my heart. I believe that it's my faith and trust in God that has brought me where I am today, because I look at guys like Isaac Hayes—they have gone through so much money. Oh, God, if I'd had the money those people have had. I often wonder would I have handled it any better. But the fact that I've never had very much and come from such poor background, somehow—I guess faith in God, and putting all my confidence in Him.

I didn't ever tell you this story, but before I ever took the chance to go down and sign with Chess Records, I had to have a revelation before I went down there. I had to have a revelation. I never would have darkened that door, 'cause I didn't have any confidence in making it, and I had a revelation that got me to get up and go down there and sign that contract with Chess the first time. And it was a thing that

I felt was God talking to me. Some people say, "Well, God don't tell you to do that." I even have a sister that's very religious: "God wouldn't tell you to go sign no contract to sing the blues." I said, "Well, I don't know what plans God has for me, but I didn't pray and ask nobody else to show me." I had been very, very sick and had been working on my feet for years, and I stayed in the doctor's office all the time because I had problems because of the kind of jobs I was doing. Uneducated and only could do manual labor. And I just started praying and asking the Lord, "Show me a better way. Show me a way I can make a living without this." I mean, I got to do this because I thought I was gonna die soon. I didn't think I was gonna live very long after what was happening to me. Things I can't go into detail with. Some things were happening to me—I just thought that I wasn't going to live too long if I had to continue to work on those jobs I was on. And I prayed and asked the Lord to show me a better way to make a living.

So all of a sudden this opportunity came, and I said flat *no.* "I can't sing by myself. I've only sung with choirs and with groups. I can't sing alone." And I was in my bed, and I felt a weight on the side of my bed. I was single—I didn't have nobody in the house with me. I felt a weight as though someone sat down on the side of my bed. Have you ever been half-asleep and half-awake and you was trying to wake up because you felt like somebody was in the room with you and you tried to move a foot or anything? If you could just move your finger, you could wake up, and you can't wake up. I was trying to wake up 'cause I knew somebody was in the room with me, and I couldn't move. And a voice said to me, just as clear as I'm talking right now, "You asked me for a better way to make a living, and now that you have the opportunity, you won't take it." And I mean, it's just like somebody spoke that to me. And the minute that voice said it, I woke up. And I started looking around—there was nobody—and I got up and walked through my three-room apartment looking, and there was nothing. It scared me, it shocked me, and I just started praying. I started praying.

The next day I went to my job—a barmaid in a lounge—and a young man that came in and talked to me every day, I was telling him, "Man, Chess Records want me to come down and sign a contract, and I am scared to death, I am petrified." He said, "Why are you so scared?" I said, "'Cause I can't sing by myself." He said, "Yes, you can. Yes, you can." And I said, "No, I can't." He said, "Stop telling yourself you can't. I've got a book I'm going to bring you." All these things was just coming. This boy brought me a book called *The Power of Positive Thinking.* And he said, "I've got another book I want you to get, *The Power of Prayer.*" *The Power of Positive Thinking* is by Norman Vincent Peale, and the other one is Napoleon Hill. He gave me one; I bought the other one. I read those books. I told you I was an avid reader—I used to read all the time. I went through those books just like that [snaps fingers]. I went right through it. I read that book, honey, I called Billy Emerson, told him, "I'm ready to go to Chess. I'm gonna take a chance." And I started applying the power of positive thinking in my life. I started dealing with it. I prayed on it every day. I dealt with it, and I dealt with it, and I dealt with it. I psyched myself up: "I can do this! Yes I can!" And I'd just go out and try. And that's how I got where I am today.

After the interview LaSalle gives me a tour of her home, showing me some of her original artwork (she took up painting a number of years ago after returning from a Caribbean cruise) and the basement studio she and Wolfe have constructed for their son, who has been recording with his rap group. LaSalle seems happy with the interest her son has shown in music, although she has told him he needs to tone down his lyrics if he expects to get airplay ("After all, I had to."). LaSalle is devoted to her son, explaining that he is the reason she tours less than she used to.

Ever since my son was born in 1980, I really curbed my traveling and stuff then. I used to go to Europe a lot. I *could* take some trips out to California and stuff. I may be gone two weeks; that'd be just about the extent of my traveling. My son is seventeen years old now, so I could stay as long as I want to. But he's in high school right now, and I don't like to be away that long. I have that sense of family, you know. Like I say, I'm a true mother and wife from my heart, and it's just a certain thing about me. I grew up that way. My mom was that way, and I can't get away from that. And I don't believe in staying away so long that your family don't know who you are. I like to know that my husband is aware that he has a wife and my son knows that he does have a mother that cares about him. So I'm there for them.

Still, on any given weekend LaSalle can usually be found performing throughout the South (Malaco Records' biggest market) in venues that range in size from nightclubs to fairgrounds. Many of her gigs are in small towns and rural communities.

I mostly work Friday, Saturday, and Sundays. I'm off this weekend, but I'm performing next weekend. I have to go to Georgia next weekend. I'm working in Athens Saturday night and some other little place I never heard of. It's near Americus, Georgia, though. I've never heard of this place, but they say it's close to Americus. I'm working there Friday night, in Athens Saturday night, and then the next weekend I go to Texas—Tyler, Texas.

LaSalle attributes her longevity to her understanding of the dynamics of human relationships and her ability to tell stories that everyone, regardless of background, can relate to.

I do "true-to-life" stuff, what I think interests people. The things between a man and woman are what interest people more than anything. I think people are more interested in how to love and how to live, and how to get along or how to solve a problem, how to get out of this situation, or how to make this person love me. I think that's what people want to hear. That's what most songs that get notoriety are about. You're safe when you're writing about a man and a woman. I don't have the greatest voice, and I don't near-about have the voice I want to have, but I have been given a talent to use the one I have. God has shown me how to use it to the best of my advantage, and it works. It just works for me. So I think that's what keeps me hanging around. People want to hear what I got to say next.

Ruby Johnson
Having Soul For It

Ruby Johnson, 1966

*I*n the words of Stax Records historian Rob Bowman, Ruby Johnson is "criminally underknown." Bowman's assessment is right on target: Johnson's career has never achieved even the relative degree of success enjoyed by the other performers in this book (including her one-time labelmate Carla Thomas). Her obscurity has as much to do with her scant recorded output (in a career that spanned the decade between the early '60s and early '70s, she released a mere ten singles) as it does with her decision to leave the music business for the financial stability of a nine-to-five job in 1974. As the collective memory of the recording industry is notoriously short, it's not surprising that Johnson's contributions to soul music have gone largely overlooked.

Fortunately, Johnson's reputation has grown since the early '90s. The event that precipitated her belated entry into the critical spotlight was the release of the acclaimed Stax/Volt nine-CD box set in 1991. The set (the first of what would eventually become three volumes) brought the glory of the Stax sound to a new generation of listeners not old enough to enjoy the music when it was originally issued. Stax music was suddenly in vogue again, experiencing a degree of popular acceptance that had eluded it even in its '60s heyday. What was thrilling about the set was the reexposure it gave to voices that had been hidden in the shadows of soul music history, confined to the dusty, off-center 45s of die-hard record collectors. Especially rewarding was the variety of great female singers in the set, a presence that refuted the long-held (though largely tacit) critical assumption that most of the worthwhile Stax recordings were made by men.

One such singer was Ruby Johnson, who was represented by four singles: "I'll Run Your Hurt Away," "Come to Me My Darling," "When My Love Comes Down," and "If I Ever Needed Love (I Sure Do Need It Now)." Two years later, in 1993, Fantasy Records (working in conjunction with Ace in London) released I'll Run Your Hurt Away, a CD of Johnson's complete output for the Stax label, including fourteen tracks that had sat in the vaults for twenty-five years. In addition to the singles listed above, I'll Run Your Hurt Away also included heartfelt interpretations of songs from Johnson's '60s club act, such as Jackie Verdell's "Why Not Give Me a Chance" and Aretha Franklin's "Won't Be Long." With twenty tracks in all, the CD ably met the demands of Johnson's new legion of fans. The irony of the situation is that Johnson, surprised to find herself the object of so much attention, had always viewed her tenure with Stax as just another short chapter in a career that never quite fulfilled its promise. In this way, her experience at Stax was little different from her earlier affiliations with V-Tone and Nebs, two labels that failed to provide her with any substantial R&B hits.

Even amidst the diversity of talent represented on the Stax label, Johnson was different. One of the most blues-oriented of Stax vocalists, Johnson delivers performances marked by relaxed phrasing that lingers lazily behind the beat. On her best records, especially the Isaac Hayes/David Porter composition "I'll Run Your Hurt Away" (her only chart hit, reaching #31 R&B in 1966), she is in perfect communion with the Stax house band, responding to its every shift in mood. "I'll Run Your Hurt Away" certainly ranks among the greatest of Stax recordings (it is also unusual for Stax in that it features a prominent banjo part). In it, Johnson's hoarse, raspy singing sustains a fairly even tone until the band hits one of its peak musical moments—those sudden bursts of feeling that punctuate so many Stax recordings. Here, on the line "I will, oh I know, I'll run your hurt away," she lets herself go, releasing a scream that seems to come from some deep recess within her. The impression is of a singer abandoning herself to the emotional demands of the song: when she hits the scream, there's no doubt that she feels it. In fact, Johnson says she is unable to sing unless she experiences this special affinity with the material and recording environment, something she calls "having soul for it."

I interviewed Johnson at the comfortable, well-decorated home she shares with her husband in Lanham, Maryland (she has lived in the Washington, D.C., area for nearly forty years). A stylish and gracious woman, she speaks slowly and chooses her words carefully. While many of her contemporaries have made periodic attempts at "comebacks," Johnson seems for the most part content in having left the industry. Only occasionally does a note of wistfulness for her former life slip into her narrative. Her observations are filtered through the perception of someone who has been out of the music business *for a long time; she grants the same degree of importance to her current job in a government-sponsored program (Foster Grandparents) as she does to her past career as a professional singer. Tellingly, her stint at Stax takes up no more space in the interview than her passionate discussions of Foster Grandparents, her religious life, and her numerous adopted children.*

Johnson was born in Elizabeth City, North Carolina, on April 19, 1936. Her formative years were spent singing in church.

I come from a musical background. My father was a great singer. He sang with his brothers in a quartet, and my mother used to sing with an a cappella group down in North Carolina. She was a soloist. Of course, we always had the church music [in our] background. I grew up in church. We sang as a family chorus, along with cousins and aunts and uncles. All of our extended family. We were just *born singers*. And I came from a very poor background. I was in a family of eight: five sisters and three brothers. And my dad left home early, so that left my mother to rear us all. And I had always had high hopes and wanted nice things for my mother. And going to school and participating in talent shows and things like that—I was always singing or dancing. So I used to hear the rhythm & blues singers. As I grew older, I liked Dinah Washington, Ruth Brown, Dakota Staton, Etta James. All of those people—they were my idols.

So I was inspired to embark on a singing career. I don't know if it was anything other than the fact that I wanted to have some of the better things in life. Of course, I was always taking advantage of the opportunity to let somebody hear me. After I finished high school, I went to Virginia Beach, Virginia, [which] was a tourist town, and there were a lot of things going on there in entertainment. I used to work in a club where I was a waitress. Every opportunity that I got I was up there on the stage. So the guy [who owned the club] actually had to make a deal with me: "You wait tables the first part of the night, and after a certain time, you sing with the band"— the house band. So that's what I would do.

The job in Virginia Beach led to work in other clubs, first in Jacksonville, North Carolina, and then in Washington, D.C.

There was a guy from Jacksonville, North Carolina—Sam Latham. He came through the club one night, and he heard me sing and he offered me an opportunity to go to Jacksonville, where again there was a lot of entertainment going on because there was a Marine base there [Camp Lejeune]. So there was an opportunity for me to sing every night. In fact, we were doing two shows a night in a club there called the Birdland. And I was there for a while, for a couple of years. Then when I left there, I came to Washington, D.C., and *again* I was in a club—the Spa. There was a talent night there, and I got up and sang with the band, and the manager there offered me a job working. So I would work there seven nights a week, because they had something going on every night.

In the early '60s, the Spa was one of the best-known attractions in Washington's then-glittering nightclub district. During her tenure there as the house opening act, Johnson appeared on bills with the likes of Jackie Wilson and Gladys Knight and the Pips. Johnson's steady weekend appearances at the Spa cultivated a following that eventually came to include record entrepreneur Never Duncan, Jr.

A gentleman by the name of Never Duncan heard me and asked me if I wanted a personal manager to sponsor me to help me to achieve what I really wanted to do. So, of course, I was delighted. Anyway, he began working with me. We produced the records right here in Georgetown—"What Goes Up Must Come Down" . . . I'll think of some of the names of the other ones, I guess, as I go along. And that's when Al Bell came on the scene, 'cause he was a disc jockey [in D.C.], and he would play my records a lot.

Never Duncan produced Johnson on one single for the Philadelphia-based V-Tone label and six singles for Nebs, a label he founded to showcase her talents. These singles, especially "Calling All Boys" (the one V-Tone release), "Here I Go Again," and "Worried Mind," became regional hits as a result of dedicated promotion by Al Bell, then a well-known disc jockey on Washington's WUST. When Bell moved to Memphis to become national sales director (and eventually president) of Stax in 1965, he decided to bring Johnson to the label, which was then beginning to hit its commercial stride. When Johnson signed with Stax's Volt subsidiary at the end of 1965, it looked as if her big break had come.

Al Bell offered me an opportunity to go to Memphis to record on the Stax/Volt label, and he ended up giving me a contract there. So that's how I got in Memphis. I was terribly excited. I thought my moment had arrived, you know what I mean? But it really didn't turn out to be the kind of experience that I thought it would be. Number one, they had their own unique way of producing and recording. I'm the type of singer that really likes to know my music [ahead of time]. Because *that* way, I can sing it like I feel it. And I didn't have that opportunity in Memphis because I was actually handed a piece of paper and told, "Hey, these are the lyrics. It goes like this." And we would rehearse once or twice, two or three times, for me to try to get the feel of the song. Then they'd say, "Let's cut it." And as far as I was concerned, that was not the best way for me to record. If I didn't know the song, I couldn't really sing it like I would want to do on a recording.

As a singer accustomed to the finely-tuned and rehearsed standards of the club circuit, Johnson was confused by the Stax studio's reliance on head arrangements. She was also unhappy with what she feels was the inadequate promotion Stax gave to the women on its roster.

The other factor as far as Stax was concerned [was that] Carla Thomas was Stax's baby at that time. So all ears and eyes and money and everything else was placed on her. And I would venture to say that they did not promote other female artists as much as they did Carla. So, unfortunately, I did not really get the attention or exposure that I wanted to get from that contract. In addition to that, I think my style was different. Carla—she had a different style of song that she would sing, and I was just a plain old blues and rhythm & blues singer. And they were not accustomed to that. I don't think they really had a girl singer on that label that actually was into the blues, that had the style that I had. So it was very difficult for them to come up with something that would suit my style and my soul. If you'll notice on that CD [*I'll Run Your Hurt Away*], the songs that I personally feel that I did the best on were recuts of [songs of] other people, because I knew those songs and I had used them through the years as part of my repertoire. So it was just like an old shoe to me. I could sing those songs with no voice at all hardly. I was just that familiar. My knowledge of those songs allowed me to be creative with my voice and sing them the way I felt them deep down within. And that's the only way that I can sing. That's the only way I can feel it. So I personally feel that because my style was different, I was just like an oddball there.

But I was, of course, excited—excited about having an opportunity and hoping that every time I'd come out of the studio that I would have the right one. And I feel that the songs that they *did* release on me, had they been pushed more, they might could have gone further. So that was just an experience I chalked up to an experience, if you know what I'm saying. And after then, I would do things locally around here, and then I got to travel and be on shows with other artists, so I did get some work with songs that I had recorded on Volt and Stax. I've been on a show with at least two or three headliners, people that were nationally known and had more exposure than I did. But I could always hold my own on stage. I tried to look like an entertainer with good taste. I always try to give the people their money's worth. I never had a problem in that area. As a matter of fact, it's the opinion of some people that I was better onstage than I was recording. I don't know if that had to do with the influence that the people had on me, as opposed to just listening to music. Or the fact that I had the live band, 'cause I did do some recording with the [pre-recorded] soundtrack. And it was always just more exciting to me just to hear the bass drum, you know [snaps her fingers] and know it was right there in the room with me. I think that helped me to produce a better record, with the live music. 'Cause it's just not the same feeling with the earphones.

Despite her discomfort with the head arrangements, Johnson clearly enjoyed the live interaction with the Stax house band. The excitement can be heard in the music; her Stax sides are the best recordings of her career. After Johnson left the label in 1968, Never Duncan produced her on one more recording session, the results of which have never been released.

We decided that we would try again to do something on our own, and we just wasn't lucky enough to come up with anything, because the fellow that was supposed to be writing for me [R&B songwriter/singer Dickey Williams], I didn't particularly care for his writing. So I guess after then I decided that I would just kind of back off and get something more stable going in my life, like a nine-to-five job. Because I certainly wasn't getting any younger. And that takes us up to the time that I gained employment with the county.

But it's a part of my life that I will always cherish. Even now sometimes, when I see the various shows come on TV and everything—oh, I'd give anything to be back out there. And actually, if it wasn't for my personal circumstances here, if I was a single lady, I'd be out here doing something on the weekends, and may still consider that once I've retired. I'm constantly approached by some of the older guys I used to work with: "Why don't you come and do a gig?" They could get me some work, but, like I said, because of my personal life. . . . Before my mother died, I was involved in her care, and she passed a year and a half ago. And now my husband is getting old, and his health is not really that great, so I don't know where he would be happy about me being out somewhere, singing, traveling. Of course he would be welcome to come, but he couldn't keep the pace up, 'cause I am a night person. My brain don't even start ticking till around twelve [laughs]. After all of these years, really, I'm a night person.

Johnson believes that the difficult conditions a performer is often forced to endure on tours would make it hard for her to maintain her home life.

One time in the very beginning of my career, we went on a tour down South, and we would do two shows in Columbia, South Carolina, and then after the show we'd pack up and travel all night to the next town or the next destination. In cars. The band, the instruments. We had our own little show one time: Bobby Parker, who was a local here, myself, dancers, and we had a comedian, so we had our own little package that we presented all around through the South, and that's hard. I didn't particularly run into a whole lot of segregation at that time, but it's not easy. That particular tour, we did about four or five cities, and we were gone, like, five days. So we would be in a city each night. It's tiring. You're grabbing what sleep you can in a car. If we were going to be there overnight, two days or something like that, then, of course, we would be booked into a hotel, so you were able to get somewhere and take care of your needs. But it's not the easiest thing. It's not half as accommodating as it is now for people—they have these luxury buses and those kinds of things when they go on tour. You had to love what you were doing.

Johnson says that she never experienced the racism that so many of her fellow performers had to face when they toured the South.

I'm sure down South there were some places that had that kind of attitude back then. That was a known fact, so you basically dealt with the situation. You didn't have to stay there forever, so we did what we went there to do and left. But I've never had any unpleasant encounters, unlike some of the other artists that I've read the background and history of. I've never had to experience any ordeals like they did, like Billie Holiday and all those old girls that's gone on. Lena Horne and all those people. I didn't encounter anything like that, never did.

Occasionally Johnson had the chance to perform at a high-profile venue such as Washington's famed Howard Theater. Before the Howard closed in the early '70s, it was rivaled only by the New York Apollo and the Regal in Chicago as a national showcase for African-American talent.

I had the pleasure of being on a show there with Johnnie Taylor. I think I was at the Howard Theater too with Jackson—what's his name?—he was physically challenged . . . Walter Jackson.[1] I was at the Howard Theater with him. We also used to play a lot of beaches—I was on a show with Jackie Wilson, Jerry Butler, Etta James, Ike and Tina Turner, Inez and Charlie Foxx. I had the opportunity of working with a lot of people who were more nationally known than I was. All of the people that I met along the way were great people. I felt there was always that competitive spirit. We got along fine in the dressing room, but when it was time for us to go on, we would try to what we'd call "burn" one another. It was wonderful. You could work and play, too. When you like what you do, that's a plus. I really love to entertain. Even though I'm not singing now, I like to entertain people and have people come into my home.

Johnson has particularly fond memories of Washington's nightlife during the early-to-mid '60s. The neighborhood centered around 14th and U Streets was the hub of the city's African-American community and featured many prominent theatres, restaurants, and clubs. In many cases, the buildings (such as the structure that housed the Bohemian Caverns, where Ramsey Lewis recorded his 1965 hit "The In Crowd") are still standing, but the scene itself is largely gone, a victim of the 1968 riots that seemed to turn the neighborhood into a ghost town overnight.[2]

Fourteenth Street used to be the strip. There was the Birdland, the Spa, and the Bohemian Caverns. There were several clubs all along the Fourteenth Street corridor. You had a variety of places that you could go and hear different kinds of music. On Saturday night, at this particular place where I was singing, the Spa, they used to be lining up around the corner trying to get into the place, and we'd end up having to do two shows. And then we would "do forty [minutes] and take twenty," and we would go to the next club a block away and listen to the other gig that was going on there. We would just visit one another, the artists that were working in those clubs. I mean, Fourteenth Street was the place to be. The Howard Theater at that time was *it*, here in this town.[3] I think that that's one era that's greatly missed by people, because it's so different in that area now, because of the safety factor—so much crime and stuff going on now that actually people are afraid to venture out. I haven't been in a club in God-knows-when, because I'm just afraid, I really am. Because a lot of clubs are not really choosy about their clientele, what kinds of people they let in. A lot of them allow these teenagers to come in, and it just makes for a different atmosphere. When we were on Fourteenth Street years ago, we weren't afraid to walk anywhere. We'd walk all up and down Fourteenth Street, didn't have to worry about getting robbed or anybody harming you in any way. It was really wonderful. It really was.

Johnson is careful not to romanticize the '60s soul scene; she also emphasizes what she considers its darker side.

There were some negative forces along the way that you had to be strong and avoid, like the drugs. Of course, back then, you didn't hear as much about drug usage as you do today. But there had always been some way to get high, pills, that kind of thing. And I was just strong enough and relied on my training and my knowledge of right and wrong and my knowledge of what those kinds of things would do to you physically and mentally. I just did not want to get caught up in those kinds of things. And it was all around me. And then I had the kind of people around me that were involved in those kinds of things, but they were very protective of me. They didn't do those things in front of me. And if I talked like I might want to experiment, they had that discouragement going right away—not that I ever really wanted to. I enjoy a cocktail or two, but I never really wanted to get involved in the hard stuff like that. And it paid off for me, too, because right here in Washington, D.C., there were female singers, and from what I can understand, I'm about the only one that's alive today. Because of their drug usage, they're all gone. I'm sad that they had to end their lives that way, but I'm just terribly happy that I was strong enough to avoid all of those traps. And I owe a lot of that to my upbringing, my poor mother. And of course, the spiritual side of my life, which I never forget because I feel that if I didn't have that help from that supreme power, I could do nothing. So as they say, to God be the glory. And I never fail to recognize that.

Johnson's religious upbringing continues to play an important role in her life. She was raised a member of Temple Beth-El, a Jewish, predominantly African-American denomination founded in Lawrence, Kansas, but with its national headquarters in Suffolk County, Virginia. Although Temple Beth-El is in every way a Jewish congregation, observing all major Jewish holidays, members sometimes refer to the Temple service as "church" when speaking to those outside the denomination.

I've always believed that Saturday was the Sabbath. That was my teaching, from a child up. My mother, father, grandparents, great-grandparents, all of them were raised in the same religious organization. We practiced Judaism even then. But people back there did not really consider us as black Jews, you know. Because I think the general idea for most of the community there was that you had to be white to be Jewish. And of course we both know that's not true. But I have been involved and adhered to Judaism all of my life. There were times in my life that I was not as involved, you know, but I have never strayed too far away from it, because God is the center of my life.

Johnson still sings in services at the affiliated First Tabernacle Beth-El Temple on New York Avenue in Washington, D.C., although not as frequently since her mother's passing.

It has been very difficult for me to sing. I'd feel it in here, but once I'd start a song, I couldn't get through it because there was a sadness that overtook me— especially in our congregation, because my mother used to attend church on a regular basis, and she loved to hear me sing. And I guess just knowing that she wasn't there—the grief was too much. So, I did get through the song today. And it came out very nice. I sang, "My Heavenly Father Watches Over Me." And we do a cappella. In fact, we have churches all over the United States and Africa, and we have a reputation of being singers. When we go to the Passover at our headquarters in Portsmouth, Virginia, we have something like three or four thousand people there at one time. It's a sight to behold. I don't think you would have ever witnessed anything or will ever witness anything like what you would see—that's true—or hear. And we have at least four or five hundred people in the choir, and we're all singing the same songs. And we do it a cappella—no instruments whatsoever. The most beautiful music you would ever want to hear. And even the little children. We just have that gift.

Outside of Temple-related events, Johnson had not performed in almost twenty years when contacted by Fantasy Records in 1993 regarding the proposed compilation CD. She confesses that she was more than a bit surprised; she had long assumed that her reputation as a performer was consigned firmly to the past.

It was just out of the blue. A young man that used to write for me when I first started recording, Dickey Williams, he called me and told me that Fantasy Records had tried to get in touch with me. He has some things out for this [record] company, so they called there to find out how they could get in touch with me. And they called and told me that they had been trying to get in touch with me for some time and that they wanted to release this CD, but they wanted to do a bio on me. Someone called me from California and talked to me two or three times by phone. But anyway, I had the opportunity after talking with them to visit California. And I went by the studio and everyone there was very nice, you know. Oh, they promised me the world, in terms of my royalties, but I have not received one penny—not one dime of royalties from this CD—and I know it's selling. I sell a lot of records overseas, I really do. In Europe.[4]

Because '60s record companies customarily treated recording and promotional costs as artist expenses, Johnson did not receive any royalties from Stax when the material was first recorded.

I really didn't get any royalties because during that time [the mid '60s] everything was expenses. You had to sell a hell of a lot of records before you were able to get a dollar for it, because they take their expenses right off the top. So Fantasy can't even use that as an excuse for not paying me, because all of that material that they inherited from Stax when they bought Stax out was paid for. They just had the expense of generating press and the CD.

There have been other frustrations: the thrill of her first album release (twenty-five years after the material in it had been recorded) led Johnson into a hastily-made business arrangement that she now feels was a mistake.

It was really exciting for me, I got so caught up in that excitement. This same gentleman that used to write for me [Williams], he was in town and he approached me with a deal of us maybe producing a master tape ourselves and financing it. And that wasn't such a wise idea. But, as I said, I was so caught up in the excitement of it all, I took the chance, but it didn't work out. We went to North Carolina and used a little studio of a very young fellow down there, over in a cotton field—but he had state-of-the-art equipment and produced a hell of a sound. But again, I didn't like some of the lyrics that this guy [Williams] writes. And then he actually deceived me too, about the material that I *did* choose to record. He had a master tape of nothing but song and music tracks, and basically what I did was choose some of the things that I felt like I had soul for—these are the ones that I would like to do. And as it turned out, he had recorded some of the ones I had picked on a CD of his own. Some of the same songs and the music tracks were on his CD, and he did not tell me. His defense was that people record other people's material all of the time, and that's true. But I think since I was financing the deal, then I should have been able to decide whether I wanted to do that or not. So I just decided to quit before I invested any more money, because I felt that if he would deceive me about that, he was not a good person to do business with, so I just let it go.

In backing away from the deal, Johnson shut the door on the possibility of getting the tapes released.

We did not do anything with what we did. There was a couple good tunes on there. On "Memories," I did not like the words that he had, so I kept the soundtrack and wrote my own words, and then we went in the studio the next morning, 'cause I had to go down to North Carolina on the weekends to record. I did a blues—"I'm in Love with a Married Man." That was on there and another one that I had always wanted to record, but my manager back then [Never Duncan] did not particularly care for the word *lord* being into a blues [song]. He just did not like that. But it was a nice blues that Dickey wrote for me years ago, "Why Did You Make Me Human?"—[sings] "Oh lord, why did you make me? Why didn't you make someone else in my place?" I did like "Memories." I think had we had *that* released, it would have gone places.

This heady period of Johnson's life did offer one thrill without any subsequent disappointment: the chance to perform at Washington's newly-restored Lincoln Theater in 1994. The theatre had once been a popular movie and live-entertainment house in the heart of the African-American community but had sat in disrepair for many years until its rebirth in late 1993.

They had a Stax anniversary, and I was booked there with Mable John and— what's the young lady's name that did "Mr. Big Stuff?" . . . Jean Knight, and Kim Weston. The four of us. That was really exciting for me. I went out and bought three gowns, just to do one show. I didn't know which one I really wanted to wear, so I bought three. And that was a good night for me, a good night. I did some of the older songs that I had used in my repertoire, and of course I did "I'll Run Your Hurt Away." I did about six songs.

The positive audience response was particularly exhilarating for Johnson, although she speaks of it with characteristic humility.

Hometown girl, I had the advantage. Each of us had our own style, but I like to keep the crowd moving, you know? I like crowd participation. There are some songs that I do that I involve the audience in. I talk to the audience. I just had a groove going, I really did. I was terribly excited about being back on the stage for the first time in twenty-some years, with all the interviews that I had. I was on the radio stations and I was on Channel 8-TV. So it was just fantastic. But Kim didn't have a good night that night. She walked off the stage. And she was telling people, "Why aren't you clapping for me? You clapped for Ruby Johnson," and that kind of stuff. I think she might not have really been her true self that night. I think she's been going through some difficulties with her life, and she's still trying to get it back together, but she has a beautiful voice, really. I think if you're going to compare voices from the '50s and '60s, she had about the best voice that night.

Although the Lincoln Theater engagement provided Johnson with a fleeting chance to revisit her former life as an entertainer, the next morning she quickly stepped back into her job as director of Foster Grandparents, a federally funded program that she operates out of the Prince George's County Municipal Building in Hyattsville, Maryland. She has held the position since 1986.

That's a very rewarding job. I'm a people-oriented person. I get on well with other people. I communicate very well with seniors because I'm down to earth. I'm always talking junk with them. Keep it on the light side. But on the other hand, they know that they have to do what they're supposed to do in terms of participating in the program.

Foster Grandparents teams senior citizens with children who need extra support and encouragement.

[The seniors] go out in the communities and work with children that have challenges in life. We call them "at-risk children." I have sixty-eight volunteers on board now. And I have fourteen sites all over the county. I just gave them their Christmas luncheon on Thursday, and they had a wonderful time. I took them out to the Old Country Buffet in Laurel [Maryland]. They had the chance to eat all they could eat or want to eat. I had some extra money that I needed to spend, so I went to Giant [a Washington-area supermarket] and bought seventy boxes of chocolates about [holds up hands] that long and about that wide. They were already gift wrapped, so it made it very easy for me.

[What the volunteers do] depends on the site that they are assigned to and the activities that are going on where they're assigned. I have volunteers in the public school that provide one-on-one with children that need extra support in learning how to read. I have volunteers that work with teen mothers. They care for their babies at Saint Anne's Infant and Maternity Home while the teen mother attends school and prepares herself for the job market. Then we have a regular day care center, where there are children there who come from one-parent families. So they're just that extra pair of hands. It's a wonderful program, it really is. It's twenty-five years old now nationally. It's just wonderful to see elderly people who have already experienced raising their families that are willing to give of their time and experience at this stage in their lives, when they could be somewhere doing anything that they would want to do. It is just so wonderful. And they are willing to give so much for what they get. And they are more dedicated than paid employees. It keeps them busy and involved, and it helps the children as well. It's almost like a prevention program in terms of the well-being of the seniors. They're sick less, they stay mentally alert longer, and they're out of the nursing homes and hospitals.

Johnson's life is busy. When she's not coordinating volunteers or working with her Temple community (one of the first times we spoke by phone she was "up to her elbows in cake batter," preparing for a raffle), she attends to the needs of children of her own.

I have four or five godchildren. And through my second marriage I inherited nine grandchildren. So there's really never a dull moment in my life, because I have a giving nature; and I am awfully concerned about the well-being of children—getting a good education and staying out of trouble and staying off of drugs. And God has been so terribly good to me, David. I mean, I'm not a rich person by far, but I am always willing to share what I have, especially with children or young people. So I'm very much involved with teenagers. It's nothing for me to get a call: "I need money for books." I had one that needed things to go to the prom. Tuition needs, some assistance with their tuition. I try to sacrifice, because I feel that this kind of positive support is so necessary, especially if you find a young person that really wants to better their lives and do something with their lives. If that phone ever rings and I am asked to assist, I try not to ever say no, I really do. And I don't expect anything back in return but that they do well. Young people have so much to fight against right now. There's so much going on. There's a lot of kids that's living in dysfunctional situations in their homes.

Johnson isn't exaggerating by saying that she offers help at a moment's notice—during our interview, she received several calls from her godchildren and dispensed advice to each one. The many twists her life has taken gives her a unique vantage point from which to offer guidance. Her reflections on her singing career are shaped by her belief in the randomness of fame.

From my perspective and with the experiences that occurred with me, I have always felt that you could be ever so talented, but it was a thing of being at the right place at the right time. It wasn't what you could do, it was who you knew, that could get you where you wanted to go. And it was just that simple. I feel like there were some female artists that reached that plateau that they were reaching for. I don't ever feel like I had that opportunity to do that because I did not have the big guns behind me as I should have had. But all in all, I don't regret anything, the time that I put into it. It's been a wonderful experience, and I was doing something that I liked to do and still like to do.

I didn't really gain anything financially. But on the other hand I did gain, 'cause it was an experience that I've always dreamed of having. I don't have any ill feelings about anything that has happened in that part of my life, because I enjoyed it. And I do believe that from the time you come into this world, your future is predestined. I believe that God really has a plan for everybody that he creates and brings into this world. And even though that may have been my desire—to be a big professional rhythm-and-blues singer—that may not be God's plan for me. Actually, when I think about how close I've come sometimes—never quite close enough to reach that level—I'm almost convinced that that may not have been what God intended for me to do. Now, I sing spirituals, and I don't mean no self-praise, but I can set a church on fire singing spirituals, and that may be what He wants me to do in life, and I'm completely satisfied with that. I'm still using that talent that He gave me. That's just the way I look at it.

I think I've been blessed. I really do. Certainly, getting back to all these things that I wanted to have—the beginning of all of my aspirations, the reason that I was wanting to travel this road. I'll tell you David, I never reached that level of international prestige, I've never really earned the money that I probably would have earned had I reached that level, but certainly I have not wanted for one thing that I desired. I always wanted a home—God blessed me with one. I mean, it's not a $300 or $400,000 home, but it's comfortable. I enjoy it, and I am very happy here. I always wanted a nice automobile—I've had that, still have a nice one. Mink coats and diamonds, I've had it, you know? Without even reaching the level in the entertainment field that I always felt that I had to do to achieve that. That achievement helps me to . . . maybe to realize that I'm not missing anything. God gives you what you need and what you desire, if you give Him a little of your time and service. Treat your fellow man right. Share your blessings. I do all of that—it comes back. I'm just happy and comfortable. Everybody from time to time has to deal with some kind of a problem, a day-to-day problem or a situation that's not pleasant, but that's normal, that's life, you know. But He gives me the strength to be a survivor, and He gives me the knowledge to know how to deal with things without damaging my mental ability or physical ability. So I'm happy. And somewhere in the back of my mind, I'll always leave that little space where, if the opportunity presents itself, I'll be back on stage in front of an audience one more time.

Carla Thomas

Memphis's Reluctant Soul Queen

Carla Thomas, 1966

As a teenage devotee of the More Better Man and the world surrounding WOL's studio at 4th and H Streets, N.E. (a world he surveyed through his large glass window facing the street), I was one of many Washingtonians treated on an almost daily basis to the music of Carla Thomas. On WOL, we heard not only the Carla Thomas, whose winsome, teen-aged voice graced hits like "Gee Whiz," but an older, more experienced Thomas whose approach to mature ballads such as "Comfort Me" and "A Woman's Love" was masterful. Her voice was smooth and gentle but always full of surprises, with a range that moved from a girlish soprano all the way down through the rich tones of a sultry lower register. "Comfort Me," in particular, sounded like a lost treasure from a time long past, lovingly brought back to life through the power of the More Better Man's universe. The record shimmered with breathtaking guitar lines, a piano part right out of church, the most beautiful backup vocals imaginable (supplied by none other than Gladys Knight and the Pips), and most of all Thomas herself, who sang with a pleading intensity that made the music sound deep and personal. At a time when much of what I had loved about Washington was coming to resemble a blasted-out hole, "Comfort Me" provided an inspiring sense of permanence. It seemed to say that what matters the most really does stand the test of time.

Despite her prominence in the More Better Man's world and in mine, Carla Thomas in the 1980s was still very much a cult figure. Though considered the top female vocalist of the great Stax label and the "Queen of the Memphis Sound," she was mostly written about in connection with her father (the legendary performer and disc jockey Rufus Thomas) and her one-time musical collaborator Otis Redding. One of the first writers to present Thomas as a great artist in her own right was Peter Guralnick, who interviewed her for his classic book Sweet Soul Music (1986). Even Guralnick's account left her somewhat underrepresented (the only female performer whose career the book explored in depth was Aretha Franklin), and it was a number of years before Thomas's contributions to soul music would be fully appreciated.

Thanks in no small part to the efforts of Rob Bowman, who interviewed her extensively for his essays accompanying the three Stax/Volt box sets and his 1997 history of Stax, Soulsville, U.S.A., Thomas has begun to receive her due. She has numerous reissue CDs in print in the U.S., performs all over the world, and is regarded as one of the architects of the Memphis soul sound. Even so, her career tends to be described in inchoate terms; in an interview for the 1994 CD, Gee Whiz: The Best of Carla Thomas, former Stax president Al Bell declared, "I never felt that Carla's potential was fully realized." Even Thomas herself says that her father is the focus of more journalistic attention: "I don't give many interviews. He does most of the interviews."

Perhaps what has kept her from achieving the notoriety of an Aretha Franklin or a Gladys Knight is the fact that, aside from intermittent backup work and the occasional guest spot (such as on Lee Atwater's 1990 album, Red Hot & Blue) she was almost exclusively associated with Atlantic and Stax. In fact, Stax's existence and the duration of Thomas's recording career are nearly parallel. From 1960, when her first record (a duet with her father entitled "Cause I Love You") appeared on Satellite (Stax's predecessor), to the early '70s, when the label began to experience the financial problems that would eventually lead to its dissolution, Thomas never strayed from the fold.

In any case, there can be no doubt that without Carla Thomas, Stax would not have developed in the way it did. "Gee Whiz (Look At His Eyes)," which Thomas had written as a poem when she was about fifteen and had then tucked away for a couple of years, became the fledgling label's first big pop success in 1961. A fetching, delicate song with a flowery string arrangement that marvelously framed Thomas' seventeen-year old voice (she would turn eighteen in December of 1960, four months after cutting "Gee Whiz"), the record reached #10 on the pop charts once it was rereleased by Atlantic.[1] Thomas never had another pop hit as big as "Gee Whiz" (although "B-A-B-Y," an Isaac Hayes and David Porter production released in 1966, came close), but the success of the record provided Stax with the recognition and capital it needed to move from a struggling little label to a major force in R&B and soul music.

Thomas, who has never married and has no children, shares a house in a quiet Memphis neighborhood with her parents Rufus and Lorene, both of whom were present during parts of the interview. Although the Thomas home is notable for its conspicuous lack of plaques, gold records, and other adornments, it's nonetheless impossible to walk inside without being overcome by the realization that one is in the presence of a great American musical family: eighty-one-year-old Rufus sits in one corner of the living room, casually going through press clippings and other assorted items stored in boxes, while photographs of the three Thomas children—all accomplished musicians—grace the walls. Carla's brother Marvell, who also resides in Memphis, is an excellent keyboardist and arranger, who has played on countless Memphis soul records (including the original recording of "Gee Whiz"), while younger sister Vaneese has enjoyed a moderately successful solo career, recently appearing as one of the voices of the "girl group chorus" in the Disney film Aladdin.

The separation between public persona and private personality, distinct in all those who have experienced stardom or something close to it, seems especially acute in Thomas. One senses in her a deep ambivalence towards interviews, although the dictates of stardom demand that she never turn an interview down (when I first called to ask if I could talk to her for my project, her response was an immediate and unhesitating "yes"). "There are a lot of people you get very personal with, and you just want to just keep right on going," she tells me. "All you might want to say is, 'Hello, I really enjoy talking with you.'" This sentiment seems an especially telling reflection of the conflict that she most likely feels. While never anything less than the epitome of southern graciousness, Thomas is reticent; it often seems as if she is holding something back. Nonetheless, many of her observations are etched with the same honest, heartfelt quality that permeates her music, which is saying a great deal.

Thomas is irrepressibly girlish as she walks into the outer living room where I'm waiting: her hair is pulled away from her face with bright, multi-colored string, and she wears tall, black lace-up boots. "I'm just a little kid!" she exclaims, explaining why, though it's late February, the Christmas decorations still have not been put away: she can't bear to take them down. During the interview, however, there are times when her youthful ingenuousness disappears and she seems heavy with the reality of being an adult. At these moments—such as her description of the difficulties associated with being a woman in the music industry—she becomes serious and hushed, clutching the tape recorder tightly in a way that gives her words a poignant authority. It's as if the contrast between girl and woman that I had always sensed in her music on the "More Better Man" show goes far beyond the scope of her recorded work: it forms a key element of her personality.

Carla Thomas was born on December 21, 1942. As a child she lived in the Foote Homes Housing Project, just a stone's throw from Beale Street and the Palace Theater. Rufus Thomas was a beloved emcee at the Palace, which during the '40s and '50s was Memphis's most famous showcase for African-American talent.

I grew up across from Church Park in the projects.[2] Beale Street was right there—it was like a way of life for us. I was around music all the time and around Dad all the time. And he would take a lot of the kids to [the Palace Theater]. He was the emcee of a lot of those amateur shows. We'd all be holding hands—Mom and all of us—and we'd go watch the show. It was interesting because people would just allow their feelings [to come out]: "Man, get off the stage!" It was just fun.

Thomas's first chance to follow in her father's footsteps as a performer came at the age of ten when she joined the Teen Town Singers. The group was sponsored by WDIA, then one of the highest-rated radio stations in Memphis and the first station in the country to adopt a full-time lineup oriented towards the African-American community (Rufus Thomas was one of the station's most popular on-air personalities). The "Teen Towns" served as a training ground for some of the best singers in Memphis: in addition to Thomas, the group at one time featured Isaac Hayes and future Soul Children-member Anita Louis.

Actually, you weren't supposed to join until you were in the ninth or tenth grade. I heard them one day on the radio. I heard them singing, and I said, "I think I want to join that group." And he [points to Rufus Thomas] said, "How can you join that group yet? You have to be in high school" [laughs].—[with resolve] "I want to join that group!"

So he talked to the gentleman at the time, Mr. A.C. Williams (we called him "Moohah"), and he said it was okay: "Let me hear her sing."[3] They had a talent show that would follow the Teen Town singers, so I did a little song on one of the talent shows. I think it was "Here Comes Peter Cottontail" or something like that. So I got my little Brownie camera. They used to give you a little Brownie camera when you won (back in those days there was a little box camera and they called them "Brownies." People couldn't wait to own a little Brownie camera. I mean, that was *it*). So they had those things there for kids, but [today] it's not that simple. It has to be a big production. But that gave me a lot of musical knowledge. I stayed in there until I was out of twelfth grade. Every Wednesday, every Friday, every Saturday out of every week.

Being a Teen Town singer required an extraordinary degree of stamina for a ten-year-old.

It was quite a schedule. I think about that now. Lord, I was sometimes late for this and late for that. I was a kid—how'd I do that? But I did it. It was get off school every Wednesday and go straight to class. Get off school every Friday and go straight to rehearsal. Had to catch the bus and go, 'cause we had moved by that time. And Saturday we had to go down to the station and sing. It was just a whole bunch of us. It was a lot of fun, it really was. And a lot of young people learned how to sing out of that group, I'm telling you.

Performing with the Teen Towns also gave Thomas the chance to sing country music, which she acknowledges as one of her earliest musical influences. She even recalls making some country demo tapes at the WDIA studio, although she doesn't remember where the tapes were sent (she thinks it may have been Tree Publishing Company, a major country music publisher owned by Dial Records founder Buddy Killen).

I used to do Brenda Lee's stuff with the Teen Towns. "I'm Sorry," all of those. I even used to do some audition tapes for her to listen to. I remember for some reason they [the WDIA staff] knew I liked country, so they'd come get me when I was at school and I'd go down there and sing some audition tapes. I never knew who they'd send them to. A lot of times I know they sent them to Brenda, 'cause that's all I cared about. Send them to Brenda. At the time that's all I really knew. As a young girl my age, she was kind of like a role model.

Thomas says her first real indication that she might one day be a successful singer came through a prediction her mother shared with her. As she relates this anecdote, she looks toward Lorene Thomas, who is watching television in the adjacent living room.

I was about fifteen years old. We were sitting watching Jackie Wilson on *Bandstand.* We were sitting there watching him sing, and I said, "Ooh, I'm so glad to get a chance to see Jackie Wilson." You know, back in those days there was that pride of seeing an African American on TV. My mother told me, "You know what? You're gonna be on there." That was prophetic, because I didn't get on *[American Bandstand]* until after I was a freshman in college. I wrote "Gee Whiz" in the tenth grade, somewhere around there. I was writing songs around the house, and she said, "You're going to be on there." I didn't make fun of it. I said, "Ooh, that will be great!" But I never will forget that. It was so true. And [speaking slowly and quietly] I think about it a lot more, because some people just don't realize that the parents are real involved in their children's careers.

After speaking Thomas remains silent, staring at her mother with what seems to be a deep sadness (although I later learn that Lorene Thomas has just recovered from some serious health problems).[4] At first she doesn't hear my next question about her early records. Soon, however, she slips with surprising ease back into the enthusiasm she displayed earlier.

My first record was with Dad, called "Cause I Love You." So it was really a fun thing. We were singing, traveling about, doing things—but more in this area, more in the tri-state area. August of '60 we cut that stuff and I went on to college that coming September. I cut "Gee Whiz" too before I left, and they released it in October, but nothing was happening because they were still promoting "Cause I Love You." Plus, you know in the record business how the Christmas records all start coming out, so "Gee Whiz" got kind of lost in there. And then there was another group that also had "Gee Whiz" out. I wish I knew the group's name, but of course—1960. I wasn't on a show with them, so I never got a chance to meet these guys. I only heard their record. But we were saying, "Oh my goodness, which one is going to do it?"[5]

So December went by, and all of a sudden I start hearing it more—I start hearing it a little more around the middle of January. Then eventually by February, I hear it more and more and more. And in the spring [of 1961] I was invited to do *Bandstand* in Philly. That was actually the first TV show as far as exposure, which was some heck of exposure.

During her American Bandstand *appearance Thomas quickly realized that television, to a much greater extent than the stage, demanded from the performer a sharp awareness of surroundings.*

I was singing, and I saw this little bench over there and I thought it was something I could sit on. It was a prop! [Laughs.] And I didn't know how the scene was going to look. They set it up while they were making me up. So I was singing, and I was going to just sit down and cross my legs—I was going to do one of my own numbers. It was kind of like cardboard or something, but they had it fixed up so beautiful with flowers all over it, and I said, "I think I'll just go sit on there." It looked so sturdy, the way they had it. They said [from the side of the stage] "Oh no! [laughs] No, no, no, please!" And then afterwards we talked about it on the interview. [Dick Clark] said, "I am *so glad* you did not sit on that. That would have been over!" [Laughs.] We all were laughing. The kids were laughing because, see, they had been in there watching them put [the set] up. That was one of the fun times with [Clark]. I'll never forget that.

Thomas credits television shows like American Bandstand *and the* Clay Cole Show *with giving African American performers the opportunity to be seen by a wide audience.*

It was very difficult at that time. There weren't many shows that African Americans were on, unless they got a real huge record. You know, you'd see Jackie Wilson or somebody like that, but some of the other artists you didn't see much of. So TV really helped.

By the time "Gee Whiz" hit the pop charts in February of 1961, Thomas was in the middle of her first year at Tennessee A&I University in Nashville.

My freshman year was really an interesting time, because people were really getting to know me and find out what I was doing. March seemed to be a big month for that record ["Gee Whiz"]. I did the Easter show with Murray the K. Kaufman, do you remember him?[6] Murray the K, Clay Cole—oh God, to get a chance to meet all these guys was just terrific.

Thomas's friends at school seemed as excited as she was about her appearances on television.

I was doing a lesson once, and somebody came around and said, "You're gonna be on TV!" [laughs]. So I ran down into the lounge and I sat there and watched with everybody else, and they said, "There you are! There you are!"

However, balancing the pressures of college life with the demands of pop stardom proved quite difficult.

It eventually got to be harder than I thought. In the beginning it wasn't [hard], because it was still a lot of fun. I was just learning school as well as the business. They were all kind of caught up together and I realized I had to buckle down to do both. Then it got to be I was getting more job offers, and that's when it got to be harder. It was harder because I would have to leave [school], but in a way it was good for a young lady because it wasn't like a hard club gig, getting off at two and three in the morning like I did later on. I did mostly theaters, three and four shows a day. You had to do maybe two numbers. Because back in those days, everybody had a share of what was going on. Nowadays, you maybe have one person that has this big fabulous show going on, but back then, those Easter shows, you had ten or twelve people on them for one show.

Thomas is referring to the "package tours" that were so much a part of the early '60s pop- and soul-music scene. At the time, Thomas says, promoters could get away with booking a dozen artists per show.

It's because we weren't making the money—especially African Americans—because we needed the exposure. We needed to be seen.

The artists themselves were in a bind: the shows paid very little, but a visible presence was necessary to prevent the proliferation of pirate artists—"fake" singers who billed themselves as the real thing. In the days before music videos, this kind of chicanery was not only feasible but quite profitable.

I remember Lloyd Price tickled me so bad. He said, "I just saw you down in the deep south of Florida." I said, "You did?" He said, "Yeah." I said, "But I wasn't down there." And he fell out laughing. But he was teasing me, because he knew me when he saw me. That's what was happening. There were people that were doing your gigs, using your name, so when people got the [visible] exposure, it was a lot better. So a lot of the '60s artists had to do a lot of promotional things, 'cause, hey, [today] you can fax a picture all over the world: "This is who this person is, this is what the person looks like." You can send it off express and it'll get there, and you don't have to worry. But back then, we had a whole lot of promoting to do. Also back in those days, disc jockeys brought the people in—they would sponsor the show. There was a lot of good relations between the radio personalities and the artists back then, and a lot of those friendships still are bonded right now. You know, then, even radio personalities had names; they were personalities just like the artists. And probably in their earlier life a lot of them *were* artists.

R&B and soul disc jockeys in the '50s and '60s entertained their audiences by drawing upon a tradition of showmanship that had its roots in vaudeville. Often the disc jockeys employed clever nicknames (like The More Better Man) through which they were known to their fans. I mention "Magnificent Montague" and Thomas's eyes roll, with a laugh ("Oh boy, yes"). Magnificent Montague was the ultimate showman but reputedly something of a huckster. In Soulsville U.S.A., *Thomas characterized him unfavorably when describing a Stax concert he had promoted: "He was supposed to pay Booker [T. Jones] and left owing everybody. He ran out the door with the money."[7] The incident underscores the fact that personality DJs like Montague were also salesmen who, like everyone else in the record business, wanted to make money first and foremost.*

And [famed Philadelphia DJ] "Butterball." They just had these names that stood out, like "Bless My Bones."[8] People'd call them by their fun names. Even the shows—[the promoters] chose the emcee to be kind of like one of those personalities. And [the emcees] would even hold the record up—[the artists] would bring the album and give it to the emcee and he would take it and say, "Got a new album out! Comin' out, comin' up, here they come!" And then they'd introduce you. So people knew that they could go out and buy a record. So it was very heavily promotional.

There was little time for mistakes on the package shows. With a dozen other artists on the bill, there was always someone who could take your place.

You had to bring your charts, you had to bring all your things, and it was very professional. You had to be very professional. Your rehearsal time was set at this particular time, and you did your rehearsal spot. You missed it, that was just too bad. If they had some time afterwards, we'll see . . . but it was very professional. You may have had twenty minutes or so to practice it, and [the band] would say, "OK, let's hit it. How're you going to start it? How're you going to end it?" And it was good because if somebody needed background and folks didn't show up or whatever, we'd just get a mike backstage and just do the background. Nobody knew who was singing background. But that taught me that *professionalism.* You've got to be there. You've got to bring your little satchel and your dress. And sometimes I only had that one song to sing, and I went off and Jackie Wilson or somebody would come on, and he went off and [laughs] then somebody . . . and I just loved those shows. It's very difficult to have a show like that now. With the '60s artists you probably could do it, because they still have that thing of family. You know, we admired each other. I think we all really admire each other. Artists admire each other. I wish we could do it a lot more openly.

Thomas says that her many tours and promotional appearances were easy—at first.

I was younger, so they weren't tiring [laughs]. If I had to do it the same way [today], it would be very tiring. If I had to go on a promotional radio tour for thirty days, go from one state to another state, and you need to be here at this particular time 'cause this is during a carnival or something, and if you're here, you'll get the most people to see who you really are and you'll pass out your pictures. Autograph sessions were like . . . the *thing.* [Disc jockeys] would say, "Hey, look who we have in the studio with us today," and you could just walk in. And then it got to be harder and harder—there were more and more artists. It got to be quite a bit harder, as a matter of fact. You couldn't just walk off the street and say, "Hey!" You had a hit record this particular time, [but if] you didn't have a hit record the next go-round, you might have a hard time getting in, because somebody has opted for your slot. You see, it's hard. It was hard in the latter part because I was beginning to understand that whole competitiveness type of thing. It wasn't a deliberate competitiveness; there were just more people out here. When you get another hot record, you've got a slot—unless you were doing a real big show with a bunch of folk and you all came down to the studio. Then it was fun—it was set up that way. But still, you couldn't just call up and say, "Hey, Butterball, I'm in town. I'll come on down there and holler at you." You couldn't quite do that anymore.

This heightened degree of competition came as the result of the crossover success that soul music as a whole experienced during the latter half of the '60s.

There were more record companies, there were more managers, there were more TV shows, more everything. But that's how we had to do it. We had to promote. [Speaking with sudden force:] We had to promote, we had to be seen, we had to be visible. And it was kind of stressful because you were doing so many interviews, *so* many. They were trying to find out so much. Singing is one thing, but talking about your personal life is another. So then you had to watch what you say, you had to learn what to say, when to say it, how to say it—although I never did too well with that one [laughs]. People'd ask me and I'd try to answer the question. It's been many a year, but . . . these promotional tours could wear you out, so it took a lot of prayer and a lot of stamina. Get up, fix up, sometimes you had to be on radio at 7:00 in the morning, so the people that were on their way to work could say, "Yeah, she *is* in town." So you had to get there the night before or something like that. It was fun, but it was hard.

I remember one of the most exciting things I ever did—and a lot of people don't know this—Wilma Rudolph, the track star, and I were doing tours together. She and a young man named Ralph Boston, they were fabulous athletes during that time, and we would all travel together. I would sing, and they would speak to a lot of the kids in the area. So to me, that was one of the most rewarding things I've done, too. So I even got the exposure *that* way, and the young people got a chance to hear my record, and they also got a chance to see people who were making history in other areas besides just music. Those little things like that helped formulate my performance, I believe. You had that big gym floor to sing in with this great big sound. I used to love performing in the gyms. Yes, boy. You could really sing. It's like singing with a group in the bathroom—the acoustics were great.

I began to learn how to sing with tapes. We hadn't been doing that, because everything we did down at Satellite, down at Stax, was live. If one person made a mistake, everything stopped. You know, a drummer [made a mistake] and I was singing, everybody had to start all over again. So there wasn't a lot of money in that, doing those things up around school, but it was rewarding. It was teaching you how to get along and really what the eventual road was going to be all about. How to travel with others and get along with others.

The culmination of Thomas's first six years as a touring performer was the legendary Stax/Volt tour of March and April 1967. Although she could only stay in Europe for a week due to a prior booking in Chicago for a civil rights benefit, the experience opened her eyes to the extent of her popularity (as well as the popularity of her Stax labelmates) overseas.

When we went overseas to Europe, the exposure got bigger. And, of course, overseas it was a lot different. It was interesting. They would come in, do an interview just like we're doing now, and put it on a movie and put it in a theater, so there's no way in the world you could come over there and not be the person that you said you were. Like we used to have cartoons that come on before the big movie? Well, they might have a [movie] special there, a whole little mini-show talking about Otis and all the other artists.

In spite of her frantic rehearsal and performance schedule during the European tour, Thomas made the most of what little free time she had.

I'm a real tourist! That's one thing that made it a little harder on me than other people, because when I got to *wherever* I was, I would immediately call someone. I'm not coming over there just to sing. Who wants to be in Paris or London and nothing's happening? I remember one time, we had a four-hour layover at the airport. Everybody was just sitting there in Paris. And I said, "I don't know about you guys, but I'm getting ready to go to the Eiffel Tower." Just like that [laughs]. And so they said, "Let's do it, but we don't have a chance to really look." I said, "Well, I don't know. I'm going." And then all of us, we got all these taxis together. And it was so funny, because French people are interesting. I think they like to see you try to do the language so they can say, [imitates a Parisian not comprehending]. I was trying to say, "To the Eiffel, to the Eiffel" [pronounced "I fell"]. Reminding me of Otis trying to say, "Je t'aime, je t'aime" when he was on the stage [pronounced "jay tom"]. And they were saying it right back with him, "Jay tom, jay tom!" The French people were saying it just like he was saying it. It was really funny. So we would be trying to use our little limited amount of French and trying to get around. Oh, it was great.

Eventually, Thomas devised a way to make the cab driver understand where she wanted to go.

I went and got a postcard. I said, "I want to do this right here" [laughs]. And the cab driver just started falling out laughing, but he knew all the time. They have fun with tourists like that sometimes. And it taught you how to be what they used to call way back then "intercontinental." It doesn't matter [that they don't speak English], because those people love the music. And you wonder—they don't understand a lot of what I'm saying, but they can understand the *feeling.* They understood soul music, 'cause they'd always want to know, "Why do you call it soul music?" And I could see by the way they responded to it, they already basically knew, but they wanted to hear it verbalized.

I ask Thomas how she would answer their question.

If you look at it, it's a whole different type of singing. You're singing from your soul. It's not like trying to be some "perfecto" thing. You just put the music together and just sing to it and let your own true feelings . . . it's not like right here I'll do a B-flat and over here I think I'll do a little so and so. It's like whatever comes out. It's a music that seems to be real close to the spiritual, the emotions. That's why it reaches those people like that. And I believe that's why that music has lasted so long.

Thomas recollects with warmth one particular reunion of the "Stax Revue" in Europe in the late 1980s.

I talked with a young man. He came backstage, and he was crying. He had these tears in his eyes after he saw the show. I think it was Eddie [Floyd] and Sam [Moore]. Dave [Prater] was gone by then, and Otis, of course, was not there. But it was just as packed—because of these memories! And the young man was crying, and he was saying, "I'm so glad you all came back over. I'm so glad you came. You all just don't know what you've done for us over here, overseas, by bringing this music back." I didn't realize people appreciated music like that.

It's that special power to move and inspire listeners that has made the music Thomas recorded at Stax during the 1960s continue to sound so fresh today. Her work retains a clarity and vividness for which the numerous technical advances of the past thirty years could never compensate. As fine as Thomas's pop hits—"Gee Whiz" and "B-A-B-Y"—were, it is her lesser-known performances— "I've Got No Time to Lose" (#67 R&B in 1964), "A Woman's Love" (#71 R&B, also in 1964), "Comfort Me," "Another Night Without My Man"—that will form her legacy. These recordings, all heartrending ballads that convey a true-to-the-moment kind of soulfulness, could never be done the same way twice. It is as if each represents a very special moment in time, durable and immune to the vagaries of public tastes and trends. I ask Thomas about one of my personal favorites, "Comfort Me."

Ooh! Do you know anything about that record?

I respond that I know the Pips are singing the gospelized backup vocals.

All right. That's what I was going to say [laughs]. Gladys too. That is one of the hardest songs in the world to sing. Without them [the Pips]—*They* were the encouragement on that song.

The story goes that Thomas knew the Pips were in town and invited them to the studio to perform on the record with her. Thomas emphatically denies this, shaking her head.

They might have been in town for a show, but I had no idea they were going to come on my [record]. I mean, they may have walked in to say hello or said, "Hey, we may run down to see you or something like that," but it wasn't like I said, "Hey, come and do the gig." No! They came just to say hi. They heard the tape, and they said, "Wow! Can we do that?" And I was, like, [gasps in disbelief]. Because when we were in school, all the young ladies would just croon—[Gladys] was singing "With Every Beat of My Heart," you know, "there's a beat for you." And I have never been able to recreate ["Comfort Me"] in my soul—I think that's what I'm trying to say. You know, I probably could sing it, but I just never was able to reproduce it in my soul.

Unfortunately, "Comfort Me" does not appear on Thomas's 1994 Best of CD (perhaps because it failed to dent the charts). The luminous "Another Night Without My Man" is also conspicuously absent. Like "Comfort Me," "Another Night" was co-written by Thomas's fellow Stax artist Eddie Floyd. Floyd's compositions often had a deep gospel flavor and were imbued with the kind of passion and urgency that Thomas no doubt admired. She wishes that Floyd, a Washington, D.C., native who spent less time in the Stax studio than many of the label's other artists, had been around to write more songs for her.

Now see, that's another thing. A lot of times, when artists would write for you, it may have been a short-lived production, because they went out on the road. Like Eddie, writing songs like that ["Another Night"]. Oh, I love that song! You know, it's in retrospect, but we would have probably done a whole lot of good songs together, because I was still pretty popular in D.C. during that time. You see, Eddie was in D.C.—that whole D.C. scene, he was up there a lot as well. So when he came down to Memphis to record, we just seemed to hit it off.

Thomas's popularity in Washington was due both to Stax president Al Bell's influence with D.C.-area disc jockeys (stemming from his experience on Washington's WUST) and to her one-time status as a resident—after graduating from Tennessee A&I in 1965, she worked on her master's degree at Howard University.

Yeah, that's my town. They used to have Carla Thomas Day, Carla Thomas Week—they had banners all up in the town. I worked on my master's at Howard. I was in American Drama.[9] See, I was always interested in drama. I was always interested in putting together productions. So I was into stage lighting and different things like that—how to make things look a certain way. That was the direction I was going into. Dramatic production.

Thomas never completed her degree, although she later continued her studies in drama at the American Academy of Dramatic Art in New York. She says that the cost of being a touring performer prevented her from finishing her work at Howard. Ironically, it was her work as a professional singer that gave her the income to attend Howard in the first place.

One ended up paying for the other. Plus, around that time was when I started going overseas. So I said, "Oh, now what?" You know, you come out of school and you have to buy a gown and you have to [pauses, reflects for a moment] . . . maybe one day I'll finish.

Although Thomas's life saw many changes of environment during the mid-'60s—promotional tours, travel to Europe, graduate school—the original Stax studio on East McLemore Street in Memphis remained a constant source of personal stability and creative inspiration. Thomas asserts that the studio was, at least during the early years, a place relatively free of tension, giving credence to Steve Cropper's observation that working at Stax was "like being in church." In fact, she frequently describes the Stax regulars as a "family."

We used to just sit there all day. Go eat, come back [laughs], finish, because that was our studio. It wasn't like it was on a time situation. We had the time to put it down, the time to mix it, level it out, get it mastered or whatever, and pay the charges. We just kind of liked being with each other sometimes, although we had our squabbles. 'Cause a lot of times some artist might come in from out of town, and we might have to opt our time and get mad [laughs]. But then, we'd always end up in the studio watching.

Thomas is referring to Atlantic Records's practice of sending non-Stax artists like Wilson Pickett and Don Covay down to the Stax studio to record. Several hits, among them Covay's "See Saw" and Pickett's "In the Midnight Hour," resulted from this arrangement, which was destined to be short-lived. In Soulsville, U.S.A., *Jim Stewart was quoted as saying he ended the practice because of the resentment of the Stax house band and performers: "It got to the point where the guys felt they were being used, so I stopped it. They weren't getting much money for that stuff."[10]*

But see, we enjoyed it too. We didn't want to give them studio time, but we enjoyed them. It was interesting. And what helped is [that] they had the same band—Booker [T. Jones] was playing just about for everybody. So it was still that whole family situation even on their material.

The Stax studio has also been characterized by writers as a place of racial harmony, a fully integrated environment situated (at least during the early years) in the pre-civil-rights South. I ask Thomas about her perception of the racial dynamics at Stax.

We didn't have much tension. Most of the tension came about as wanting to do it our way, but that's with the artist thing. It was relatively free of *racial* tension, but we still had our problems. I mean, when I first started out singing, I was the only little chocolate drop around. I traveled with Steve [Cropper] and Packy [Axton] and all that bunch. And they [the press and members of the public] would always ask us, "How does it feel being . . . ?" I'd come out, and it was the Mar-keys playing behind me, you know.[11] So we went everywhere like that. I think later, because there were other people involved in our company, there was a lot of that other kind of tension—competitiveness tension. And then there probably was a lot of [racial] stress on Jim [Stewart], on Al [Bell], and on a whole lot of the others. We were *still* in the South in the '60s. Even though we could get lost down there in that studio, we still had to come out.

Thomas believes that the racial climate at Stax was affected by the cadre of outside producers and other characters who began to infiltrate the sanctity of the Stax environment during the late '60s, breaking up the cohesiveness of the "Stax family."

Later on, there was a lot not only with racism, but I have a feeling a lot of that comes about as a result of competition. The more and more people get involved more and more, that's what happens. It could be said to be a racial thing when it may be just . . . that can just be used as a word, when it's just, "Hey, I want the money."

Her experiences at Howard University also made Thomas forget some of the day-to-day racial inequities of life in Memphis. Whenever she returned to Memphis, she was forced to reacquaint herself with the qualities—both good and bad—that make the city unique.

It was sort of like a culture shock, in a way, to be back here. But one thing I give Memphis, they love their music. They *do* love their music. And I love my roots. I love the spirit of where I came from. I love the sprit of *this*. Because if I'm going to get it together, I'm gonna have to get it together here. I'm gonna have to get it together *through* here, where all the pain and suffering and whatever there is. There are people who come from everywhere all over the world. It's amazing how they want to come *here*. They want to feel the spirit of whatever got you to be whatever you were. Even with that history of racism. And you know, I've been around where there might have been some [racial] stirs and different things, but I've also encountered a lot of problems from some of my own folk, so, hey.

Many of Thomas's difficulties resulted from what she feels were the personal challenges she faced as a woman in the music business.

You know, [there was] not just racial tension, but personal tensions. Being an artist, being a woman—that's tension in itself. [Speaking softly:] A woman—and see I didn't realize this, I was just so excited—a woman really needs someone, a strong person who cares about their talent and sees the talent. And they don't want to just exploit it, which is what you do to talent, but using the word in a positive way to let people see all the sides of you. A lot of things come with success, and some are not very easy—trying to overcome all the barriers that come up against you as a result of trying to be out here and be successful. But I tried not to allow that to bother me. A lot of my problems were trying to juggle the school thing. That was one of my first *big* hurdles. And then trying to have a personal life. It was very difficult.

A lot of people think it's so easy—just get out there and walk around. And it's hard. It's hard with relationships too. Like with guys. They look at you on a stage and they think [suggestively], "Hey. . . ." But you're a person. You got to get up in the morning. You got to fix up, or *not*, as the case may be. It's very hard. And it's also a type of business that needs a lot of nurturing. And I think—maybe somebody wouldn't like what I'm saying, but anyway—I think men are used to being nurtured by women in this business. I don't mean women *in the business*, I mean men who are in the business are accustomed to having women go, [makes swooning sound], right? *That* kind of nurturing of men. But it's hard sometimes on relationships when women [performers] have *men* going, "Ooh-hoo" and *they're* in relationships. It's a whole different kind of thing—it's an ego thing. I don't even know if it's jealousy. It's like someone says, "ooh!" [and the boyfriend/husband says], "Who is that?" He's somebody who probably bought a record. And to understand takes a very special person.

Singing in front of a live audience raises some difficult questions, such as how to negotiate the boundary between performer and spectator.

There's a lot of fear out here now about getting a little too close to people, and it's well-founded, in a way. Like a one-on-one, being in the audience with people— you can project to the audience, but actually *being in* the audience, like in a club, you have to be a special type of person to be at a club. I'm serious. It's an intimate environment. And it could be rough if you get too personal. There are a lot of people you get very personal with, and you just want to just keep right on going. All you might want to say is, "Hello, I really enjoy talking with you."

In spite of her personal reservations, Thomas is a magical club performer. In 1990, I saw her perform at Anton's, a now-defunct club that was located on Pennsylvania Avenue in Washington. In this intimate setting, Thomas was the consummate entertainer, sounding confident and assured. Her voice was, if anything, even richer than it had sounded on records twenty-five years previously. The highlight of the set was a touching version of "Gee Whiz," in which Thomas provided the sole accompaniment on piano. Most impressively, Thomas did not attempt to recreate the sound of the original record. Instead, she rearranged the song entirely, underscoring the words with deep soulful chords. The effect was not of a forty-seven-year-old woman trying to sound like a seventeen-year-old girl, but rather of a forty-seven-year-old reinterpreting the lyrics and music through the accumulated life experience of an adult. Her interpretation added complex layers of meaning that I had never before considered.

That was one of the most enjoyable times of my life. Actually, it was one of the most luxurious times of my life too. I had a wonderful stay where I was. It's fun being picked up by a limousine every night. Especially for a club gig! [Laughs.]

The appearance at Anton's came at a time when Thomas had long since ceased to be a full-time performer. By the '80s, she was spending much of her time working with Memphis-area schoolchildren, a part of her life that she still cherishes.

We have what we call an "artist in the schools" program, and I worked with them for about ten years. The artists go in with their pictures of the era and say, "Look, this is what we did." And then [the students] send you letters, the cutest little letters. It's all so rewarding. They're those little things that really keep you going in this business. To some people they may seem very minute, but to me it's real important.

I taught [the students] performance and style. How to be whatever *you* are. Yes, we have a lot of heroes and we have a lot of people we look up to as role models, but next year you're going to like somebody else. They all holler out who [the hot artist of the moment] is. I say, now I'm going to watch and see if you still have the person's name in about six months or a year. And I've noticed also—now this is tension, you talk about tension—what they used to call an oldie is now a three-month old record. It's scary.

As an "oldies" recording artist, Thomas is particularly sensitive to the ethic in American culture that overvalues the new and underappreciates the past.

I think that's America. I really do. And it's amazing what the young people will bring out of you with the questions they ask. Sometimes I ask them who they like, and some [when hearing the answer from their classmates], they'll say, "Booo!" I say, "Now how would you like for someone to boo you? Think about it." You know, we talk about little tiny things like that that can be so important. And I say, "You ever thought about a person like Michael Jackson, and look where he is now, and all the stuff you've read about him in the last thirty years? How he *got* to be thirty, with all of this mess? But he got there. And he still can move, he still can do his step and groove." I say, "It's that point from where you started to where you are and what's going on in between there that's important." You may not even hear from him for a while. But a lot of times, where you all may forget him, there's another group over here that's wondering where he is, and they're out interviewing, like you're doing with me. You see what I'm saying? So these things keep us going, and this is what I try to tell them.

Thomas hopes to continue her work with children by exploring different avenues of performance and instruction.

I still would like to do an album for children, and *with* them too, because I have a lot of songs I have written. But it's kind of difficult to know which road to go into because that's a whole different area as far as promoting it, but it is a category now [in the Grammys]. But I'd have to be so much more perfect—when you're putting together something like that for a curriculum that people are going to hear to inspire them.

I'd like to go back into the schoolroom with more of a focus on music but teaching them as far as speech is concerned too, because that seems to be still such a problem, even in the late '90s. Kids have trouble speaking [and] speaking up. They're a whiz at the other things, but the verbal communication. And that's why I say I was blessed coming up that we had to do so much promotion. They had to see you talking. And [if] we were scared, we just couldn't be.

By the time Thomas was working with the Artists in the Schools program, much of the Memphis that she had loved as a teenager and a young woman was gone. Beale Street deteriorated during the '60s and '70s, with the ultimate act of destruction—the demolition of the vaunted Palace Theatre—occurring in 1973. Even more disheartening for Thomas was the loss of the original Stax studio building on McLemore Avenue, torn down in 1989 ostensibly to make way for a church parking lot (over a decade later, the site remains dormant and rubble-strewn).[12] Given that the original Sun studio across town has been profitably revitalized as a museum, the demolition of Stax was not only historically disrespectful but fiscally foolish. As we discuss the loss of the Stax studio, Thomas breaks into a famous Joni Mitchell song.

[She sings:] ". . . put up a parking lot." Maybe that's what it's going to be, but I wish it would be some kind of landmark, more than just a sign that says this is where it used to be. I hated that [the demolition]. If they could have just kept . . . but you know, it was coming down from the inside. A lot of things had happened, and I think if [other Stax artists had] all been here and sort of got a good rally going—a rally-around-the-building sort of thing. But it's hard for one artist to do it, you know. Now *that* may be harder for '60s artists, 'cause we weren't accustomed to doing that. We were only accustomed to singing. We weren't accustomed to running up against all that political stuff. But the artists nowadays, they will. But they have more people behind them. So it was very difficult to see what had happened and to know it had happened so quickly. You know, even though somebody may not like something somebody did, the preservation of the music itself brought millions of dollars to this town, and the notoriety it still brings. It still does.

Of course, Memphis has historically been blessed with a unique ability to jump back on its feet after difficult times, and the current musical scene reflects this resilience: a revitalized (albeit somewhat homogenized) Beale Street boasts several clubs and other venues in which great local music can be heard on any night of the week; legendary producer Willie Mitchell has continued to make records, working out of the same studio where he recorded his classic '70s sides; the original Sun studio attracts pilgrims from all over the world, and the "new" Sam Phillips Recording Studio (the second Sun Studio, built in 1960 after Phillips moved from his original studio at 706 Union Avenue) has produced great albums in the '90s by singers such as Charlie Rich and Gwen McCrae.

Through all of the city's ups and downs, the Thomases have persevered. Rufus Thomas is now recognized as a living cultural treasure, with his own Tennessee state historical plaque in front of the old Palace Theatre site. The record of his achievements is beautifully encapsulated in a glossy booklet that Carla gives me, "Hoot and Holler: The Life and Times of Rufus Thomas in Pictures." At first there is some question as to whether or not the copy I am taking is the last one. As I protest that I don't want to deplete the supply, she interrupts, "You better keep that book," settling the matter. As we are discussing the book, Rufus Thomas (who has been upstairs during much of the interview) comes down to talk.

Carla: He was reminding me of a lot of things I had forgotten.

Rufus: People keep up with more than you do anyway. They can always tell me something that I've forgot. 'Course you remember it when someone reminds you. Then you say, "Oh yeah! I remember."

Carla Thomas laughingly admits that her father is right. She says that she is often surprised by the respect and love that fans have for her music, adding that it's easy to forget how much others appreciate her contributions.

You know, a young lady was telling me, she said, "Carla, you may not even realize this, but your being sixteen, seventeen drew a lot of the sixteen, seventeen-year-olds who felt like they had talent too." And you know, a lot of times we want to feel like we haven't done anything, we haven't really contributed much. And it takes sometimes people to help you see that maybe you did.

In the end, dwelling on the many ways in which the Memphis community and the world at large have changed in the past thirty years is unnecessary. What matters is that the music that Carla Thomas created in the 1960s has survived. In another thirty years, it will still sound just as remarkable.

That's it. It'll never die. It'll always be there. And I'm always reminded by that man that came backstage with those tears in his eyes. I'll always see his face—those are the kinds of things that make you want to keep keeping on.

Part Two

Detroit

W

While the Detroit sound is inextricably linked in the minds of music fans to Motown's classic '60s recordings, this once-thriving industrial city had always supported an active musical scene prior to Motown, spurred on by famous nightclubs like the Flame Show Bar and the Twenty Grand, as well as legendary entertainment spots like the Greystone Ballroom and the Paradise Valley, or "Black Bottom," district. The city has long been a haven for African-American performers, and was home to one of the first integrated musicians' unions in the U.S. Later, in the '60s, a number of small soul labels managed to thrive in spite of Motown's encompassing presence: Bob West's Lu Pine label, Ric Tic (which Motown eventually purchased), the Atlantic-distributed Carla (which scored a big hit in 1966 with Deon Jackson's "Love Makes the World Go Round"), and Karen all attained a moderate degree of success utilizing the cadre of excellent musicians active in Detroit.

The Motown Sound itself has too often been denigrated by hard-core soul fans, but even though it was clearly marketed with a broad pop audience in mind, the music Motown created in the '60s remains viscerally exciting and influential. Further, Motown contributed enormously to the musical life of the city, both directly, by employing some of Detroit's most talented musicians, and indirectly, by cultivating a vital musical climate in a city whose fortunes were in many other ways beginning to decline. Motown's move to Los Angeles in the early '70s left a void in the city that has never been filled, although great music continued to be recorded throughout the '70s on other Detroit labels such as Westbound and Holland-Dozier-Holland's Invictus and Hot Wax. Further, Detroit in the '70s boasted a first-rate studio in United Sound, patronized by artists like the Dramatics, the Dells, Millie Jackson, and many others.

Today's Detroit probably boasts more underutilized musical talent than any city aside from Memphis. On any given night in one of the city's many small clubs, great bands can be heard producing a tight, lean, spare sound that is both hard-driving and intelligent. The city still has its share of great local singers such as Laura Lee (now back to singing gospel after a successful soul career), Alberta Adams, and (as we shall see) Bettye LaVette—many of whom are hoping that the recent legalization of gambling will help them find work in the new casinos. Whereas in the past Detroit was all too eager to ignore its heritage (the demolition of the Greystone in 1980 is still recalled with sadness), the city today seems prepared to value the many treasures that remain. In the downtown district, for example, half a dozen historic theatres sit in vacant but good condition, awaiting expectantly the benefits of a second economic boom. In spite of hard times, Detroit will continue to play a vital role in the preservation of R&B and soul music.

Bettye LaVette

Buzzard Luck

Bettye LaVette, late 1960s

*B*ettye LaVette is the quintessential cult singer. While few know about her, those who do are fiercely devoted, and with good reason: LaVette is one of the most gifted vocalists in all of soul. One listen to great performances like "Let Me Down Easy" and "Right in the Middle (of Falling in Love)" and you too may be tempted to place her alongside Otis Redding and Etta James in the soul pantheon. Although any attempt to compare her with other singers would do her a great disservice, first-time listeners often say she reminds them of Tina Turner or Mavis Staples.

While elements of both of these fine singers can be heard in her performances, LaVette is often a deeper, more complex vocalist than Turner, and she has—at least these days—more technical stamina than Staples. LaVette can shout with the best of them, but she can also be disarmingly gentle and restrained. On any given recording she will move from one extreme of emotion to the other, covering every gradation in between.

None of this is to say that LaVette's career adequately represents her abilities as an artist. For, unlike most of the other singers profiled in this book, she has never enjoyed the benefits of a durable recording contract, releasing only one non-compilation album in nearly forty years in the business.

Instead she has recorded singles on some fifteen different labels (she is one of the few artists who has recorded for both Motown and Atlantic), resulting in a mostly out-of-print body of work characterized by a disparate collection of producers, material, and sounds. Listeners who take the time to sort through her assorted recordings—"Feelings" and all—will be amply rewarded, for LaVette (who is sharply critical of her work) has never given a weak performance.

Bettye LaVette was born Betty Haskin in Muskegon, Michigan, on January 29, 1946. Both of her parents had migrated from Louisiana with the hope of achieving greater economic opportunity in the industrial North. Her father, whom her official bio claims "daydreamed about Betty leading a glittering life, either as a singer or in the circus," died when she was twelve. Unlike many of her contemporaries, LaVette does not come from a church background and has no formal music training—a fact that has sometimes made her an outsider when dealing with other performers (LaVette is living proof that great singers are often born and not made). She has been married and divorced twice, has one daughter (who works as a schoolteacher) and two grandchildren, for whom she wakes up at seven each morning to take to school.

On the morning of our interview, LaVette decides that a good place to meet would be the Elwood Grill, a historic, art deco bar that has sat for sixty years across the street from Detroit's famed Fox Theatre. Since we have never seen each other, she asks me over the phone what I look like. After I describe myself, she responds, "I'll probably be more conspicuous. I look like a gangsta rapper." When I arrive at the proposed meeting spot, the Elwood Grill is clearly closed for business. A newspaper article in the window explains that the structure will be moved, providing a new site can be found, to make way for a new stadium that is to be constructed on the mostly-vacant block (the historic Gem Theatre is already in the process of being moved to safe territory just two blocks away). When LaVette arrives, looking youthful and trim but very little like a gangsta rapper, we decide to move to a brick-oven pizza restaurant that is housed in the same office building as the Fox. As we cross the street, LaVette asks me what I've seen so far in Detroit (I've been there for two days). When I reply that I have visited the Motown Museum, she snaps, "All white people want to go to the Motown Museum when they come to Detroit!" LaVette's response, while somewhat tongue-in-cheek, suggests that the legendary label is the source of conflicted feelings. While Motown virtually ignored her during its '60s heyday, she finally wound up there for a brief stint in the early '80s. Naturally, Motown is one of the topics addressed once we begin to discuss the career that LaVette describes as "a series of misadventures."

I have a menu fetish.

Bettye LaVette's confession comes during the middle of a conversation about the great R&B singer Jackie Wilson. I ask her to explain.

I just love menus, and if it's a really interesting menu with a lot of interesting stuff on it I . . . just go on and talk and I'll answer you, but I'll be reading the menu. I'm not trying to decide, I'm trying to read the menu.

We resume our discussion of Jackie Wilson, focusing on his debilitation in a coma and subsequent early death. LaVette, in dark sunglasses and every inch the star, keeps her eyes fixed on the laminated, brown-paper menu.

Well, he used himself up so much. I mean, he just completely used himself up. He would have just died anyway, if that [the stroke that led to his coma] hadn't happened. If he hadn't continued to have a modicum of success and had just gone down really bad, then that could have killed him too, but if he still had the success where people were giving him money and drugs—either way it went he was gonna be dead. He and Little Willie John were destined to die. You could hear it in their voices.

I ask LaVette about some of her early musical influences, then retract the question when I notice that she is still scanning the menu.

That's all right, 'cause I'm not reading word for word, I'm just trying to see the gist of the menu. I haven't been in here before. I think that probably more men have influenced me than women. I think that there's something in me that's always known that women and I weren't going to be the best of buddies [with a sly grin]. I like men and they like me. And I set it up that way. I don't even try to make girlfriends. I try to make men-friends. I like them for personal friends, for lovers, for everything. My father and I were much closer than my mother and I, and I'm just a man's woman, so that always makes for lots of women enemies. And the few girlfriends I've had in this business were pretty much like that early on.

But Etta [James] is who I wanted to be when I first started singing, in terms of females. I mean, that was the first female that really attracted me. Etta had all these records, and I just thought she was really wonderful. And then when I came into my own, I just kept the respect for her, but I *stringently* avoid even any memory of the way she sung. I don't listen to her music or anything. I don't listen to music at all, actually. I'm not a music enthusiast. People are always very surprised when they come to my house. They never hear me humming, never hear any music playing. I am a television enthusiast. I watch everything on television. I just finished watching this documentary that was on PBS about the travels of Lewis and Clark. I like that kind of stuff. And when I go out I really don't like to go and see anybody do anything. I'd rather just sit there and drink and talk and eat.

But my influences have mostly all been men—Clyde McPhatter, early-on a singer called Dee Clark [of "Raindrops" fame], Ray Charles, Marvin Gaye. In fact my show used to consist of Marvin's records and whatever two I had. As soon as his songs came out, they were automatically a part of my show. I think I've got to be the only black woman in the world who has never sung "Respect." Or "I Will Survive." Or "Get Here If You Can." I've never sung those songs.

I remark that it seems unlikely she ever will.

You know what? I'm *trying* to sing "Get Here If You Can" now. I'm trying to sing it, but I don't want to. Something in me won't let me sing it, I don't know. Now I don't do Aretha's music because I just feel like it's been done. I mean, that's it. You know, it's done really well by her. And I'll do something by Barbra Streisand because I can interpret it so differently, you know. Every once in a while I will like something by Gladys Knight so much until I'll just have to do it—maybe she didn't quite phrase it the way I would have and I'll do it. But I don't really do songs by living females. Most of the songs I do by females are by dead females—Dinah Washington, Billie Holiday—on my show.

Knowing that LaVette has a weekly cable television spot ("What's Going On With Bettye La-Vette"), I ask if she is referring to her TV show or her club act.

Oh, the television show, it's just a talk show. But I've been with the cable company now for about six or seven years, so if I come up with a musical production idea I want to do, I can do it. They [the cable company] told me, "Come up with the specials, write them down the way you want them and you can do them." And I thought I would come up with one every week. I've only come up with two in six years! I love television so much, I wouldn't want to be on there just to be on television. I wanted it to be really interesting. But the specials were fun. And I find they were much more fun to do than making records. I enjoyed it much more: telling everybody where to stand, how they were going to pose, and thinking of my own scenes and choosing the songs. I don't have as much of that ability in music because I don't read [music], you know. So I have to do a lot of listening and call for a lot of help. And the television thing is just making a story move. So it was really fabulous. I'm having dreams now of going to Hollywood and becoming a Holly-wood *producuh.* Motion *pictuhs,* don't you know [laughs]. I did one special with me and all of the female blues singers that were available that were singing in Detroit when I started singing. I had Ortheia Barnes, Alberta Adams, Johnnie Mae Matthews, who was my very first producer, who just kept holding the production up and I had to cut her out of it—but I really wanted her. She was one of the first female producers in the country probably. And I really wanted her in the special, but she just never would show up. She never did pay me for my first record; she didn't show up for my special.

Johnnie Mae Matthews was a semilegendary figure on the Detroit R&B scene of the '50s and '60s, influential both as a performer and producer. Matthews met LaVette (at this point still Betty Haskin) through a mutual acquaintance who was very well connected in the club world.

I wanted to be a groupie, so I was hanging around the singers. I had met this little girl whose name was Sherma Lavett—Lavett was her middle name. And she knew everyone who had ever done anything bad or who had ever sung a song. I said, "This is my girl here. I love it." Should've had my butt in school. I loved her. They called her Ginger and *everybody* knew Ginger.

Once Ginger introduced the sixteen-year-old Haskin to Matthews, everything happened very quickly. Impressed with the maturity of Haskin's voice, Matthews rushed her into the studio with a catchy song entitled "My Man—He's a Lovin' Man."

Johnnie Mae did this thing on me in one weekend. I learned it through that week, we did it that weekend, we changed my name that Sunday, they put it out that next Friday, and it all just happened like that. Atlantic bought it the next week. And I had no idea how big all of that was. I thought it was wonderful, but I had no idea what it really meant or what I was supposed to do, and nobody was telling me.

Much of LaVette's confusion resulted from her complete lack of experience as a singer.

When "My Man" came out, Johnnie Mae heard me sing and said, "Oh, she's got a great voice." She gave me a few little pointers. Basically the voice was there, and they just let me apply it to the song. They didn't even tell me what key it was in or how to count a song off. The first time I went on stage and the musicians said "count it off," I was like [makes puzzled face]. You know, I hadn't been in talent shows. I'd never sung before in my life, before that week. [LaVette emphasizes this point with a laugh and a pause] I had never been Bettye LaVette before, and I had never sung before. I mean, I'd *sung*, but not in front of any kind of audience or with any group.

Once it was picked up by Atlantic in 1962, "My Man—He's a Lovin' Man" went all the way to #7 on the R&B charts. It remains the biggest hit of LaVette's career. On the 45 the young singer was listed as "Betty Lavett"—the first of several alternate name spellings she has used throughout the years. The record became a staple for club performers and was covered by Tina Turner on a live album recorded for Kent in the '60s.

I have never heard Tina's version. I heard Ortheia Barnes sing it when it was first out.[1] She was a little more bluesy and a little more audience-trained. I mean, she had at least sung in church—I hadn't even sung in church. So when I heard her interpretation of it, I was very intimidated 'cause I knew I couldn't sing it that well.

I am surprised to hear of LaVette feeling cowered by the vocal prowess of another singer; LaVette would seem to be the last performer who should feel insecure about her talent. Much of her self-doubt is rooted in her belief that her records were poorly produced, with little consideration given to the qualities that made her unique. There is some credence to the notion. After a second Atlantic single, LaVette was thrust into the trajectory that would become the standard pattern of her career: recording briefly for a series of labels without the benefit of a solid producer, an album or a long-term contract. Her next such situation was at Robert West's Detroit-based Lu Pine label in 1963, then home to the Falcons (who, with Wilson Pickett singing lead, had a hit with "I Found a Love" the previous year).

Robert heard "My Man" and he said, "Oh yeah, she can sing," so he gave me another song to sing. And then the next producer heard that and said, "Oh yeah, she sings good on that, let her sing this." No one ever said, "Listen to this song, see how this does." Instead they said, "Oh, I know just the song for her," based on what they had heard. And it kept getting farther and farther away from me and more like these songs these people were writing. So I never had a chance to develop a "me." I've never really had very much to say about any of the music that I've done, and I've never liked any of my records. They all sung me; I didn't sing any of them. I took a lot of direction, and no one was directing me. I never learned any of them properly, other than "Let Me Down Easy," which I thought was a wonderful record, and it just happens that rhythm and blues had not gone pop. It went right the year after with Aretha Franklin's "Respect." But mine did as well as it could do.

"Let Me Down Easy," a #20 R&B hit released on the small, New York-based Calla label in 1965, is still LaVette's favorite of her records.[2] A deep blues song with a haunting string part (provided by noted arranger Dale Warren), the record featured her most soulful performance to date—miles away from the youthful impetuosity of "My Man," recorded just three years earlier. The fade, in which she repeatedly shouted "Please! Please!" was particularly effective. More than any of her previous

records, "Let Me Down Easy" showcased the qualities that would set LaVette apart from other singers: a blistering intensity modulated by moments of deep, heartfelt reflection. It was this combination of the aggressive and the vulnerable, the spontaneous and the meditative that proved so striking. More than that, there was the quality of the voice itself: a moody, sultry instrument marked by a distinctive catch (or in singer's terms a "thing") that made her instantly identifiable.

Having moved to New York prior to signing with Calla, LaVette remained there for several years trying to build a successful career in the world's most competitive city. However, no further hits resulted from the association with Calla, and she eventually decided to move back to Detroit. It was there that she met her future manager, Jim Lewis.

So I guess about 1968, after "Let Me Down Easy" and New York kicked my booty and sent me back home, I met Jim Lewis, who was the assistant to the president of the musicians' union here in Detroit. And that just became a life-long friendship—his life long. He passed away about nine years ago. But he just brought the Bettye LaVette out. The first thing he had to tell me—'cause I'd do these records and people kept spending this money, so by then I thought I could sing—he said, "Well, you can't" [laughs]. I mean, this man had been with Jimmie Lunceford and with Count Basie and had come up with people who really could sing, who really knew they could sing, who were really good musicians. And I really wasn't very good. I had these records and my voice sounded pleasant, but a Sarah Vaughan or somebody could have blown me right off the stage. I wasn't that kind of singer. So he intimidated me with all those people and showed me how long they had lasted, and when one of my records would flop, he'd say [as if to prove a point], *"See."* I mean, he was just . . . I think he gave me *one* compliment. But the first time I ever had any insurance in my life, he got it; the first car I ever had, everything. He really just brought the person out. There had been nothing but this little recording person, and that was all. He really brought the bitch, the woman, the singer, all of that out of me. He knew it was there, and he wasn't going to let me just flit it away, acting a fool, which is what I was doing.

And so now, if I never have another record as long as I live, I can sing. And I can sing anywhere. I realize that I do have my very own sound—we don't know for how many more days, the way these girls are coming out of grade school now—but right now I still do have a little bit of a handle on sounding like me, and I'm hoping that I can get something out in the streets, if I can only get one in before the deadline. But honey, these little people that you see standing on the television digging between their legs and pointing and carrying on—late at night, they know they can't outsing me, and if they never admit it, they know it. And I knew it too. I knew I could not outsing these people. The records were selling and people liked me, but the people who counted knew that I wasn't that hot. I was pretty cool and could grow, but I wasn't that hot.

LaVette's next (and, unfortunately, last) top-30 R&B hit, "He Made a Woman Out of Me," came during her tenure with Silver Fox, a joint venture between Nashville entrepreneur Shelby Singleton and Leland Rogers (brother of Kenny and the producer of Little Esther's 1962 comeback hit, "Release Me").[3] Recorded in Memphis in 1969, the record was one of LaVette's finest. The lyric—about a young country girl seduced into having sex for the first time—was decidedly sexist and might even have seemed campy in other hands ("I used to tease Joe Henry, I guess I teased too hard/Then one day it all happened, right in my own back yard/Joe Henry had his way. . . ."), but LaVette turned it into a powerful account of liberation through sex. Her performance was perfectly timed (right down to the "Ooh . . . Lawd" in the bridge), building to a marvelous, improvised climax full of hortatory, twisted "Whoa-oa-oas." The sound of the record was hard-core southern soul, with darting horns, stinging guitar licks, and heavy, churning percussion. Not surprisingly, the song was banned on many stations and consequently never got the airplay it deserved (even when it was covered soon after by country performer Bobbie Gentry).

LaVette was signed to Silver Fox through the influence of Kenny Rogers, who had been impressed with her cover version (for another Detroit-based label, Karen) of his first hit, 1968's "(Just Dropped in) To See What Condition My Condition Was In."

The company [Silver Fox] was in Nashville. And we didn't want Shelby to come in the studio, so we went to Memphis to record. But Leland Rogers, who produced that stuff on me, had been my national promotion man when I did "Let Me Down Easy." And Kenny Rogers came to Detroit to work in a nightclub with the First Edition. I took him my copy of "What Condition My Condition Is In," and he was just thrilled about it. And at the time he was broke as well, but he said his brother was starting a new company in Nashville and he wanted to send ["My Condition"] to him. So when he sent it to Leland, he [Leland] said, "Oh, I know her. I love her. I worked on 'Let Me Down Easy.'" And he and his brother fell out for a very long time because Kenny was doing so bad then, and Shelby Singleton was doing well and Leland was doing well with him, and Leland didn't give Kenny any money for bringing me to the company and Kenny felt that he should, and they fell out for a long time—until Kenny got big and called on Leland to help *him*. They were really kind of ripped about that. I'm glad I was involved in that! [laughs].

Leland—not being the best producer in the world—*was* a singer-lover, and so he had a great deal of respect for the female voice and would kind of force whoever was doing the arrangements to kind of listen to me a little bit more. And then by us doing them with the band right there, the tunes tended to kind of go the way that I went because I was there singing with them. So it kind of pulled them a certain way. But still, to ask any singer to scream the way they had me scream down there was ridiculous. They couldn't have wanted me to sing any more. [Laughs, imitating Rogers:] "You got to do a little holler right there." And I thought that was my strong point, you know. Well it *was*, because if I was stylizing and phrasing, it wasn't deliberate—that was just the way it was coming out. I had nothing to do that I knew I *could* do but holler. I knew I could holler, so I was happy to do that.

Since we are talking about recording in the South, I ask LaVette about the kinds of racial situations she observed there. She explains that segregation, while outlawed by the time of "He Made a Woman Out of Me," was very much a reality during the tours of her early-'60s career.

We had no place to stay at all in the South when I first started singing, other than rooming houses. But there was a place in Atlanta, Georgia, called the Forrest Arms. I don't care how big you were, if you were black, this is where you stayed. And the two telephones were in the courtyard—the hotel was built around a court-yard—and sometimes you would go down there in that courtyard at two or three o'clock after the clubs closed and there would be me maybe and Ben E. King stand-ing, waiting to use the phone, and John Lee Hooker and Gladys Knight, 'cause that was the place where everybody stayed. And you would have just been surprised, the mire we were living in [laughs]. But we thought it was good. It was the biggest black hotel, and Mr. Forrest, who owned the place and also sold corn liquor, is who Jimmy Reed is talking about when he sings "Big Boss Man," 'cause he called him "Boss Man," and he would wake him up all during the night to get another half pint or whatever. Then they would have to go back and get, like, a dollar or two dollars together to get another half-pint. You know, they would never just come and get, like, a gallon or something. They were getting just two dollars' at a time. So he would say, "Boss man, boss man!"

In addition to participating in tours that took her throughout the South, LaVette was also a prominent performer on the local Detroit music scene. By the early '60s, Detroit's nightlife, although still vibrant, was showing incipient signs of deterioration (signs that would point to the eventual decay of the city itself). I refer to one of our earlier phone conversations in which LaVette had lamented the loss of live-performance venues in the city. She responds with a vivid description of the Detroit of her youth.

I mean, just look at the books that have been written about Detroit in terms of the music and the nightlife. There are more stories written about our pimps and whores, who were nationally known, than almost any other city—New York or any other city. The street life and the night life here was just so fabulous at one time. When I started singing, many of the big nightclubs were on their last leg. They went out with the '60s, so I got a chance to work at all of them maybe once. You know, the Flame Show Bar and Phelps Lounge, and I did the Twenty Grand several times, but that was on its way out too. It had maybe ten years to go when I started singing, but each year was worse and worse and worse. I only had the opportunity to work the Flame Show Bar once, just before it closed. And I don't think I even had the opportunity to go there [as a patron] but three times. Because before I started singing, I wasn't old enough. I wasn't old enough *after* I started singing, but I had a legitimate reason for being there then.

LaVette had no ambivalence about being thrust into an adult environment at age sixteen.

I always wanted to be grown. Always. I never got my clothes dirty when I was a little kid. I never wanted to be a little kid. So the adaptation was very easy for me. I always wanted to drink, stay up late, cuss, all of that. I fell right into it! And was helped a lot because I was the youngest. A lot of things that happened to other singers didn't happen to me. A lot of bad things *did* happen in terms of personal stuff, intimate stuff, but by and large I was with some very dangerous people who were very cognizant of me and very protective of me.

I ask LaVette how her mother felt about having her teenage daughter perform in nightclubs.

Well, it was a step up. My family had never had anything or done anything. No one in my family, as far as we can see, has ever been in show business. And as a tot my family always had card parties and they sold corn liquor, so it was always people who drank and stayed up late all the time. So doing this without doing something that was against the law was really a step up.

During the years she spent as a teenage performer at local clubs, LaVette became acquainted with many of the artists recording for the burgeoning Motown label. Once she began to date Motown executive Clarence Paul, she became one of the only outsiders allowed a glimpse inside the secretive world of Hitsville, USA. She suspects that the autobiographies written by former Motown artists and associates gloss over the harsher aspects of the era.

All the books that have been written really haven't been forthcoming. I haven't read any of them, but the things that I hear on TV from the writers and excerpts that I've heard—from Martha Reeves's book, from the Temptations's book, from Berry Gordy's book—it all sounds like we were all just young, bright-eyed people waiting for Berry Gordy to come along and discover us to make us famous. And it really was not like that at all. None of these people were young *or* bright-eyed. They were never young, almost. All these people were grown by the time Motown started. They weren't virgins, and they had all been drunk at one point. I don't know anybody that came over there with a smidgen of innocence but Stevie Wonder. And we soon corrupted him.

I mention Michael Jackson.

Well, I'm not even talking about what happened after the time Michael came. They went on to get some real young people, but those original people were never young, and all of the people that we hung around with here in the city were very bad people. *Now* they seem that way, but then everything was so segregated— the ministers and the drug dealers all dealt together because all the blacks were in one place. So it sounds very bad now, some of the people that we dealt with and knew personally and came to our house and we went to theirs. It sounds bad in retrospect, but that's who they were and that's what they did, and no one's writing about any of that. It all sounds so very innocent. That's not the group I knew.

LaVette explains that drugs were pretty much taken for granted as an inherent element of the scene, with heroin the only substance carrying any sort of stigma.

If you were strung out on heroin, that was a no-no. The only people we knew that messed with any heroin were Esther Phillips and Ray Charles. But *that's* when you were messing with *drugs*. Other than that, the other stuff was not "drugs." And I guess just before Motown got to be really big, the people who were messing with cocaine, like Jackie Wilson and Little Willie John, they had graduated into kind of a "white thing," we called it. So they were dealing with a heavier kind of drug, you know. But then right after "Respect," when everything black started to go national, then we all started too. We had cocaine dealers that were on the road with us. They went from town to town with us, and then they would fly back here and get more drugs and come back. It was just after people started losing their homes because of the other financial things—not because they messed it all up with drugs. They were making enough money to buy the drugs, you know. But when other things started to fall down and the groups started breaking up, it became more apparent that they needed to leave it alone, and then we all did. I guess everybody still kind of smokes joints, but nobody . . . I mean, you just *had* cocaine. *Everybody* had some cocaine. Everybody knew several drug dealers. We had known these people from the beginning of our career. The numbers men and the drug dealers—these were our fans.

LaVette's reference to the sometimes-murky relationship between artist and fan makes me recall a remark she made during one of our first phone conversations. My sister was about to get married, prompting LaVette to quip, "Wish her good luck for me. Tell her it's [marriage] almost as hard as being an R&B singer."

It *is. Especially* if you're an R&B singer [laughs]. You invariably marry a pimp or a fan. And either one of them is just really bad. So it takes a while to find someone that's secure enough with themselves or is generous enough to not take advantage of you. It's hard doing anything, unless they're doing it with you. It's hard to go to school or have children or be married, unless they're with you. And then you've got to really be kind of soul mates, you know, and feel the same way about music.

Another thing, when you talk about trying to be married, people do not know the extent that these young women go to get into these guys' rooms. And I just know some awful stories. There were hotels that we could no longer stay in because Jackie Wilson's show had just come through or because Sam Cooke's show had just come through. And they had just caused so much trouble we couldn't even stay there. They used to do just awful things, but they didn't seem awful then. They just seem awful now.

LaVette asserts that there were also plenty of male groupies.

It was always what they called "stage-door Johnnies." The guy that would years ago be standing backstage with the flowers or the diamond bracelet, he was there with the cocaine. It was "Pretty Rick" and "Fast Eddie," and these people were pimps or drug dealers or numbers men, and they would be there in their El Dorados waiting for Diane [Ross], me, Florence [Ballard], Martha [Reeves]. Everybody that we were messing with was out of the same group, and there was nobody that was really notorious. If a cop got killed, the streets stood still until they found out who did it. Everybody got involved and helped. These people did these awful things, but they took care of their mothers, and they opened community centers, and they didn't cuss in front of grown folks, and they didn't carry guns. But they were the sleaze of the earth and they did really bad things. And most of them are dead now, and no one mentions them at all. No one mentions that those were Berry Gordy's running partners, or that I used to go with them and that Martha used to go with them and

Martha and I used to go with some of the same ones all over the country, because there was a little nightlife group. And everybody knew them all over the country.

By the time LaVette finally got to Motown, Florence Ballard was dead, and Ross and Reeves had left the label. Tell Me a Lie *(1982), her one album for Motown, was something of a mixed bag. Recorded in Nashville with an excellent band, the album featured, in songs such as "Right in the Middle (of Falling in Love)" and the countryish title track, some of her best material to date. The former song in particular is an unacknowledged classic: a magnificent performance in which LaVette seems to pick up where the late Otis Redding left off. Once again, her voice, timing, and extraordinary improvisatory ability are on fine display. With the Muscle Shoals horns contributing punchy riffs, the song was one of the best R&B records of the '80s and pointed to a soul-retro style that would later gain prominence on Etta James's great* Seven Year Itch *album. Other songs, such as the obligatory Motown covers—"If I Were Your Woman" and "I Heard It Through the Grapevine"—were less inspired, although LaVette's performance was strong throughout. Furthermore, the album suffered from poor promotion and distribution, so that very few people ever saw a copy. LaVette's description of her experiences at Motown give an indication of why her career there was not successful.*

The deal was actually all done by phone. I never went to the company but once. I was living in New Orleans, and [producer] Steve Buckingham, whom I had worked with before, had done something for them—I don't know what it was.[4] But anyway, in the interim, they told him that Diane was leaving Motown. She hadn't left yet; she would be leaving in a very few short days, and they wanted to fill that void and they didn't want to fill it with a kid. They wanted to fill it with somebody that was already well on their way. And he, just thank goodness, thought of me, because they gave me more money than I had ever made up to that point. And then it was going to be *Motown.* By the time that the Supremes got to be big, *everyone* wanted to be with Motown. I don't care where you were. It was such a clever little thing [with sarcastic sweetness] and they were all *"family."* Everybody was really kind of envious of them after a while. So by the time that I did do this thing, I was very pleased that I had something on the Motown label. I was very glad, and I'm very proud when I see it. I just wish it had been the real Motown [the '60s Motown].

But it was strictly out of the blue. It was not a sought-after thing. I'm telling you, as they call it in the country, I have *buzzard* luck in my career. I knew that the album was not going to sell. It was going too many different ways. But I didn't know that in words then. I didn't know *why* it wasn't going to sell. I just said it wasn't good, you know. And it was Steve Buckingham's production, and I didn't want to insult him— he had been so nice and he had thought of me. Lee Young, who was then chairman of the board, told me, "Don't worry about it and don't voice your opinions around the rest of the people at the company." He said, "Let's get this out. Let everybody know you're still around and you're back. And the next one, maybe you can coproduce, or at least have much more to say." And then they fired the man! In the middle of my album, they fired him. They said, "Take that shit off the air!" [Laughs.] I said, "*Please* give him another chance." 'Cause he was so enamored of me. You know, he had been Nat "King" Cole's drummer.[5] So this man had worked with Nat "King" Cole, and what he thought about the rest of those little people that were there at the time, other than Stevie Wonder, was nothing. So I had a really good shot, 'cause the man knew that I could sing.

In an example of Motown's poor presentation of the album, LaVette's photograph did not appear on the cover. Instead, the cover sported a photograph of two fine-featured model types: one male and one female. Her back is turned, with her face in profile. With his arms around her waist, he can be seen discreetly slipping off his wedding ring in anticipation of the transgression to follow.

I hadn't been married very long, and they just thought that it would look so bad for me to be standing there in this suggestive pose.

I remark that they could have just changed the pose.

Couldn't they have just put my picture on smiling? You know, change the scene? And they were so set on that scene, of the guy taking the ring off. They really wanted that scene on the album. I would have raised hell about everything if I had known they weren't going to give me another shot. I was, kind of, "Okay. Well, okay, that's fine [with compliant resignation]. I like that too." Steve would give me this darn song like—you heard that album?—this "Seen One, Seem 'Em All" [feigning enthusiasm]. "It's . . . oh, it's just *wonderful. I've always* wanted a song like this one!" But I'm steady, knowing I'm on Motown now, and this was my first album, you know. I had had fifty singles. So I wasn't going to blow anything. Fired the man [referring to Young]. *Fired* him. So after that, it's just been catch-as-catch-can, just doing gigs here [in Detroit]. Fortunately, they never forget in Europe, so I get a chance to go there.

I ask LaVette why she thinks that Europeans often seem so much more receptive to soul music than Americans. Her response is only partially a joke.

'Cause they've got good sense, and they realize they can't sing as good as I can [laughs]. I really don't even know. We're such a disposable society. And we're such a wonderful society. I mean, we have so many *wonders,* until nothing's wonderful to us. And then when you talk about audiences here in Detroit—I mean, everybody in Detroit lives next door to one of the Temptations or one of the Supremes or somebody who's become legendary. So they aren't that impressed.

Like many soul artists, LaVette has relied on theatre as a potential creative outlet whenever record deals have become scarce. In 1978, she starred with Honi Coles (and later Cab Calloway) in the touring production of the hit Broadway musical, Bubbling Brown Sugar. *In an interview for the* Michigan Chronicle *designed to promote the show's Detroit opening that September, LaVette displays the same type of self-deprecating wit that she employs twenty years later in our interview. She admits to the writer that before receiving the offer for the show, she had wanted to retire: "I had been in this business for seventeen years, and nothing was happening with my career at the time—I mean nothing." At the end of the interview, she says she's changed her mind: "Listen, I don't know what was on my mind. If Barnum and Bailey called tomorrow, you'd better believe I'd be learning to ride an elephant."*

LaVette says today that despite the rigorous performance schedule of eight shows a week, she still found theatre less strenuous than touring as a singer.

[A theatre performance] only lasted an hour and a half, two hours tops, and you've got thirty or forty people to say something every time you say something. Or you sing a song, and then you don't sing another one for twenty-five or thirty minutes, so it's very easy. The *rehearsal* of a theatre show is more arduous because you rehearse nine hours a day, seven days a week for maybe three or four months. But then after that, I found it got boring easily because you'd have to stand in the same place every night and say the same thing.

Working with the other cast members, however, was a different story.

I've never sung in a group, and I've never been in a choir, and I found it annoying that every time I went somewhere, all these people were there. They got on my *nerves.* When I got dressed and got ready to go somewhere, I couldn't go until everybody else was dressed. The people were wonderful, they were, but I found theatre to be very gospel-like, and they always wanted me to hold hands and pray or hug. Honi and I—and when I was doing it with Cab Calloway—we always just kind of got away and got drunk.

I did a show that [Motown producer and former husband of Kim Weston] Mickey Stevenson wrote. This was before all of these gospel shows started going around. This was one of the first. And Johnny Brown from the television show *Good Times?*—he was the star of the show. And it was called *The Gospel Truth.* It was about a church that was struggling, trying to get big, and the minister had two wayward children, and they come back at the end—of course, they've seen the light. But there were some fabulous songs. *Fabulous* songs. It was well written, and it was before it got just really outrageous the way it is now, with *God's Gonna Tell You Something* and all kinds of stuff like that. There are just a gang of them: [adopts evangelical tone] *Don't You Hear God Calling?* and just everything.

But they [the cast members] would pray before they would go on. *Bubbling Brown Sugar* was really more like a Broadway show, more like people in show business, but *The Gospel Truth* was strictly people who had come out of church, and I was really the only strumpet in the show. Mickey probably wouldn't have even hired me except that the producer and owner of the show [Mary Card] was my very best friend, so she said, "I'm hiring my friend, whether they all like it or not." 'Cause I think Mickey, of course, wanted to hire Kim Weston, and they didn't need us both. So Mary said, "Well it's my show, so use Bettye."

But they would be praying, and I'd be walking past them going to the sidelines to wait for the curtain to go up, and when the show started to close, I mean, every week it was just this gloom—that's another thing I don't like about theatre. With a record, it just flops, but this—it drags on and there's this gloom, and everybody gets scared and when is it going to close? And they were, like, "You're the reason that this show is going to close because you won't pray, and I think you're just with the devil." I said, "That's all true, and this show is *definitely* going to close, in a matter of days now" [laughing]. They hated me! They hated me. I went and got this sweat-shirt made, and it said, "Everybody has to believe in something . . . I believe I'll roll another joint!" [Laughs.] And they hated me. Now some of these people *had* been friends with me. You remember a group called Hodges, James, and Smith? They were in it—all three of them. One of them is from here, and I had known them from years ago when Mickey Stevenson and Clarence Paul had started a company together, so some of the people *did* like me before the show. They all hated me when it was over. Oh! I had a wonderful time.

And then Mickey Stevenson had gotten so mad he wouldn't let me go on. I was understudying, but Mary made them pay me the same thing they were paying the girl [the lead]. When he said, "Well, I can't pay. She's an understudy," Mary said, "But she's a star. She's just out of work. You gotta pay her the same thing you pay the girl." So when Mickey got mad at me 'cause I wouldn't pray and wouldn't let me go on, I was just making two thousand dollars a week for nothing. I was just hanging around, fucking with everybody. [Laughs.] It was awful. I had a great time!

During the pause that follows this story, LaVette asks me to check on the time (she has to pick up her grandchildren from school later that afternoon). Since we still have half an hour, I ask her about a singing contest that she won in New York in the late '60s. Reputedly, she beat out hundreds of other contestants to perform the vocals on a TV commercial for Schaeffer beer.

Oh, the Schaeffer beer commercial. Now this guy Jim Lewis that I was telling you about, who thought nothing of me but thought everything of me—the guy that was my manager. I would never have entered a talent contest. I had had five or six records. I was above that! He said, "You ain't nobody. You better try to get in this contest." He put me in the contest, and I won. And they played it for years, and it was such good royalties.

LaVette had never received royalties up to that point, and she has rarely received them since.

I know that Shelby Singleton has to owe me something. I sent him a letter saying that their particular group of records have been released everywhere, a million times. I said, "It looks like you could send me something." So he sent me a statement—a debt— for $10,000! And the stuff with Atlantic [the early '60s tracks, such as "My Man—He's a Lovin' Man"], I signed, saying that they wouldn't owe me anything else. Everybody had told me, "They haven't put anything out on you. You should leave them." I didn't know anything about it, so I went to New York—the first time I had ever been to New York (I knew that's where I had always wanted to be though)—and I stormed into Atlantic: "I want a release from my contract!" And I think they probably said, "Do you know where you are?" And Jerry Wexler told me, "We have a new writer/producer." I don't know if he used the word *producer*, 'cause that wasn't a big word then—they weren't that important. But he said, "We've got him doing a lot of things and he's doing some things for Scepter too, but we want to put you with him. We want to see what kind of sound we can get out of your voice on a white producer. So if you would just stay in the contract just six more months till we can get to him and see if we can get another record out of it. His name is Burt Bacharach." [Laughs.] I said, "I don't care who it is. I want a release from my contract." Well, I mean, nobody knew who in the fuck Burt Bacharach was then. Who knew? Everybody knew probably, except me! So Jerry Wexler gave me $500. They didn't owe me anything. He said, "You poor baby. Here, I'm going to give you this. You're gonna really need it." And that man never lied. Never lied.

It wouldn't be the last time LaVette signed away her royalties to be free from a contract. In 1978, she left the small, New York-based West End label after recording a mid-tempo disco song, "Doin' the Best that I Can," that later turned into a huge hit on New York's gay club scene.

I was doing *Bubbling Brown Sugar* and trying to get something to go again at Columbia[6] because [head of the R&B music division] LeBaron Taylor was still there. So LeBaron turns me over to yet another promotion man in black music for Columbia who says there's a young boy whose name is Cory Robbins who wants to start a company, and he wants a black singer. So I go and meet this kid who is eighteen at the time, and he couldn't even snap his fingers on beat. I said, "Oh, this is really bad." But I said, "Okay, I'll do this." I liked the song. And then, every week that I came back, they had added a little more to it, a little more echo. I said, "Naw, this is not going to be good. I'm gonna let y'all go on with this. Let's just tear up the contract." I said, "I don't wanna do no disco. Give me a release from the contract." They gave me a release from the contract and made me sign a paper saying they didn't owe me any money. They sold 150,000 copies in Manhattan. Just in Manhattan. [Laughs.] I get a quarter. But since Cory now has Profile Records, I stormed into his office one day about three years ago. I said, "Just give me $500 'cause." He gave it to me.

And I had said, "This little boy ain't gonna never do nothin." I made some really dumb decisions! I had no faith in these people. But these people didn't have any talent! Burt Bacharach didn't have an inch of talent until he met Hal David. And Cory had none. Cory just liked black people moving around and gyrating; he had no sense of music. And I didn't want to be tied up in that forever. I had no idea he was going to meet other people and start a really big company. [In exasperation] Oh! But I left him to go down to Atlanta to do this thing with Bonnie and Buddy Busey. Does that sound down-home or what?[7] They had introduced me to Steve Buckingham. They had the Atlanta Rhythm Section, and they were all involved with Jimmy Carter, and I said, "Oh, this is going to be great." Steve and I went to the company and the doors were locked, and we have never heard from the people again. So when he got this thing with Motown, he felt he owed it to me to try to make it up.

Other short-term associations with fly-by-night record companies abound, such as the one that produced the unpromisingly titled "Trance Dance" (1984), her lone single for the Street King label.

That was Steve Buckingham again. I never even knew who they were really. They just met Steve, and I think the Motown thing had just not happened, and they said, "Let her come and try this 'Trance Dance' thing." I kind of slip up under the table and hide if that comes on.

LaVette's most recent label association has been with a New Jersey-based company, Bar None Records. So far, only one single has been recorded (a demo version of Etta James's "Damn Your Eyes"), and it doesn't look like any others will follow.

With the people that pressed up "Damn Your Eyes" for me in New Jersey, I would be the only black artist that they have at the company—it's a small company. And when they see me, they think Tina Turner, and I don't necessarily want to do that. I think they were, like, "Here's a powerful voice that's a rhythm and blues singer that we want to apply to these very white rock 'n roll tunes." We went through maybe a hundred tunes, and I couldn't find one that I really could hear anything that I could do with. We dragged around with it for almost two years, and then I guess we kind of said, "We ain't doin' nothing here."

Unfortunately, the single is not available for widespread release, and anyone searching in a record store would have a hard time finding it. Since LaVette had financed some of the money for the session herself and had not finished paying for it, her then-manager (from whom she is now estranged) bought the rights, preventing Bar None from doing anything further with it.

This guy [the ex-manager] has caused me so much trouble. I thought that I was going to have a deal with [names a southern label specializing in blues and soul] because the owner and I have known each other for thirty years. I sent him "Damn Your Eyes," and he said (this is the thing to show you about the buzzard luck I was talking about), "Oh, this is fabulous. This is the best thing you've ever done. Write down the songs you think you might like to do in an album. We'll get you down here right away, da da da da da." I don't hear anything from him.

At the time, LaVette blamed her manager for ruining the deal, although she now believes internal problems within the company were the cause.

He had called there [the record company] and started saying a bunch of things that weren't true, like "Bettye's got to have blue curtains in the dressing room and bear rugs on the floor." All kinds of stuff. I mean, he's much ado about nothing. Just a grandiose type of person. I'm thinking about maybe trying to get back in touch with [the owner], but I don't really know what the situation is there [at the record company] and my feelings are too fragile right now to get caught up in another ruckus, but I felt really good about that and really safe about it. Oh! I was as excited as the time when Atlantic was going to put this album out on me that Brad Shapiro had produced, and then they just called and said, "We changed our mind." I said, "What?" I got up under the dining room table and stayed three days. I just stayed under the dining room table. I was just devastated. I mean, it was like my whole family had been murdered. I couldn't believe it. And that was *all* they said. "We decided not to do it." We had done the rhythm in Muscle Shoals, and we did the strings in Miami down there with Brad Shapiro, and the background was done in New York. I mean, they put a lot of money into it. Sent me a stack of plane tickets to go on the road and promote it. Told me to send the tickets back. Decided not to do it. I was just devastated. I mean, I got to Muscle Shoals Sound, I got Brad Shapiro. I said, "I've practically got Aretha and Wilson Pickett in my back pocket here with me."

LaVette is referring to her second stint with Atlantic (the third, if you count the four singles she recorded in 1968 for the Atlantic-distributed Karen label) in 1972. Only two singles from the proposed album, Child of the Seventies, *were released; neither succeeded in charting. Although the album still has not seen the light of day, one of its singles, a version of Joe Simon's "Your Turn to Cry," turned up on a 1992 compilation entitled* Atlantic Sisters of Soul. *LaVette delivers a characteristically nuanced, delicately shaded performance, even if the song is marred slightly by the penchant of Brad Shapiro— then only a year away from hitting commercial success with Millie Jackson—for heavy string charts.*

I think [the album] was the best thing I had done up until then. And especially "Your Turn to Cry," which I thought was just excellent. I liked the way I sung it, I liked the arrangement, I liked the way it was played. I really liked that. I just hated that it had been someone else, and I wish it had been my original song. But I really liked it and I liked the attitude that Brad Shapiro had given to the album, the direction he had taken. It's the first time I had ever sung soft. I think that would still be the kind of album I would be after now, but only if I could apply myself to each one of the songs, instead of going the way that each one of the songs went. I would bring the songs to me. But the songs were very good and very well cho-sen—we went through hundreds of them to get the ten. I just knew that that was *it.* This is it, y'all.

Although she keeps her sense of humor firmly in place when talking about her career, LaVette nonetheless feels deeply hurt by her inability to find sustained success as a recording artist. She is, however, heartened by the "comebacks" many of her once-obscure contemporaries have experienced and periodically allows herself flashes of hope.

It's just been a series of misadventures. Really, misadventures. But any one of them could have been fabulous. But they've kept me meeting other people . . . I don't have an agent. That was one of the drawbacks of Jim being my manager. He felt that the people in today's business were so flighty. He said, "Soon as one of those little records come out, they'll call you. You don't have to call them." So he never established a rapport with an agent. He wanted me to have the agent who was booking Tony Bennett and Sarah Vaughan and those kinds of people, and those people weren't interested in me. So I have no long-lasting relationship with anyone who knows anyone, anyone who books anyone. I think that would be my biggest drawback now. I have absolutely no one saying anything for me. And at this time it's kind of hard for me to just get out and hustle. And then every step you take toward hustling, it takes away from the thing you really want to present. I don't like the back-room deal thing at all. That part of it I hate. I am used to someone else putting the music together and someone else counting the money. I hate those two things. So if you find any agents in your travels that want to bring someone up from the crypt. . . .

If I ever make any more money, I will never be broke again. And I haven't made any money since I made up that decision! [Laughs.] But I know that I don't know how to do anything else. I've never done anything else. I don't even know how a cash register works. So when I don't do this and there are no patrons, then I don't have any money. You know, only about two percent of the people in the world can sing. It's very much like a parrot talking. It's not that it's so difficult to do, it's just that either you can do it or you can't. And I think that that's a very special thing, and I can't believe that people would like me the way they do—I've never had a bad review, never had an audience turn their back when I'm performing, so I can't believe I'm not supposed to do this. I won't accept that. I can see them carrying me away to the loony bin, saying, "I'm supposed to do this!" But I can't believe I'm supposed to do something else. Why don't I know how to do anything else? Or why don't I do anything else as proficiently as I do this? I cannot understand why. Well, I understand *how* things got to be the way they are, because those early steps that you make are the ones that come back to haunt you. And certainly many of them were made wrong. But just the way all of these old people are coming out of the crypt now and working everywhere, I don't know why I can't find anybody that will help.

Before the interview is over, LaVette gives me directions to the Piercing House, a small club on the outskirts of Detroit where she has a weekly gig.

So you think you got it? 'Cause we can go down there together—I don't want you wandering around Detroit now, so go through that. It's just a little bitty place.

We're going to keep doing it until this stupid man decides, "I can't afford this." He can't afford it, but he likes it so well and he wants it to go on. He's had the club maybe two or three years, but this is the most money he's spent and he really doesn't need to spend this kind of money, but he likes it and he wants the club to be impressive, and it's really just a little joint. I mean, he could put some guy in there playing guitar. Of course, I won't suggest that!

We wind up the interview exactly where we started: talking about Jackie Wilson. LaVette says she considers sleeping with Wilson and the legendary dancer (and erstwhile Bubbling Brown Sugar *co-star) Honi Coles two of her greatest achievements and adds, only half-jokingly, "I'm considering putting it on my resume."*

I am so proud of that. I really am. Those were the sexiest men I have ever met in my life. And Honi was like almost eighty, but I'd have to knock the dancers out of the way—the young dancers hanging out at the dressing rooms when he'd come through. I'd say, "Get out of there!" [Laughs.] He was a sexy old man, believe me. Well, I'm going to have to go and pick my grandchildren up from school, come back, and turn into Bettye LaVette. From the scullery maid, then grandma, to Bettye LaVette!

As we part after leaving the restaurant, LaVette turns around one last time to warn me to be careful in Detroit—"I don't want you wandering around!"—before heading home to get ready. That night at the Piercing House she gives a spellbinding performance, ably backed by a tight band that includes Rudy Robinson, her musical director for the past thirty years. She is dressed to kill in tight, black pants and a matching jacket. The club is very much as she described it: small, with the bandstand only about ten feet from the bar. In addition to the barstools, there are several tables lining the sides of the room. The effect is tight, intimate. The club's size allows LaVette to engage in direct interaction with the audience; on her version of "Feel Like Breaking Up Somebody's Home," she interpolates the line, "Wanna start some shit *here" and moves from table to table, whispering the expletive in the ears of selected patrons as she goes along. On another number she engages in a similar repartee with individual audience members, but this time the banter is more suggestive. Getting to me, she jokes, "This child needs to get back to school!"*

During the intervals between sets, LaVette sits at one of the tables, freely conversing with the club's regulars. The closeness of the space contributes to the warmth and spirit that she obviously shares with the others in the club. It also fosters a bit of tension when a woman sitting behind us, well-intentioned but obviously unused to relating to singers, keeps telling her things like, "You know who you sound like . . . ? and "You remind me of. . . ." LaVette takes umbrage at first ("Why does everybody have to sound like someone to you?"), then backs off by explaining to the woman that no singer wants to be openly compared to another: "You may think it's a compliment, but it's not" (and in truth, there really is no one who sounds quite like LaVette). Although the scene ultimately blows over, the momentary antagonism makes me recall LaVette's earlier comment about her relationships with women.

LaVette launches into her version of "Let Me Down Easy" after requesting of the audience, "Allow me to engage in a bit of braggadocio." She then introduces me and says, "He's doing his thesis on me." She proceeds to give a smoldering reading, marked by a personal pain and anger that go far beyond the bounded meaning of the lyrics. By the song's end, when she is shouting the word "please" again and again, she is stooped over, with tears coming from her eyes. There is not a sound in the tight, crowded room. LaVette seems in another place entirely, getting in touch with thirty-five years' worth of frustration and loss. In the brief moment after the band has wound up the coda and LaVette has straightened up to face the room, she seems embarrassed by the fresh tears. It's a moment in which she suddenly appears very vulnerable, unable to summon her usual defenses: humor, sarcasm, attitude. "You know," her drummer later tells me, "Bettye's got a heart of gold." For those in search of a textbook lesson in soul, LaVette's performance of the song and the exposed moment that followed it would have provided them with all they needed to know. Soul is something that no amount of braggadocio can conceal.

Part Three

Philadelphia

Philadelphia has been active in record production since the early '60s, when the small Cameo label, along with its affiliated company, Parkway, achieved a remarkable degree of success with a series of novelty records on artists like Chubby Checker ("The Twist") and Dee Dee Sharp ("Mashed Potato Time"). Philadelphia was further notable for being the home of *American Bandstand*, the television program on which all-American (and in its early days, all-white) teens danced innocuously to the latest pop records. But it wasn't until the mid-'60s, when a number of R&B-oriented record labels started to spring up, that Philadelphia began to make a name for itself in the soul field. A pivotal year was 1965, when a Catholic schoolgirl-turned songwriter named Barbara Mason had a top-five national pop hit with her third release, "Yes, I'm Ready." What made "Yes, I'm Ready" different, aside from its highly personal tone (a quality shared by nearly all of the best soul music), was its use of strings. Unlike many '50s pop recordings, in which strings were layered on as "sweetening," the strings in "Yes, I'm Ready" sounded like an integral part of the arrangement: they complemented Mason's winsome vocals in an almost conversational fashion, acting in tandem with the male backup singers as a second voice.

It's not surprising that strings would become one of the most salient features of Philly soul as it matured during the '60s and grew to national prominence in the early '70s. The string section of the Philadelphia Orchestra, headquartered at the venerable Academy of Music, has for centuries been considered among the best in the world; being locally based, the Orchestra's string musicians were easy to hire for recording sessions. The use of strings also provided the chance for Philadelphia producers to emulate the highly successful Motown Sound then exploding in Detroit. By the end of the '60s, Philly soul was also becoming known for another musical trademark: its intense, propulsive rhythm tracks, a development that points to Philadelphia's role in the disco phenomenon of the next decade.

Although the Philly Sound was still rather nascent during the '60s, several highly important soul labels were established to exploit Philly soul's new commercial potential, such as Arctic (upon which "Yes, I'm Ready" appeared), Philly Groove, and Gamble. The latter was started by the songwriting and producing team of Kenny Gamble and Leon Huff, who had worked on many of Arctic's releases and by 1968 had begun to find commercial success with their production work for the Intruders, the Soul Survivors, and Jerry Butler. In the '70s, Gamble and Huff would become the masterminds behind Philadelphia International Records, the label that brought Philly soul to its commercial apogee and made worldwide stars of the O'Jays, Harold Melvin and the Blue Notes (featuring Teddy Pendergrass), the Three Degrees, and Billy Paul. At the same time, Philly Groove producer Thom Bell was honing a softer, plusher brand of Philly soul for groups like the Delphonics and, later, the Stylistics.

Key to the distinctive Philly Sound was the presence of the core group of musicians that first coalesced on Arctic's releases and continued to play together throughout the '70s, including Ronnie Baker (bass), Norman Harris (guitar), and Earl Young (drums). These musicians initially developed their unique sound at the small Virtue Studio (where many early Philly soul records were recorded), then moved to the Sound Plus Studio after it was bought by engineer Joe Tarsia and renamed Sigma Sound in 1969. It was at Sigma Sound that the most famous Philly records, including Harold Melvin and the Blue Notes's "Bad Luck," MFSB's "T.S.O.P." and the Three Degrees's "When Will I See You Again" were recorded. The studio eventually achieved such popularity that, by the early '70s, it had become the destination for a number of non-Philadelphia acts seeking to capture some of the city's musical energy: in 1970 alone, Dusty Springfield, Wilson Pickett, and the Sweet Inspirations all recorded hits there.

The popularity of the Philly Sound declined in the early '80s, supplanted by newer movements such as the Minneapolis Sound of Jimmy Jam and Terry Lewis. By the middle of the decade, Philadelphia International ended its long-standing distribution deal with CBS and began a new one with Capitol/EMI, but was still able to come up with top-notch songs like "Do You Get Enough Love?", a 1986 hit for Detroit native Shirley Jones. In recent years, Gamble and Huff have continued their efforts to restore Philadelphia International's status as a major force in contemporary soul. Regardless of the final outcome of these attempts, the music Gamble and Huff and their Philadelphia counterparts produced in the '60s and '70s will go down in history as some of the finest soul ever created.

Barbara Mason

A Lot of Life in a Short Time

Barbara Mason, 1965

The first edition of The Rolling Stone Record Guide *called Barbara Mason "Philadelphia's true first lady of soul." Starting with her first record in 1964, Mason (born on August 9, 1947) helped define the burgeoning Philly soul sound, often keeping several paces ahead of her contemporaries in pop and R&B. In the early-to-mid '60s, while Mary Wells was still singing the praises of "My Guy" and Lesley Gore was busy throwing tantrums in the middle of parties, the teenage Mason was writing songs with lines like "My life is all mixed up, God bless the child can't earn a penny for his own cup / Because I'm so untamed and I'm so wild, and they call me the trouble child" ("Trouble Child," recorded in 1964 but written a year or so earlier). Later in the '60s she came to exemplify what critics of the next decade would call the "singer-songwriter." Idiosyncratic, occasionally oblique, Mason's songs were vehicles for her own unique musical personality. Although her signature song, 1965's "Yes, I'm Ready," has been covered by everyone from Gladys Knight to the Lettermen, no one has been able to recapture the combination of innocence and precocity, hesitancy and resolution that Mason brought to her original.*

By the time the early '70s ushered in a new degree of social and sexual awareness in soul music, Mason was recording songs that dealt frankly and unapologetically with dissatisfied, stale relationships

("Bed and Board") and the desire for a lover outside of marriage ("You Can Be With the One You Don't Love"). In addition, she became the first person to record in the "heavy breathing" disco style, which later made Donna Summer a household name, with her 1972 cover version of Curtis Mayfield's "Give Me Your Love." "Give Me Your Love" even predates Sylvia's "Pillow Talk," the record often considered to mark the beginning of the heavy breathing sound. Although chiefly remembered for "Yes, I'm Ready," Mason's popularity with the R&B audience has always been high: out of the top 500 artists listed in Joel Whitburn's Top R&B Singles: 1942–1995, she ranks an impressive #222.

Mason's vocal appeal is considerable, although hard to explain. The winsome, sometimes flat quality of her singing (what the same Rolling Stone entry referred to as "her off-key cooing") is partly responsible for the coy, girlish sound of her early records. These recordings—"Yes, I'm Ready," "Oh How It Hurts," "Sad Sad Girl"—are notable for their honesty, simplicity, and melodiousness. Mason endows the songs with a palpable emotional pull; she sounds as if she is revealing something deeply personal about herself, even if she still seems a little unsure of her full capabilities. Her later recordings (for the Buddah label) reveal a more mature vocalist with surer senses of pitch and timing and a salty, sometimes bitter tone. Her vocal range opens up considerably, and she proves that she can go through an entire song without once straying off-key. In light of her '70s records, her occasionally shaky intonation seems more like a device that can be turned on and off at will, something she employs to give special coloring to her often quite moving interpretations.

Ultimately, what makes Mason so memorable is the strong artistic current that courses through her work: the sense of a performer communicating her deepest feelings through song. If there is one emotional quality that characterizes her music more than any other, it is sadness. Mason often seems beset with an acute melancholy that finds its voice through her moody tone and the odd line or phrase whose precise meaning is unclear. For example, in one of her earliest compositions, "Girls Have Feelings Too" (recorded in late 1964), she sings, "Just because in life everything went wrong/The people say that the girl, she won't live long." The song's title conveys a standard adolescent bid for respect, but the lyrics suggest that Mason is aiming at something much deeper and darker.

In other compositions, the sorrow of Mason's characters is more clearly articulated. "Poor Girl in Trouble" (1967), which Mason wrote with a young Kenny Gamble, depicts a young woman voicing her regret at not having thought twice before marrying: "I should never have married so young, but I was so young and dumb. Oh what am I gonna do?" Addressing the husband who abandoned her (the song also implies that she is pregnant), she turns sharply accusatory: "All the harm is done; you couldn't stay, you had to run." Mason imbues the line with a painful sense of disillusionment and innocence lost; this could be the dark flip side to the dewy-eyed romanticism of "Yes, I'm Ready."

I got in touch with Mason through Jamie Music, the Philadelphia-based publishing, record, and distribution company that handled her '60s recordings—still in business after thirty-five years. The staff at Jamie kindly offered to forward a letter, and within two weeks there was a message from her *on my answering machine. During our first conversation, I found Mason to be a fascinating talker and an engaging storyteller. I was happy (although not surprised) to find that the highly developed artistic sense that I had always felt in her records was very much evident in the way she described her work. She said that she had "lived each song" she sang and that she had always viewed the songs she wrote as stories, adding that, "as I got older the stories got more interesting." We also talked about singers we both admire, such as Carmen McRae and Billie Holiday (Mason says that she listens to music "twenty-four hours a day"). We ended our conversation with Mason promising to mail me a compilation CD of her work that I had been unable to find. When I offered to send her money for it, she quickly demurred: "Just knowing you're someone who understands and appreciates what I'm trying to say is payment enough."*

For the interview, Mason drove from Philadelphia to meet me at my office in the Miller Theatre at Columbia University. Dale Wilson, who manages Mason and handles all of her business affairs, accompanied her and offered some interesting insights during the course of the interview. The two women have worked together since the early '80s. Mason, a petite woman with an excellent complexion and a perfect set of straight white teeth, comes off in person as warm, gentle, and talkative. Her observations are characterized by an infectious sense of wonder, as if she can't believe so much has happened to her. The ingenuousness of her personality makes it all the more surprising when she punctuates her speech with the occasional flash of bravado. At such moments, one gets a taste of the sort of brash confidence that was surely required of someone who at eighteen became an overnight star.

I'll just start from the beginning. Let me go back to maybe the age of twelve years old. I basically listened to a lot of R&B radio because that's all we had to listen to in those days. We had transistors and we'd put little plugs in our ears and walk around listening to music.[1] One of the biggest R&B stations in our town was a station called WDAS. Every kid, every adult listened to that station. So I grew up listening to people like Curtis Mayfield and naturally all the Motown stuff. Again, this came before I began to become a professional singer. In the summertime when I was out of school, they would give talent shows right across the street from where I lived at a playground. [The playground] was called Francisville, and I lived on Francis Street. So I would audition for the talent show, and they would pick me. I had three other people with me: a guy and two other girls. So we would dress up and do the talent show, and every time I would do the talent show, I would win. But I really didn't think of anything about becoming professional because I'm still twelve years old. But each year I would go around to *different* playgrounds, and I kept on doing more talent shows to see whether if this section of town likes me, maybe another section of town [will].

Now, I come from what they call the north side of Philadelphia, so I would go to the west side of Philadelphia, and everybody'd like me over there. And wherever I went, people would like *me*, not necessarily the people that I was with. I would say to that, "Gee, you can't have me without my group." I mean, I really thought that we were hot, right? The group really wasn't doing that much. I was writing what I'd call at that time maybe poems and putting a little melody to it. I had no formal training. I don't come from a musical family; no one in my family came out of a gospel church. My mother probably could have been a singer. If I sound like anyone or have any particular style, it would be my mother's voice.

One of these "poems" was "Trouble Child," which eventually became Mason's first record. It was released in 1964 on Crusader, a small label owned by Weldon Arthur McDougal III, a Philadelphia-based doo-wop performer. The record, featuring castanets and an "uptown" production style in the manner of the Drifters, is strikingly mature for a sixteen-year old singer. I ask Mason how she came to write a song that dealt so convincingly with juvenile delinquency.

The songs that I wrote really reflect my life. I was a teenager, and I did things that teenagers do: I stayed out late; I got disciplined a lot. I just decided to write this song called "Trouble Child" because I figured there were a lot of other troubled kids doing things that I was doing. And a gentleman by the name of Weldon Arthur McDougal III (who really discovered me) came to me one day because of the female group that I had. A young girl that lived what we call "across town" ("across town" would be like across a street called Broad Street; once you cross that you're on the other side of town, so to speak), she and I—in fact she sounds so much like me—we would sing. There was a group out of Philadelphia called the Larks (now there are two sets of Larks—this is the Philadelphia Larks). This gentleman by the name of Weldon was in the Larks, and he also had a partner named Bill. Bill lived next door to my friend—we call her Kissy, but her name is Geraldine. So Geraldine said, "I believe someone will be able to get us in the record industry." I said, "What's that?" I mean, we were just used to doing little talent shows. She said, "Well, they want to hear us put our voices on tape." I said [with hesitation], "On tape? Okay." And we had in those days big reel-to-reel tape recorders, so we put our voices down, and it's almost like the rest is history.

This gentleman Weldon heard me and asked me if I wanted to do a club date. I said, "I have to ask my parents. I've never been to a club to sing." He said, "Well, just get up there and sing. What do you do?" I said, "I do 'Moon River.'" "You do 'Moon River' by Andy Williams?" I said, "No, the one by Jerry Butler." But look, that's what we were listening to. I knew that Andy had it out, but I'm listening to R&B radio, and they were not playing Andy Williams. I knew that Henry Mancini wrote it, but I didn't know what writing was. So I would listen to Jerry's version and I would do what he did, but I would do it in my style. And I did this particular "Moon River" at this club that night, and I got a standing ovation, along with my girls. After the engagement, Weldon came to me and said, "Listen, would you like to make a record?" I said, "Sure. We go downtown to the penny arcade on Sundays and I make records." He said, "I'm talking about for the whole world to hear you." I said, "Get out of here! What about my girls?" He said, "Oh no, I can't . . . they don't have it." So we haggled back and forth about me and my group. I took Weldon to meet my parents, and I asked my mother and father if I could make a record. They said, "Do you want to make a record?" I said, "Sure, but Mom, it also means I'm going to have to come out of school." I had one more year to finish high school. My mother and father looked at me and said, "It's up to you." "I'm gonna come out."

Next week, we went in, we recorded "Trouble Child." It was what we called a "regional hit." It might have done well in Philadelphia, Baltimore-Washington, big hit in Florida, and a big hit on the West Coast, and then that was it. Nothing international. But I'm still with Weldon McDougal. Now he says, "I have a disc-jockey friend that's on the major stations that has money. Can you still write songs?" I said "Can I *write?* I've got so many . . . I just call them poems." He said, "Name some of them." I said, "I have one called 'Are You Ready?' I have one called 'Girls Have Feelings Too.'" He said, [incredulously] "'Are You Ready?' For what?" I said, *"Love!"* He said, "How old are you?" Now by this time I'm gonna be like sixteen going on seventeen. And he said, "Well okay, I'll take you to meet my friend at the radio station, and you'll audition for him. If he likes you, since he has the money, then you'll make your second record."

The disc jockey was Jimmy Bishop, a record entrepreneur and producer who would define the course of Mason's career for over a decade. Known as "The Bishop" to his many listeners on Philadelphia's famed WDAS (where he also served as vice president of programming), Bishop during the '60s was a bona fide local celebrity. Mason approaches the subject of Bishop gingerly, often referring to him during the interview as "my manager." Bishop was so impressed with the teenager's sound and songwriting that he decided to make her the primary artist on his Arctic label, distributed nationally through the aforementioned Jamie Records.

We went in the studio. Well first of all, I auditioned for Jimmy Bishop. Jimmy—I *guess* he liked me, he acted like he did. He decided, okay, we'll take this little girl in the studio. He said, "So what do you have?" I said, "Well, I have this song called 'Girls Have Feelings Too.'" He said [skeptically], "Okay, well go on and do it." It was a smash, David. Now I'm getting more markets—you know, Baltimore, Washington, they went crazy. Naturally, Philadelphia. He's a jock on the station, he manages me, I get instant airplay. He has friends all across the country that instantly go on the record.

"Girls Have Feelings Too," also recorded in 1964, gave an even clearer indication than "Trouble Child" of where Mason's future lay. A dark, atmospheric piece, it was one of the first records to feature the swirling strings that would eventually become a Philly soul trademark. Although it only reached number thirty-one on the R&B charts, it served to place Philadelphia pop music on a different artistic plane. Whereas before the city had been known mostly for poorly recorded and hastily produced dance records, here was something different: a record that seemed to channel the confused emotions of a highly unique singer. Mason's performance on the record is extremely impressive; at one point she holds the word life over the course of many syllables, a surprising feat of breath control for one so young.

As important as "Girls Have Feelings Too" was to the history of Philly soul music, it failed to establish Mason as a successful performer. That honor would go to Mason's next recording. "Yes, I'm Ready" is one of those magical records that strikes a responsive chord with all those who hear it. Featuring a memorable, melodic hook (the male voice sings, "Are you ready?"; Mason answers, "Yes, I'm ready") and a string part that Mason says was influenced by the score of the film version of Picnic, the record told the story of an inexperienced girl making her move into the mysterious adult world of romantic love. The song was a smash hit (aided no doubt by the influence producer Jimmy Bishop held with his fellow disc jockeys), going all the way to #2 on the R&B and #5 on the pop charts. "Yes, I'm Ready" made eighteen-year-old Barbara Mason a star, and the record remains a staple of oldies radio stations. It's the one Barbara Mason song that every pop fan knows. Here, Mason describes its genesis.

My manager [Bishop] said, "I want to ask you a question, Barbara. You've written about three or four songs which we've recorded. Can you write *one* more song that would make *everyone* in the world know you?" I said, "Yeah, I already have it." He said, "What's the name of it?" I said, "It's called 'Are You Ready?'" He said, "You have to make everything first person." I said, "Why?" He said, "'Cause I'm gonna make that the singalong" [the male part]. I said, "Sing what?" I had no idea what he was talking about. He said, "Let me ask you right now, 'Are you ready?' What are you going to say?" I said, "Yes." He said, "Yes *what?*" I said, "Yes I'm. . . ." "That's it! That's the title!"

I said, "Oh, okay . . .[with resignation]. I don't like it, 'cause *I* named it 'Are You Ready.'" He said [skeptically], "And by the way, how'd you write this?" I said, "Well, I'm in love with Curtis Mayfield and everything Curtis does." Curtis wrote "The Monkey Time" for Major Lance. And the line in "The Monkey Time" is [sings] "Are you ready?" Same melody. In the house where I was raised, we had a big upright piano, and I would just tinkle away, messing with the chords. And I would listen to what Curtis had done with that and kind of invert it for me. And as Major was saying, "Are you ready?" I was saying [speaks more slowly, emphasizing each syllable], "Are you *rea*-dy?" I slowed it down to fit me, and all the lyrics just came naturally. And that's how "Yes, I'm Ready" came about. And then naturally we needed a follow-up, which was "Sad Sad Girl," in which I took the same melody, did it a different way. *Same* melody. I must have used that melody a million times. But I know how to take the same melody and sing kind of against myself. I don't know how I do that.

Although "Sad Sad Girl" sounded too similar to "Yes, I'm Ready" to become as big a hit (it went to #12 on the R&B charts), it was a worthy follow-up with an especially lovely string part. Both records showcased the expertise of musicians Norman Harris, Ronnie Baker, and Earl Young. Mason was particularly fond of Harris and remains sad about his untimely passing in 1987: "My dear Norman. We grew up together. I can see us twelve years old together running around Philly doing talent shows."

In 1965, Mason was still a record industry novice, unprepared for dealing with the demands of sudden fame.

I didn't know what was going on, David. "Yes, I'm Ready" is out, I'm still living at home, and I'm opening up the Sunday paper and looking at the charts—the number one records. And I said, "Boy, who is Billboard? . . . [excitedly] Mom, there's my name— Barbara Mason!" 'Cause that's my real name. She said, "Yeah, what does it mean?" I said, "I guess the paper picked my record." I had no idea. I mean, they weren't teaching me anything about the *business* end of the record business. So I just kind of enjoyed it. My mother went out and bought a big stereo, and we put my records on—the little 45 with the blue label with the penguin.[2] The next thing, I looked around, "Yes, I'm Ready" was just . . . they could not press up enough records to meet the demand. The company was too small. Now the distribution was great, but it seems I was becoming too big for the label. But I continued to stay there for some time, because there are a lot of 45s on Arctic that we did cut.

After we cut "Yes, I'm Ready" and it became so large, then the managers came back and said, "We need to do an album."[3] So I'm starting to know what albums are, because I've seen other peoples' albums.[4] I said, "Oh, okay. Well, what songs would you want on an album?" They said, "Well, have you written any more things?" Because they know that now if I'm writing they can have all this publishing, and I don't know a thing about publishing or any of that stuff. I said, "Yeah, I'll bring some other things." And [referring to a copy of the Yes, I'm Ready album] you can see the things that I did write on there and the things that I didn't write. And they said, "Do you do any songs by other people that are out?" And I like a lot of male songs, as you noticed on there. The Joe Tex thing, the Solomon Burke thing—I would listen to that kind of bluesy stuff—and they said, "Can you sing Solomon Burke?" I said, "Oh yeah, 'Got to Get You Off My Mind'? I sing that with the radio all the time." They said [with disbelief], "This 'Misty' thing—you do 'Misty'?" I said, "Yeah, and plus I do it in kind of a jazz thing." So they hired a famous jazz arranger from our town, a guy by the name of Leon Mitchell. And Leon did it with the big band. So now I'm singing live with all these one hundred musicians, guitar players, and violins and horns and everything, and I'm just doing "Misty" the way that I hear "Misty" in my head. I would listen to Sarah Vaughan and Dinah Washington and Ella [Fitzgerald] because we had a little small recorder with a fat spindle on it, and my mother would play that stuff and I would just fall in love with it.[5] So I would just sing along with the records that she would purchase. And when it got time to do the album, when [the managers] came, I said, "Here's all the songs for the album." There was nothing that they ever had to do for me, in terms of my material.

The Yes, I'm Ready album, released as Arctic 1000 in 1965, featured a full-color photograph of Mason against a bright yellow background. Sporting the kind of high bouffant wig popular in the mid-'60s, she rests her chin on her hand and parts her lips in a vague, aloof smile. Already there is a dreamy, elusive quality to her image and appearance. The album contained all of the singles she had released up to this point (including "Trouble Child," which had been leased from Crusader Records) along with some standard mid-'60s album filler: "Misty," the Solomon Burke song, "Moon River," a Supremes number, etc. The brief liner notes (uncredited but probably written by Jimmy Bishop) called Mason "the greatest talent find of 1965," saying, "Barbara is endowed with the God-given talent to pen and perform songs in a unique manner. Her approach to song writing is as different as is [sic] her unorthodox style of singing." The album proved that Mason was her own best writer—her own compositions are marked by a level of personal commitment absent in some of the more conventional material.

So by this time I'm really getting pretty seasoned, and they [her managers] said, "You know what, we're going to have to send you on tour." I said, "Oh Lord . . . tour? What's *that?*" I just thought maybe like touring around the city. And to a degree, going back to "Trouble Child" for a minute, I did a couple of little local things—clubs, so that people could get a chance to see me. People knew me well from the neighborhood, so when I would go somewhere, everybody would come to see me, you know. But then, by "Yes, I'm Ready" becoming so huge, they said, "No, you have to go on a *national* tour." I said, "Okay, what does that mean?" They said, "We'll sign you up to a booking agency." I said, [gasps in disbelief]. It was so much, David. I could not, you know, comprehend anything that they were saying. I said, "Well, okay. What do I have to do?" They said, "Just be Barbara. Just keep doing what you're doing. Don't change a thing."

But now all the time I am developing. My style is getting ready to blossom. There's not another female that I know in the industry that I sound like or that sounds like me. I've never tried to sound like anyone. I did a show at the Coconut Grove [in L.A.] some years back, opening up for the Four Tops, who are friends of mine, and they needed an opening act. The Tops, they asked for me, which I thought was the greatest thing in the world. So they put an act together for me. And one of the songs that I did was "When I Fall in Love," the standard. The press gave me such a wonderful write-up, and they said that, to them, I sounded like Dinah Washington. I'm talking about the *L.A. Times* and every major publication in Los Angeles came to see the show and said that I reminded them of Dinah Washington. I said, "Well, great." Because you don't know what I have, so you have to compare me with someone. So that's greatness. But it didn't make me go out and buy a bunch of Dinah Washington records or try to be Dinah Washington because she *was* the Queen. You know, Aretha is the Queen but Dinah was *the* Queen. Because I've heard Dinah do notes that she kind of talk-sings, but then she can sing. And I don't particularly talk-sing, but there are things that I can do that I know that other people don't do.

When I was on Buddah Records many famous people would stop by, and one day I was up there and Chaka Khan came by, and I introduced myself. She said, "Please, you need no introduction, I know who you are. I love you." She said, "I tell you Miss Mason, you are the greatest female ballad singer that I have ever heard." I said, "You know me?" She said, "*Please!* 'Yes, I'm Ready' and 'Bed and Board.' " I said [in disbelief], "You know 'Bed and Board'?" She said, "Miss Mason, *please!*" And I thought it was just the greatest compliment, coming from someone of her caliber who I *did* come before, but when people pay me those kinds of compliments it just means so much to me.

The national tour Mason embarked upon in 1965 was the beginning of an extremely busy and exciting period of her career.

We did what we called the "chitlin circuit" in those days. I did a southern tour. The first tour that I probably went on, I went on the road with Gene Chandler, Joe Tex, Joe Simon, The Royalettes (I loved them, the Royalettes), a guy named G.L. Crockett.[6] I can't remember who else. There weren't a lot of us in those days, and there weren't many females doing what I did, like a "Yes, I'm Ready"-type thing. Fontella Bass, she was out; I went out with her. Inez and Charlie Foxx, who I loved; I went out with them. Went out with the Temps a lot, went out with Little Anthony. The tours were basically headlining what would be, say, a B.B. King tour. Awesome tour. Then I would go from there to a Curtis Mayfield and the Impressions tour. Go from that to a Jerry Butler tour, then come back from that, do a Jackie Wilson tour, then Dick Clark would call for me to come out to the [West] Coast and I would do a lot of things for him.

I went on a Dick Clark tour with the Turtles. I took my mom with me to travel. We went all throughout New England, out in California. I only had really one hit. You know, the major hit, which was "Yes, I'm Ready." Dick came to me one night and he said, "Barbara, you've got to do another song. Can you do 'Shake' by Sam Cooke?" I said, "Of course, I know 'Shake'!" And I had a dress that was like chiffon, but it was *tiers* of chiffon, and every time I'd shake, the dress would shake. It was a perfect dress. I did a show at that time which Dick had, aside from *American Bandstand,* which was called *Where the Action Is.* I shot that on location, performed in front of the Chinese Theater [in Hollywood] there with Edwin Starr. And I really got a chance to see the other side of the coin, so to speak—the pop side. I came from the R&B side, and they didn't have any indication that "Yes, I'm Ready" was going to go so far in terms of reaching a universal appeal.

I tell you, David, the tours that I did in my day, we would do fifty one-nighters, okay? Now we'd have only the time off to travel to the next [engagement]. I don't remember ever having a day off to just sit anywhere and rest. And I loved it! I had my own little station wagon and I had all my junk, like cookies and comic books and whatever I liked, in the back of this station wagon, and they would hire a driver for me. They'd also hire a lady to take care of my hair and my make-up and my clothes, so there were basically only two people that would travel [with me]. All the other business was being taken care of back at the record company.

I ask Mason if she encountered any racial prejudice during her mid-'60s tours.

You know, you speak of Billie Holiday. Now here I'm coming along, and I'm talking about before civil rights was passed, and so we went through the same things, where we would book a whole hotel, get up there—and by this time now I *am* on a bus with Dick Clark; Dick would have buses for us—we'd get up there and we were not allowed to stay (we being myself, my mother, the gentleman that sold the books—we were the only three blacks on the tour.) I'm touring with Dion and the Belmonts. And so [the Belmonts are] saying, "Well, gee, if Barbara doesn't go in, then we're not gonna go in." So then Dick said, "You know what, I've gotta start trying to get you guys at the Holiday Inns." And Holiday Inns could not discriminate. And so from then on there wasn't a problem. Naturally, sometimes we would stay on what they call the "black side" of town, which wasn't as nice as the other side of town, but for us that wasn't a problem. We were just happy to do the music. And I was playing in the larger venues, every major auditorium you could think of. I loved it. And the South has been a cornerstone for me, and if I were to really put a southern tour together, I'm sure now I could go right down there and do well.

Mason is accurate when she attests to her popularity in the South. Her records received excellent distribution there as a result of Jimmy Bishop's influence with the southern disc jockeys. For example, in Soulsville, U.S.A. *Rob Bowman writes that Bishop plugged the Astors' 1965 hit on Stax, "Candy," in exchange for Memphis disc jockeys' avid promotion of "Yes, I'm Ready."*

I ask Mason if she ever had a chance to record in the South. She responds with the story behind the creation of her biggest '70s hit, "From His Woman to You" (1974), an "answer record" to Shirley Brown's 1974 R&B smash on Stax, "Woman to Woman."

Did we do the South . . .? [tries to remember]. You know what, David, yes I did, I recorded in Memphis, Tennessee. I'm so glad you brought that up. We were just listening to that stuff coming up here too. My manager [Bishop] got a call from a lady by the name of Bettye Crutcher, and she said, "I have the answer for Barbara Mason to Shirley Brown's 'Woman to Woman.'"[7] He said, "Okay, fine." I mean this was a guy that never really asked my opinion of anything. He just said, "You know what? You're going to Memphis and you're going to record the answer to Shirley Brown's record." Now I knew that Shirley's record was gold by this time. I said, "What could I be doing to Shirley's record? How would it go?" I flew in that night with one of my promotion men from Buddah. In fact, I was on the road promoting the *Transition* album, which wasn't doing anything. Nobody wanted to hear the *Transition* album [Mason's 1974 "protest album"].

So we get the call. I was in Atlanta at that time doing a lot of record shops, going around shaking hands, signing autographs. And Jimmy Bishop calls and says, "You've got to get out of Atlanta tomorrow and go to Memphis." "Oh lord," I said. "Okay, fine. For what?" He said, "*You're* going to do the answer." I said, "What answer, what?" He said, "It's called 'From His Woman to You.'" I said, "*Who*, from *what?*" He said, "Just meet me. *I'm* driving, 'cause I'm bringing a friend with me." He brought a friend with him who didn't like to fly. So I flew in to Memphis from Atlanta. Get to the hotel that night, and Jimmy Bishop was such a nut, too [laughs]—excuse my expression, but each state that he was in he called me and woke me up: "I'm in North Carolina!" I said, "If you call me one more time . . . !" Because I have to do this session tomorrow, which I don't have any idea of how the track sounds or anything.

We get to the town, we go over to the studio, I meet Miss Crutcher. There were only two people there. If you look on the record, it says Lester Snell and Bettye Crutcher.[8] Lester on keyboards. They had already done the track. They didn't have my key or anything! Because usually sometimes I would give the key over the phone. No keys! They put the track up, and I said, "Let's cut it." I heard probably about eight bars. I said, "Let's cut it now. Immediately." I did it in one take. I'd never heard it. She put the lyric in front of me on the stand. She said, "Jimmy Bishop, this time you will *not* produce Barbara Mason. She's in *my* hands." Of course, he didn't like that. He never wanted anyone else to do me but him. He said [with hesitation], "Well, I hope it comes off great." We sold so many records. Believe me. We have a saying in Philadelphia, I was selling records like the subway.

It is significant that Mason's "From His Woman to You" story centers on being free from Bishop (who had, up to this point, produced many of her records) and her feeling of vindication when the record did so well (it went to #3 R&B and #28 pop). The account reflects Mason's ambivalence towards Bishop: she's thankful because he did so much to promote her music, but she's also resentful of his attempts to oversee each aspect of her career. She feels that his control prevented her from making certain decisions that would have proved beneficial for her future. Mason's frustration again becomes apparent when we talk about her popularity overseas—she has more records in print in Europe than in the U.S.

I've never been overseas. The only foreign country that I've ever performed in was Brazil. The managers that handled me felt that it was not feasible for me to go there. Why they thought that way was really ridiculous, but I *will* be going in the future. Because I know that they would just love to see me. I got a chance to do a lot of interviews for the publications over there, but for them to physically ever see me, they never have.

We discuss the esteem in which Europeans hold American soul performers.

They know *everything.* And you know to me, David, they cherish us. I don't want to put the United States down. I mean, I had to get my start somewhere. You're from here, and there are many more people that know probably as much about me as I know about myself, or even more. I mean, you might tell me something and I would say, "Oh yes, I forgot that." I mean, I knew it happened, but so much has happened in a thirty-year period that it would take me the rest of my life to put it all down. So it's just been quite a ride.

Jimmy Bishop—he had a lot of weird ways of thinking about me, about my career. Maybe taking me to a certain level and then stopping. It was his idea that I not go to Europe, which I thought again was totally ridiculous. I could have had my feet in so many doors over there. Now I get statements from every country in the world. They know me from here to Japan, and for them not to have ever seen me, it wasn't a good thing. But I'm still here, I am still able to perform.

A 1975 article on Mason in Soul *magazine substantiates her claim that Bishop had some unusual ideas about the development of her career. In it, he avers that "it's important to build the right image . . . [Mason] will not play a club, even if they offer her a lot of money. . . . I do not think it's the right career-type move for her." Many of Bishop's decisions still rankle. Mason's voice resonates with hurt as she gives the following account of an early '70s Apollo engagement.*

I had to do a performance at the Apollo, and that particular time my band didn't show up so I couldn't go on. All the people walked out. Every fan. I was sitting outside in a car, waiting for my musicians to come, and my manager [Bishop] said, "Well, you won't be able to go on." [The show] was called "The Buddah Family," with myself, Gladys Knight, Melba Moore, the Five Stairsteps, all of us, and I literally sat in a car and heard people say, "Barbara Mason didn't come. That's who *we* came to see. We're going home." I had all the stuff from Arctic out, and then I had hits on Buddah, so they were coming to see a whole collage of things. And I didn't come. And [the emcee] explained that her band got whatever, but [the audience] said, "Well, can't she sing with another band?" And I still don't know why he didn't let me go on with someone else to back me up. Because I could have pulled it off.

In spite of Mason's increasing frustration with Bishop's management, her Buddah years represented her artistic coming-of-age. Mason signed with the label in 1971 after a brief, unsuccessful stint with National General, a California company whose primary business was movies. Buddah (which had distributed National General) was at the time moving away from the production of the "bubble gum" pop music for which it had been known during the previous decade and was trying to make inroads into the R&B and soul market.[9]

With Mason's second single for Buddah, the marvelous "Bed and Board" (1972), a new persona was established. Gone was the image of the sweet, unworldly adolescent. In its place was an experienced, somewhat cynical adult who has seen her share of romantic disappointment. Composed by Flax and Lambert, a Philadelphia-based writing team, the song featured the memorable hook line, "there's so much more to love than bed and board." Mason's singing was different as well. The pain of a live-in romance gone sour was movingly conveyed by the tart, biting quality that had crept into her voice. This was the sound— world-weary and sly—that would characterize Mason's output for much of the decade.

The year 1972 also brought Mason what would be one of the high points of her career: the chance to work with longtime-idol Curtis Mayfield. Although already an R&B veteran as lead singer for the Impressions, Mayfield had just reached what many consider his artistic peak with the Superfly *soundtrack, one of the most influential albums of the '70s. Mayfield produced a superb single on Mason, a version of Superfly's "Give Me Your Love" backed with one of Mason's own compositions, "You Can Be With the One You Don't Love." The former represented another stylistic breakthrough for Mason. Singing at the top of her range, with her voice double-tracked in several spots, she had never sounded so slyly funky. "You Can Be," on the other hand, was a lush, rich production that created a particularly evocative setting for Mason's tale of lovers planning their first extra-marital assignation. If anyone still thought of Mason as the green teenager of "Yes, I'm Ready," the "Give Me Your Love" single surely proved otherwise.*

I am the first female artist that Curtis Mayfield ever had a hit on. After me, then he did Mavis [Staples], the Staple Singers. He did Gladys [Knight] from the *Claudine* movie. But I am the first artist—female—that ever gave him a hit, with "Give Me Your Love."[10] That's an interesting story on that. I was on Buddah. Neil Bogart was heading it up then, the CEO of Buddah Records. And he decided it would be a brilliant idea for me to cover "Give Me Your Love." Curtis had already brought it out from the movie *Superfly*, so Jimmy Bishop said, "Why not? Let's give it a try." Never asked me—"I know Barbara can do it." So we have to fly to Chicago to do this now. We have to go to Curtis's turf. And I've already known Curtis all these years from traveling. And it's such an honor. I said, "Curtis Mayfield, now again, Jimmy Bishop is *not* producing me." Curtis Mayfield said, "Barbara's in my hands." This is great; this is just what I wanted—to let someone else bring out some other things in me. Because if you're with one person forever and forever, maybe it would have made me kind of stagnant. But me working with a genius like Curtis Mayfield, it's like working with Smokey Robinson or Stevie Wonder. What could they have brought out of me?

So he has his own record company, and it's made like a little house—two stories. I go in and we hug and kiss, and he said, "Now go downstairs to my studio." I said, "Curtis, you got the studio here, in your office? Oh wow!" And he talks—you know how Curtis talks real slow and easy and quiet—said, "I took the liberty of doing the track without your key." I said, [nonchalantly] "No problem!" He said, "God, I hope it's the right key. I put you in *my* key." I said, "Oh lord." 'Cause now I've got to come off a little like Curtis Mayfield. If you notice the sound, it's not the same sound you heard on early Barbara Mason. I'm in another world. And I love it, David! So we go in the studio, put the track up, and Curtis goes to sleep! Here's the control [carves out imaginary space]. Spaced out, you know? He's, like, [mimics Mayfield falling asleep over the control board]. He nodded out, right? So the engineer is saying, "Sing, Miss Mason." I said, "What about Mr. Mayfield?" He said, *"Sing!"* One take. What you hear, all voices—you hear other voices?—*all* me. Everything! Everything that you hear. No background. I did every single thing.[11] They wake Curtis up. Jimmy Bishop is upstairs with Curtis Mayfield's manager. "Come down, come down, we got a smash!" I was just sitting there. [Confidently] I knew it was a smash.

But when we finished, Curtis said, "I must ask you. Did you happen to bring a B-side with you?" I said, "You know, Curtis, I did. It's called 'You Can Be With the One You Don't Love ('Cause the One That You Love You Can't Be With at All).'" He said, *"Huh?* Can you play it?" I said, "Oh yeah, give me a Fender." A Fender 73. The famous Fender 73 [electric piano]. I played it, and he said, "Um, can you cut that today?" I wrote that at home, just thinking Curtis might need a song. I mean, I figured Curtis Mayfield might write me something great. I said, "Gee, Curtis will probably write me a great B-side." But he was one of those unselfish people, and I love him.

"Give Me Your Love" became a Top 10 R&B hit, spurring Buddah to issue an eponymous follow-up album, the bulk of which (aside from the two songs done in Chicago with Mayfield) was

recorded in Philadelphia at Sigma Sound. The cover featured Mason in a provocative outfit and pose designed to capitalize upon her new image. Soul magazine described it in the following way: "Barbara, in pearlized nail polish and oversized men's shirt tails from which slim, sultry thighs are seen, stands invitingly on the album's front and back jacket."

Once we put that album together, Neil Bogart decided that my album should be on Sunset Boulevard, so he takes and buys as big as that window there, a whole billboard, and puts the *Give Me Your Love* album on Sunset, as you're riding down Sunset Boulevard. The way they had it, you couldn't miss me. For six months, he just left me hanging there. And it was the most marvelous thing that has ever happened in my career. I'm so sorry [that he left Buddah] because he was so inventive, innovative. I mean, discovering Donna Summer.[12] He had so many great plans for me. Once he left Buddah, of course those plans went out the window, and another guy by the name of Art Kass, who was the accountant, took over the record company. And accountants do not know how to run record companies. They are accountants. If you do hair, how can you do something else, right? So things started really to get kind of messy at Buddah.

So [Bogart] left, and I said, "Gee, maybe I could have been Donna Summer." At least he had great plans. It was his idea for me to do the Bitter End [in Greenwich Village]. They were playing the *Give Me Your Love* album in Spain, and he decided for Jimmy Bishop and I to do what now would be known as a video of us coming through the Bitter End doors and pretending like it was this great huge crowd edging me on. And he took that particular film and sent it to Spain, and it was one of the biggest things in Spain; and I've never been to Spain, but I certainly get a lot of residuals from Spain today. So he had a lot of wonderful ideas for me. And I always think that it's good to hear other people's thoughts, you know? Somebody can see me another way. To be seen one way, and you yourself know that there are many facets to you. Someone else must know something else about me too that I don't know. I know it's there, but what is it?

So that was one of the highlights of my career. But it was Jimmy Bishop's brilliance to put me on Buddah. Of course, he knew the people at Buddah. By him being a disc jockey, he was playing all their product. So it was a perfect blend. I mean, he knew exactly where to put me. Arctic couldn't handle me anymore because I was selling more records than what they could really press up. Although they had national distribution, they still couldn't do it. And I've never been with a major record company. I've been with major *independents*. It was better, because you got greater concentration as opposed to being with a Columbia or Epic—not that I wouldn't have liked to have been over there, but that's not how my career went.

In 1974, Mason released Transition, *a concept album that remains one of her personal favorites. Mason describes it as the album where she "looked at the world and saw it going to where it is now." Although it sold poorly, it was one of the first attempts by a female soul artist to record a "message" album. Composed mostly of her own songs,* Transition *addressed such issues as inner-city violence, the destructiveness of war, and religion.*

[With] the *Transition* album, I said, "Well. . . ." I'm looking at the world and all the things that had happened: Dr. King had been killed, Robert Kennedy had been killed. I was trying to reach out to the public, my fans, to show them, "Now this is the way I'm feeling at this time, and you know what's happening, so I'm gonna put it on a record and I hope you buy it." That's not what they wanted to hear. I wrote the whole album in a day with the exception of the last tune, which was called "Sunday Saint (Weekday Sinner)." The other I think nine songs I probably wrote in about three hours in my home, on my little Fender Rhodes. I still love my Fender Rhodes piano. I just started writing all the stuff that you hear. Everything on there. It just came like this. Everything came.

There's a tune on there called "Trigger Happy People." And "Trigger Happy People" were all the people that go around shooting people for no reason, which they're doing today. I mean, we just lost Versace for no reason, you know? Or whomever else dies by the hand of a gun. My first inclination was Dr. King, who had been gunned down for no reason. My second was Robert Kennedy. And I put those particular names in the song too. On the cover you will see an illustration of each song. You'll see soldiers with guns. I wrote another tune on there called "People Don't Believe Enough in God." That song, the illustration will show dice, it'll show gambling, it'll show all the things that people do and they kind of forget about God, you know. One line I have in there, I say that "first thing they want to know when they meet you is what sign you are." Because in that era, people were saying, "What sign are you? Are you a Leo? Are you a Gemini?" You know, everybody was into signs.

I mention that I remember Mason telling me she was an astrologer during one of our previous phone calls.

I'm not an astrologer per se as much as I know a lot of things. I just know. You know how you just know that you know that you know? So when I meet people I do ask them what sign they are.

Here Dale Wilson steps in for the first time, adding, "You were in that era. And you talked about it in your songs."

Right. It came right out, and people could relate. You know like, "Hi. What sign are you? [And upon learning the sign] Oh, I don't want to deal with you." Another tune on there I have is called "The Devil Sure is Busy." And he is. It's about him doing a lot of things. And I name a lot of cities that he's in. I name Philadelphia naturally—that's where I'm from. I think I named Texas, I think I named California. I named some major cities where he does a lot of things, where people do a lot of things. And basically, I tell you, if your mind is idle, that's when he's *most* strong. There's a tune on there called "Half Sister, Half Brother." Now someone wrote some liner notes about me and said that that record was about incest. It's not about that. I don't know how they read that.

Here Mason and Wilson start to talk at once.

Wilson: It's about a child that may have. . . .

Mason and Wilson: the same father but a different mother.

Mason: A half brother and a half sister.

Wilson: A lot of people don't know that term.

Mason: Yeah. It might mean to you maybe a stepfather or stepmother. Well, I didn't want to write stepfather, stepmother. It doesn't make sense. It doesn't ring right, it doesn't feel right. So I said, "Half Sister, Half Brother." So they thought it meant something else.

Wilson: They thought it was incest.

Mason: And I never. . . .

Wilson: And it may come off that way, but it's not.

Mason: If you listen to it, David, the lyric clearly explains that a woman has a child outside of marriage. . . .

Wilson: And that child has other brothers and sisters by the same father.

Mason: By the same father. It's really clear, all in my lyric. Plus, I got a chance to play on this album. They let me play keyboard. I don't know what I was playing. They probably mixed me out, but I thought I was doing something. So I really had a lot of fun cutting that album. But I noticed in going around the country, trying to promote it, they would put it on in the record shops, people would, like, [makes a motion as if to say "forget it"]. They really liked me singing love songs and, you know, broken hearts. I was going totally [in a different direction]. But if Curtis had done it, they would have eaten it up. But I was not Curtis Mayfield. But now that album, *now*, it is of its time.

As Mason attests, Transition *was a commercial failure; not one of its singles succeeded in charting. Her last album for Buddah, the underrated* Love's the Thing, *brought her back into the spotlight in 1975. In his notes to a 1996 CD release of Mason's work for the British Sequel label, John Ridley wrote, "The disc [is] a classic, right up there with Millie Jackson's* Caught Up . . . *on* Love's the Thing *[Mason] found her real voice."*[13] *The album featured two hit singles, the aforementioned "From His Woman to You" and "Shacking Up" (#9 R&B). The latter song features a protagonist who defends herself against the talk of neighbors who don't approve of her living arrangements. It's one of Mason's strongest performances, one in which she unleashes a great deal of hidden vocal power.*

After Love's the Thing, *Mason left Buddah and split with Bishop. Significantly, she did not record again until 1977, when she released a poorly received disco album with Philly soul-man Bunny Sigler. In a 1981 issue of* Blues and Soul, *Mason addressed in particularly candid fashion her sudden disappearance from the record industry and the dark period that followed: "The important thing is that it hasn't left me feeling bitter—not even towards the person who caused it all. We had many successful and wonderful years together. My biggest mistake—and I'll never make it again!—was in mixing business with pleasure. There's no denying that if it hadn't been for him, I would have never made it in the first place. And that's why it took me such a long time to believe that he would have said those terrible things about me." Today, Mason is more reticent when approaching the topic of her relationship with Bishop; clearly, what's past is past. Nevertheless, there is still a certain poignancy that arises when she discusses the time they spent together.*

I tell you, David, I did not even know what I possessed. I just kept on doing whatever I was doing, and no one was telling me whether I was good or bad, other than my public—maybe for the reasons that Jimmy Bishop came up with. He felt that it was better not to feed a person's ego, because they might get a little crazy. He did not know that to feed mine would have only made me greater. Because if you tell me that I'm great, I'm going to go out and do greater things. It's not going to make me say, "Oh, great," and then I'm going to stop. Let's say you're here at the theater, and you call me in to do a piece in a play that you've written and you just have me in mind, and you say, "I bet Barbara Mason could do this." And you call me up and say, "Barbara, can you come to New York? We've got a small bit." When I get finished with it, it'll be on Broadway. I mean, I've wanted to do movies, I've wanted to do films and Broadway and things like that. I never got a chance to do that, but I know I can do it. Old age that I am, I *know* there's nothing now in the field of entertainment that I cannot do. I know it within my own heart.

Here Wilson inserts some thoughts of her own.

I don't really think she has, like she said, a clear understanding of the importance of what it was like. She still doesn't really realize how hard it was and why all the things happened the way they did, because it was a man's world at that time, and that's the reason why Jimmy Bishop said, "You do this, you do that, you do it that way. I'm going to be the producer." But [looking at Mason] you just took everything for granted. Because he got her at such an early age, and I think that a lot of the females, even the ones that weren't songwriters in those days, were caught up in the same thing. And they didn't even know the difference until ten years later, and they said, "Well wait a minute, I'm the one doing this, but. . . ." They really didn't understand what was going on.

Mason: I just enjoyed doing the music, writing it, creating it. And also, not so much listening to myself on the radio as much as seeing myself make someone happy in the audience. I might see a person say, "Oh wow! When 'Yes, I'm Ready' came out I was just in high school," or "I got married off of your record." I got that particular joy in that, but the other part of it I didn't even know. But I would think, David, that Mr. Bishop knew. He saw. He saw the greatness. He gave me the greatest compliment that he has ever given me, right on Broadway. We were right on Broadway. I was at a restaurant one day eating, and he came in and I had not seen him in many years. And he sat down, he said, "Barbara, I'm going to tell you one thing. There will never come another female like you, before, nor after you. And you will retire out of this industry when *you* want to. They'll never be able to retire you." And I said to him, "Why didn't you tell me that when we were together?" He said, "Then you wouldn't have given me all the great things. You wouldn't have done what you did." He was so afraid that he was going to lose me and lose what I had, when I had all this stuff inside of me. And now it's even greater stuff there, David, now.

When you interview me, I'm living my life again. Because everything that you're asking me about . . . my songs are life songs. They're not songs that I just sat down and put pen to paper. I actually lived everything that's on that record. Any records that you ever hear, even songs that I have done of other people, you will find me somewhere in there.

Mason remains thankful to Bishop for not getting her involved with drugs.[14]

Fortunately for me, I was never led that way, into the drug era. Jimmy Bishop was not a drug user. Sometimes we are a product of our environment. Most of the time we are. And because *he* did certain things, *I* did. I did whatever he did. I'm not saying that I would or would not [have used drugs]. Thank God, I did not. Because that can also cut off your longevity. I probably wouldn't be sitting here with you today in my right mind or knowing what's going on. I do have him to thank for that. But again, there has not been a song that was not selected for me, nor that I have written, nor that I will ever sing or write that is not my life. I must do my own life on records. If I cannot do it on the stage, I have some great film ideas. I'm going to get into that area also. You brought up a film that I did.

I had mentioned earlier that one of the '70s soul fanzines claimed that in 1971 she had acted in a movie with '60s teen star Troy Donahue. Mason's description of the process behind the film gives an indication of its budget.

I was asked to go to Atlanta, Georgia, a place called Stone Mountain. And I did a film for a guy by the name of Michael Thevis. Little did I know that Michael Thevis was a pornography king![15] But the movie I did was called *The Last Stop*. And Troy Donahue was in it. I didn't know Troy was going to be in it until I got to Atlanta, and I was so thrilled because I was a big fan of his from his surfing [movies]. So I get down there and they wanted me to dress in a certain type of clothing, and I didn't have it on hand. So I called Mr. Bishop and I asked him would he bring some of my things back from Philly. I said, "Would you pick up some dresses? They want me to look a certain way, and I have some things but it's not what they want." So he brought all my stuff down. He was shocked. He said, "I didn't even know that you could act." I said, [coyly] "Oh, you didn't know that?"

I played like a Miss Kitty from *Gunsmoke*. So I was a black Miss Kitty. And the director had written out a script. I closed the book. I said, "I don't want to do that. This is how *I* want to do it." What I had to do was, first of all, I controlled the tavern. And everybody came in, and I had girls that worked for me. You know, I was the lady of the house, of this tavern. And one night, I had a poker game. Somebody made me mad. Now I was only supposed to take the cards and toss them on the table and say, "Look. . . ." [hits edge of desk]. I took the cards and mashed them in the lady's face! And the director said, "It's not in the script!" I said, [sweetly] "Oh it isn't?" I knew it wasn't. I said, "Oh, I thought I saw that." He said, "You're a tricky one. Have you had any formal background?" I said, "Yeah, I've *been* to college. I *know*, I don't *need* a script." And the movie was shown in the Atlanta area and really nowhere else. But that was my one debut. I don't know where that movie is. I wish I could find it, 'cause no one has ever seen it. It just shows me in a whole 'nother light. I always knew I could act, because to me, performing on record is acting, to a degree. I mean, different inflections that I do in my singing. You have to have drama. I don't get up to a mike and just sing. Like a Billie Holiday. I can see Billie now, closing her eyes, singing a song, coming up from the depths. So I don't just get in front of a mike and just sing. Or when I perform, I don't get onstage and sing and, "Goodnight everyone." I give you a full, whole thing.

Mason hasn't been able to find many songwriters who can write for her or who understand her particular brand of singing.

It's hard to write for me. I don't know why. There's a gentleman by the name of Frank Alston, Jr. On this particular album, *Piece of My Life* (which Mason cut for the Philadelphia-based WMOT label in 1981), I was in the studio recording and I was not lacking songs. We were finished, but this gentleman walks over to me. He said, "My name's Frank Alston and I have a song for you." I said, "Well, I'm about finished, but what do you have?" He sings this song in my ear, David, called "I'm So in Love With You." He sang two bars. I told my producer, "I'm cutting it." Of course, we got into a whole riff. Guy's name was Butch Ingram. He said, "I don't want to record it. I don't like it." I said [with a tone of revelation], "*He* actually could write for me." And this particular gentleman [Alston] got killed this past January. And we were friends, and he was a great guitarist, a great songwriter. He was able to write for me and we could do things together. He would come over and we would just mess around. He might play a lick, I'd do a lyric. I'd do a lyric, he'd play a lick, you know.

But as I said, there haven't been many people. And I'm not saying that people can't, you know. When I decide to do jazz, I'll probably be doing a lot of standards. I've written some jazz instrumentals in my head. I don't read music, so everything I do comes from up here and I have to have someone transpose it for me, which isn't a problem at all—there are so many great musicians out there. But I think what's lacking now, David, in the industry is there are not a lot of great writers. You know, something happened to our writers. And I think the industry is getting ready to change back to good music. They're looking for us. And if I'm one of those people, you know, I'd be so happy.

Knowing that much of Mason's recent work focuses on writing and publishing more than perform-
ing, I take this opportunity to ask about her current projects. After a momentary glance at Wilson for
assurance, she explains the details of her latest endeavor.

We're about to hopefully sign an administrative/publishing deal with Gamble
and Huff of Philadelphia International Records. Gamble and Huff have been friends
of mine for thirty years. Most of the piano you hear on my records, Mr. Huff is
playing, and most of the background singing, Mr. Gamble helped in that area as
well. So we've always been friends. We're not that much different in age. We did
not grow up in the same neighborhood, but we're from the same city. I was asked
[about a possible publishing deal] by one of his administrators, a lady by the name
of Connie Heigler. Connie Heigler and I go back. She used to pay me my money
when I was seventeen years old, working for Queens Booking Agency.[16] So whenever
it was time for me to go get my check, I went to Connie Heigler, never knowing
Connie Heigler years later would be working for Mr. Gamble. And she and I have
remained friends and in touch with each other. She asked me one day if I'd like to
come on board with them. I said, "Well, come on board with what?" She said, "We
know you have a hundred songs in your house. Forget what you've already done." I
said, "Well, Connie, if you put it that way, I have a hundred and one. Believe me, I
do." She said, "Well, would you like to come with us?" I said, "Would I? Yes!" And
we have been talking and negotiating for about two years. So now, Ms. Wilson has
just gotten a call from Ms. Heigler saying that when I go home, my contracts should
be in the mail.

Wilson: The agreements. The agreements will be in the mail.

Mason: Whatever they are—contracts, agreements. They should be in my mail-
box by the time I get home, because she said at the end of this week. So that is
going to give me, David, a vehicle now to take songs that I have written—kind of
like what a Babyface has done. He started out as an artist; I started out as an artist
and performer. Let these songs be heard on other artists. I'm not saying that I won't
want to ever do them, 'cause I'm dying to do them. But I would love to hear someone
else interpret me just to see if I am that good. And there aren't many black female
R&B songwriters left, if in fact there are any around anyway. I'm not patting myself
on the back, but that was a gift that was given to me, and I intend to use it until my
last breath. I am honored to be with them, but I'm sure they're honored to have me
with them as well. So that's what we've basically been working on, and, yes, I have
written things that will blow your mind. Some things are pop, some things are

R&B, my country & western things. Because back in 1976 I signed a writing agreement with Mr. Gamble, just to see if I could write for some of his artists. I hate to say this, but I did more writing for myself than for any of the other artists. And so I came up with all these songs. And he wound up owning the songs and then selling them over to Warner Brothers, so Warner Brothers has a lot of my material also. So maybe one day they'll bring it out in commercials or movies or whatever. But I've never ever stopped writing.

Mason's songwriting is abetted by her excellent memory; she can memorize a song after hearing or looking at it once.

If you show me something, I have, like, total recall. That was one of the highlights of my schooling. If we had something to memorize for class, I could do it. I was the best speller in my whole school. I won a spelling bee when I was thirteen years old and I represented the Archdiocese of Philadelphia. And it was quite an honor for me. I mean, I knew I could spell, I knew I was good in English, but that was all leading up to my writing. I'm only thirteen, I had no idea. And so I was always just doing things, leading up to where I was going to be—as they say, my niche in life. I didn't ever know what I wanted to do. I loved music, but God, me on record? I said, "Forget it." I wouldn't dream of doing anything like that. I mean, I came from a regular black neighborhood, a regular black family. I have two sisters, or I had two; one died. Mother and father, uncles, aunts, cousins: regular. Going to Catholic school, going to mass, doing the Latin. I had no idea I'd be sitting here today in 1997. So I guess it was my destiny.

I always liked working on the spur of the moment, sometimes without a rehearsal, because it's so natural. I like the kind of excitement of it all and not knowing what's going to happen. I've always worked like that. And it just comes, David. And it can come at any time. People say, "Do you have a down time when you write?" "Do you write when you're broke?" "Do you write when you're sad?" They say when things are going good, you can't write. I don't know for me. Dale, what would you say? A lot of people say that you have a down time, or sometimes you get writer's block. Would you say that I could write at any time? Just say, like, we're gonna be maybe doing things with Gamble and Huff. Do you think all this will inspire me to do greater things? Am I inspired that way?

Wilson: I think this new project with Gamble and Huff will inspire you, but I think in the past other things inspired you. Things that were going on in your life. And it seems to me that you write better when things are worse [laughs].

Mason: If they're better, I don't have anything to write about. I mean, who wants to hear about when you're on top of the world?

Wilson: It doesn't have the same feeling as when things are going bad.

I remark upon the sadness that I have often sensed in Mason's music.

Yeah, there was a sadness. And I stopped writing those kind of songs. I've written love songs, but they're different kinds of love songs. Like, I finished a song some years back called "Love Will Find a Way." And it has a jazz feel to it, it has pop. So again, whenever I evolved out of something, that's what I wrote about. And I guess it's not good being sad all the time. As I said, I should write my life, just how it evolves.

I tell her I am reminded of what she told me the first time we spoke, that she saw her songs as stories and that as she got older, the stories got more interesting.

You know, it was like writing a book. I have some novels in mind that I want to write one day too. And these novels will probably not so much . . . they'll probably be me, but there'll be many "me's." There'll be other people, you know. There could be guys. There'd be many things that I could write about. I haven't lived a long time, but I've lived a lot of life in a short time, whereas some people have lived a long time and lived no life. So I've lived all this stuff in this little bit of time that I've been on earth, and I remember everything from since I was two years old, things that happened as a child. Growing up with my grandparents, with my parents, just being kind of a loner. As a child, I would create things. I probably was doing some directing when I was small. I would have playmates, but I would make up things and say, "Okay, you'll be this and you'll be that." They said, "Well, why are you sitting over here?" I said, "Because I am the one in charge." Not really wanting to appear that way, but I probably had that ability and didn't know what I was doing. And so my first chance at a crack at it was to be a solo artist, to show that I could stand on my own. Now it's in the pot, and it's boiling now. It's getting ready to boil over, because I can tell. Dale, wouldn't you say so?

Wilson: Yes, as far as writing. . . .

Mason: As far as *everything*. It's getting ready to come apart at the seams.

Wilson: You're ready. You're definitely ready.

Mason, unconsciously echoing her most famous song, responds, "Oh yes, I am now, yes." Wilson, always taking care to approach Mason's prospects with judicious consideration, adds, "You're ready for this new project. I think you're ready for something new, period. Other than personal performances, even though she's madly in love with performing."

Mason adds her immediate assent: "Oh yeah, that's one of my loves." She still longs to perform and record, although Wilson has clearly worked hard to steer her career in a different direction.

Wilson: It took a long time to encourage, persuade, convince: this is now the way to go as far as publishing, getting your songs out there. You have a hundred songs, let's get them out there, you know? Don't just let them sit. Performing is fine, recording is fine, but let's face it, longevity is in publishing. And I think it was time. You can always go back to performing. I don't know about the recording; you can go back to that if you really want to, but to see the young people today, they do need songs. And to see them perform something that Barbara wrote maybe six, seven, eight—how many years ago?— would really be fantastic, you know? On commercials, on movies. Did you tell him about the Caress commercial?

Mason: I don't think I did tell him about the Caress commercial. Well, I thought I'd save *something*, so we'd have more to talk about! Yes, the Lever Brothers people decided in 1991 to take "Yes, I'm Ready" and use it for their Caress soap. I might be able to sing it for you, David [starts to sing]: "Makes me feel so good, like I knew you would. Yes, I'm ready." And that's the way it went.

As she glides over "knew" and draws out the second syllable of "ready," Mason's voice is as fetching and distinctive as ever. I remark upon how good she sounds.

Well, I didn't sing it. They used someone else, but it was fine.

Wilson: It was aired that year on the Grammys.
Mason: We saw it, we heard it. It was awesome.
Wilson: You know, that kind of thing she doesn't think about. I try to remind her, "I know you're performing and you're a singer, [but] you are a *songwriter*." And these things are very important. A lot of people don't know these things.

In an effort to insure control over the rights to her own work, Mason makes periodic trips to Washington to check on the copyright status of her songs. The most recent visit was in August of 1997, around the time of her fiftieth birthday.

We didn't want my songs to go into public domain, which means they would be up for grabs. Anyone could have taken them. And if somebody had stolen "Yes, I'm Ready," that would have destroyed me. So I started reading more information, and BMI was sending out packages to all of its writers about, "You've got to go to

Washington and renew your stuff." And so while I was there, I started opening up this file. I said, "Dale!" There's my name and there's this long list of songs I had written. I had no idea. So we just went back again this year. Of course now, we've got the computers in, so I can just sit there and just punch up everything. And now I can even punch up my own publishing company, Marc James Music.

The publishing company is named after her son with Bishop, Marc James Mason.

He's twenty-eight. A little older than you. They keep telling me this is the best time of my life. Diana said it, so I'm coming out—[laughing] more than one way. Every time I heard her sing that, I said, "When am I going to be able to say that? Where they say, 'She's doing this, she's doing that.'" And then all of a sudden everybody's saying, "Oh, we always knew it!" And I'll say, "Well, you never told me." But it's coming, David.

Mason says that her publishing negotiations with Gamble and Huff have been the target of some skepticism within the business. She mentions a booking agent who has been openly dismissive of her efforts.

He doesn't really believe we can pull it off. First of all, again, we're in a man's world: publishing. How many women—*black* women we're talking—would you know of that could pull off a publishing deal? That I could make my publishing company one of the biggest publishing companies in the country. Everybody I see that owns a big publishing company, it's owned by a man.

While she has focused mostly on publishing and songwriting in recent years, Mason has at the same time come to a greater understanding of her contributions as an innovator of Philadelphia soul music. She says the awareness of her influence began to dawn on her during the '70s.

I knew that I was the originator of the Philly sound. And it was never so much said, but I knew in my heart that there was no one else before me, because if you go back to, say, the Chubby Checker era or the Dee Dee Sharp era or the Orlons, who were from Philly, that was a whole 'nother type of music. Fabian, Dion, and all that came from that era [the early '60s]; I was still in school. So the beginning of a new form or type of sound was really with "Yes, I'm Ready." It could have started with "Girls Have Feelings Too," but for me to be recognized would have come with "Yes, I'm Ready." And each artist that came after me used the same musicians. If you listen, they had the same sound that I had. So where do they draw from? They don't sound like Dee Dee Sharp with the "Mashed Potatoes" or the Orlons with "South Street." They sound like me. So I have to be the originator.

Mason also says that she no longer shies away from acknowledging her past successes as a performer. She will gladly talk to any passersby who happen to recognize her.

You know, I didn't used to do that a lot. I'd see somebody on the street and they'd say, "Are you Barbara Mason?" I'd say, "You know, a lot of people say I look like her." I don't know why I did that. Why'd I do that, Dale? And you'd say, "Stop doing that!"

Wilson: Actually, at the time, they would catch you at the weirdest times.

Mason: I might have been in the supermarket, shopping. I'd say, "Wait a moment, no. But you know what? I've heard her music and I think she's wonderful." I've stopped doing that now because I finally found out how important it is for me to acknowledge who I am. I went to Sears one day to pay a bill, and the lady said, "I've got to ask you. Now I see you have a *J* in the middle, but could you possibly be. . . ?" I said, "I am! I am!" She said, "Oh, you're so forward. What's wrong with you?" I said, "I didn't mean to get so excited, but I *am* her. Do you want to know anything about me?" So I've learned now that it is important. That's a blessing that God gave me. I shouldn't just keep it hidden. He's got something for me to do. There's something else I'm supposed to be doing, you know? I have not completed this whole cycle of my life yet. I did part one.

I just feel that this vehicle which has been given to me—if Mr. Gamble and myself can pull this off—will be my "in," and the rest is history. Because as Mr. McDougal came to me when I was sixteen and said, "You want to make records?"— now I'm being given this next step. It is incredible. I was fifty years old on August ninth. And I look at it and say, "fifty? That's a scary number." I sat in Rock Creek Park and cried and looked at the Potomac River going up and down, and I said, "There's my life. It's like the current." And these were tears of *joy*, to say, "It's getting ready to get scary now." I'm going for a ride. I can tell.

Part Four

New York

The soul music recorded in New York shared many of the basic qualities of Memphis and Muscle Shoals soul but added a layer of uptown sophistication through the use of strings and the pop-oriented vision of producers like Burt Bacharach, Jerry Ragovoy, and Clyde Otis (resulting in a style often described as "New York pop-soul"). In contrast to the South, New York studios did not employ standard in-house bands; rather, the musicians were hired on a date-by-date basis, with the musical arrangements usually worked out in advance of the session. The resulting sound was arguably more workaday and prosaic than the loose, spontaneous style favored in southern studios, but what New York soul lacked in imagination it made up for in the quality of songs and the professionalism with which it was executed. Further, a number of New York-based soul producers such as the late Bert Berns (whose productions include Erma Franklin's original version of "Piece of My Heart" and Freddie Scott's galvanizing "Are You Lonely For Me"), Juggy Murray, Jerry Wexler and Bobby Robinson brought to their records a genuine understanding of the spirit behind the music. Many of their productions rank with the best Memphis records for unmitigated funkiness.

Key to the success of the New York pop-soul sound was the presence of a core group of marvelous backup vocalists, arguably (along with Memphis's Rhodes, Chalmers, and Rhodes) the finest background singers in the history of soul. "The Group" (as they were informally known before officially becoming the Sweet Inspirations) included at various times Cissy Houston, the greatly underrated Judy Clay (both former members of the gospel group the Drinkard Singers), Sylvia Shemwell, and Dionne Warwick's younger sister Dee Dee. The Group's distinctive vocals, marked by Houston's soaring soprano, appeared on records by a staggering array of artists: Solomon Burke, Aretha Franklin, Esther Phillips, Garnet Mimms, and Betty Harris, just to name a few. Each of the Group's members was also a standout lead vocalist; at various times Houston, Warwick, and Clay all pursued solo careers without much commercial success—a sad reminder that the '60s New York soul scene was populated with supremely talented but underutilized artists.

The city's soul music industry was largely centered around two geographical areas. One was the West '40s and '50s, where numerous small soul labels such as Scepter, Sue, Shout, and Calla had offices (many were located in two famous edifices, 1650 Broadway and the nearby Brill Building). Also in the neighborhood were several top-notch recording studios that brought a level of technical advancement and polish to soul music production that was absent from the more pieced-together studios of the South. (Like the head arrangements they created, many of the southern studios had built themselves from the ground up, one section at a time.) The other area was Harlem, where in 1953 local entrepreneur Bobby Robinson had initiated a series of small labels including Red Robin, Fire, Fury, and Ember that spotlighted burgeoning artists like New Orleans R&B singer Lee Dorsey and the pre-Motown Gladys Knight and the Pips. Robinson promoted his releases through his record store, which featured speakers that broadcast the music directly onto 125th Street.

Of course, the most famous label specializing in New York soul was Atlantic. Founded in 1947 by Ahmet and Nesuhi Ertegun, the sons of a Turkish diplomat, Atlantic came to rule the soul era in much the same way that it had dominated R&B in the '50s. Many of the label's artists, including Solomon Burke, Aretha Franklin, Don Covay, and the late saxophone great King Curtis, were recorded in the Atlantic studio, located at 1841 Broadway. From this position, Atlantic was able to take advantage of not only the producers and musicians working in the Brill Building scene but also the talents of Jerry Wexler, who had been brought to Atlantic as executive vice-president in 1953. Wexler became Atlantic's chief creative force in the '60s, producing classic recordings and signing artists such as Franklin and Wilson Pickett to the label. As has been noted, Atlantic also established links to southern soul through arrangements to distribute smaller, southern-based labels and by sending its artists to southern studios to record.

Always at the forefront of the newest musical trends, New York producers began to focus on other styles such as funk and disco as the soul era gradually waned in the '70s. For Jerry Wexler and Atlantic, this change was noticeable in an even more sophisticated approach to production (evident in the work of Roberta Flack, Donny Hathaway, and the later Atlantic releases of Aretha Franklin) as well as an emphasis on album-oriented rock acts like Yes and Led Zeppelin. Sadly, many soul artists who had been Atlantic stalwarts during the '60s—Joe Tex, Wilson Pickett, Percy Sledge, Solomon Burke, Barbara Lewis—left or were dropped from the label, never to regain the success of their earlier careers.

Fortunately, the scope and variety of the New York entertainment industry bene-fitted many locally based soul singers during the '70s by offering them work in nightclubs and professional theatre after their recording careers had declined. Singers such as Chuck Jackson, Baby Washington, and Maxine Brown still make the New York area their home and have continued to hone their craft through appearances at local theatres and nightspots. The undiminished presence of these great singers stands as a testament to the enduring vitality of the New York soul sound.

Maxine Brown

Story of a Soul Legend

Maxine Brown, 1964

Deftly coupling a gospel-rooted performance style with a sophisticated, pop-oriented sensibility, Maxine Brown is one of the finest proponents of New York pop-soul. Unlike other singers who exemplified the "New York sound" (such as Baby Washington, Solomon Burke, and Lorraine Ellison), Brown was as influenced by the pop vocalists of the '40s and '50s as by her upbringing in the Sanctified Church. In hits like "Oh No Not My Baby" and "All in My Mind," she exhibited the lyrical sensibility of the great pop singers, revealing layers of meaning through clear, direct interpretation. On other records ("Gotta Find a Way," "Ask Me," and "Oh Lord, What Are You Doing to Me"), she employed gospel techniques such as melisma, shouting, and sermonizing more liberally. Often she would sing the first part of a song "straight" (free from extra stylistic flourishes) but would display flashes of gospelized mannerisms in later verses or choruses.

For example, at the start of "Ask Me" (1963) she sings gently, bringing the abjection of the lyrics into sharp relief: "Would it ease your pain if I hurt inside, would it build your pride . . . then would you ask me to be your girl?" On the second verse, she changes her approach altogether, filling the line "If I gave you my shoulder to do all your crying on . . ." with sudden urgency. On "all," the shout that resides just at the edge of her deceptively smooth voice makes a sudden appearance. It's an explosive moment that catches the listener unawares, one that demands sitting up and taking notice. This interac-

tion between the control of her pop instincts and the spontaneity associated with her gospel background gives many of her records a rare immediacy.

Although Brown is regarded as a legend in the R&B and soul community (she is revered by a loyal group of music fans who have fond memories of her recordings and performances), mainstream success—extensive commercial airplay, consistent chart action—has often eluded her. Several critical publications have bemoaned this situation, most notably the 1992 edition of The Rolling Stone Record Guide: "Though she's had only three hits of any magnitude, Maxine Brown must be considered one of the truly gifted singers of her generation who, with the right breaks, might have established herself in the same rank as Nancy Wilson in terms of versatility and depth." In recent years, however, Brown has performed with increasing frequency, proving that her talent and professional flair have not diminished.

Youthful and energetic, Maxine Brown retains the reputation for style and elegance that has lasted her entire career: she was one of the first R&B sex symbols of the '60s. In fact, critics have often seemed as interested in her appearance as her singing. In a 1980 review of a performance at Marty's in New York, a Variety critic wrote, "These are earthy and provocative songs and she has the gown and figure to go with them." Although Brown has always been puzzled by the emphasis on her looks ("I wasn't trying to exude sex. My songs certainly didn't say so"), there is no doubt that her sense of style was admired by her peers in the music industry. Carla Thomas remembers the time Brown visited her on the campus of Nashville's Tennessee A&I University (where Thomas was enrolled) in the early '60s, dressed to the nines and escorting a well-groomed poodle. Brown was the object of much admiring attention by Thomas's friends, who viewed her as a mysterious, glamorous visitor from the adult world.

It would be inaccurate to suggest that Brown is chiefly remembered for her appearance; her marvelous voice and powerful performance style brought her equal admiration. Virtually every singer I interviewed for this project had something positive to say about her. Already an experienced performer by the onset of the '60s (she had worked as a professional gospel singer since the mid-'50s), Brown had an onstage polish that many other singers longed to acquire. Ruby Johnson, for example, told me that Brown's first big hit, the self-penned "All in My Mind," was a staple of her own club act in Washington in the early '60s, while Barbara Mason expressed the admiration she had for Brown as a Catholic schoolgirl in Philadelphia long before she herself began to have dreams of recording.

Brown's narrative style is seamless and flowing, much like her singing. Upon first impression, one notices a wonderful guilelessness to her personality; it seems hard to believe that someone who has spent so many years in a tough and competitive industry could be so warm and open. As she begins to recount the ups and downs of her forty-year career, however, a sense of frustration and bitterness occasionally slips out. The surprising twists that her life has taken—the excitement as well as the *disappointments—are all present in her stories. During our interview sessions, I was amazed at the clear, vivid quality of Brown's narrative as well as the depth of her memory (despite her claim that she is losing it). In many cases, old press clippings and other "props" that I had brought along triggered humorous responses (when she saw a 1981 interview in which she was quoted as "waiting for the right record deal to come along," she laughed, exclaiming, "I'm still waiting!"). The atmosphere was very relaxed: she made lunch (Brown is an excellent cook), and we listened to tapes of new songs she has composed with her writing partner, Rebecca Murphy. She hopes to have the chance to record some of these songs for an English record company that has expressed interest. One song in particular, "Walking Through the Raindrops," is a beautiful evocation of the dizziness of being in love, full of tenderness and capped with soaring choruses. It's the kind of song most pop singers would kill for, yet it's hard to imagine anyone doing it as well as Maxine Brown.*

Early Life and Career

Brown, who prefers to keep her age a secret, was born in the rural community of Kingstree, South Carolina. The story that she presents here begins after her childhood move to Queens, New York, in 1945.

I came from the Pentecostal Church, the Holy Rollers—any word you want to call it. And my mother had gotten into that and she took us along with her—us being my sister and myself. And we'd all go to church, and I was brought up in the church and learned how to sing there. And there were about five young people in the church, and I always found myself being a leader even back then. So I could bang the piano a little bit and played by ear and I figured, "Let me form a little singing group here with the five teenagers that we have in the church." And we were doing pretty good, but my pastor's wife said, "Oh, no." We were singing songs at that time by the Ward Singers, the Caravans, Sam Cooke and the Soul Stirrers, and all those people. We were doing those kinds of hip songs. But my church was a little bit more straight-laced, and they'd rather do more hymnals and things like [sings] "rescue the perishing, care for the dying"—unrhythmic-type songs. We would sing outside and do the great gospel songs like "Surely God is Able," by the Ward Singers. When we found out that we weren't allowed to sing those kinds of juicy gospel songs, I kind of held back.[1]

Not long after that my mother passed. And I was just turning seventeen when she passed. And alone, really alone, 'cause my sister was married. And I had to bury my mother, and we were on welfare. The undertaker—he knew all of us kids in the neighborhood when we were coming up, and he was very lenient in his price. I had a cousin here in New York at the time, so she assisted me along with this undertaker. And he felt so sorry for me because my uncle came up from Philly and wanted to move my mother's body to South Carolina, and I had no money to go. So the undertaker gave me a hundred dollars and pressed it in my hand and told me, "Here, your uncle doesn't look too [financially] stable. You better take this and put it on you." And I did. He says, "As a matter of fact, stick it in your bra, and don't let anybody know you have this. This is your money, because for some reason I just have a feeling that he's not very stable." And sure enough, he wasn't. So we went and buried my mother.

I should write a book, because part of my going back South to bury my mother has another story. This goes back several years before I first arrived in New York. We were kidnapped, my sister and I, oh yeah. From my father. We were kidnapped from school and brought to New York, and that's what I'm doing in New York to this very day. Because everybody writes, "She arrived in New York with her mother, and she sang in church." That's where the story always starts. They think I just packed up, made a trip to New York. No, I was kidnapped. We were kidnapped from school, and the teacher helped. She was the one responsible for assisting my mother, who I did not know at the time, to get us out of there.

Brown says she is not yet ready to describe the circumstances that brought her to New York in greater detail.

I don't think I want to write this story until after my father passes, 'cause we're speaking now. He'll be ninety-one next month. So the story starts before you see everything in print. One day I'll try to write it if I could remember most of it, 'cause it's pretty horrible. When my acting teacher heard my story, he kept making sounds like this in his throat [makes gasping sounds], and he says, "My God, your story is worse than Billie Holiday. The only difference with you is you weren't associated with drugs." But he said it's the same kind of downtrodden type of lifestyle. And pretty rough.

So after my mother passed, a friend of mine from Brooklyn came over. She heard that I wasn't singing anymore and she came and got me, and we formed a group called the Royaltones. She was the leader and I was the tenor—I was used to singing background.[2] And we became famous around Brooklyn. From there, this guy named Professor Charles Taylor heard us and became very impressed with us. He took us in the Apollo Theatre with him to appear on a show with the Caravans, the Ward Singers, and Sam Cooke and the Soul Stirrers. That was my first time in the Apollo Theatre, but I was in the background. This had to be '55, '56, or something like that. If my mother had lived, I would never have been in show business because she would have been totally against it. And we didn't make any money and we didn't do it for the money, 'cause I had a job. I went to school to Central Needle Trades, and I sewed and tried to design clothes. And that was my trade.

After completing her program at Central Needle Trades, Brown went to work for the Lilliette Brassiere Factory. The gospel group having disbanded, she was approached by a fellow performer who had recently "crossed over" from gospel into pop and was starting his own group. Although she had never performed secular material, she was persuaded to audition for an open spot in the group.

They [the members of the group] said, "You sing all the parts, so all we have to do is teach you the harmony." I said, "But I don't know anything about rock 'n roll. I don't know the style of rock 'n roll." They said, "We'll teach you." And they did. They taught me rock 'n roll, 'cause I only knew gospel. And my favorite singers at that time were Patti Page—since we couldn't listen to the "devil's music" [laughs] on the radio, I listened to singers like Patti Page and Les Paul and Mary Ford, all that great harmony and things like that. That's who I would listen to back then. And the Andrews Sisters. I came up listening to pop music. That's why I was never a dirty type of gutbucket blues-soul singer. I think that's why, 'cause my influences came through the route of listening to Dinah Shore, all those people.

The group broke up after three of its members were drafted into the army. Brown and the other two remaining members renamed themselves the Treys, later becoming the Manhattans (no relation to the Manhattans of "Kiss and Say Goodbye" fame). The frustration that Brown experienced while performing with the Manhattans, in addition to the effects of a terrible public humiliation, led to the composition of what would become her first big hit.

While in the group [leader Freddy Johnson] says, "You know, I do all the work, I do all the writing, and none of you guys contribute to the writing. Here!" He gave me a song title, "Maybe It's All in My Mind," and he took the paper [imitates throwing paper] and he threw it at me. He said, "Here, finish it!" Ooh! That thing irked me so badly because he didn't say, "Would you finish it? How would you like to learn how to write?" He didn't say anything like that. He just threw it at me. I was so angry with him. And I was angry with him and every other man who did me wrong—the type of situation I'd been through up to this point in my young life, starting with my father, so all that stuff building up in me.

So I'm sitting at home one night and I'm thinking about my life. I was just engaged to a guy and I got jilted: in the true sense of the word, jilted. He didn't show up for the wedding; everybody came but him. He was in the service and was stationed at Fort Devens. I made all these wedding plans. I bought this cute little wedding dress that was high in the front—what they're using today—high in the front, low in the back, a cute little wedding dress. I was going to have it in my landlady's house. And the whole ceremony, they did the whole number, and he didn't show. I started thinking about my father, this guy, everybody else I can just add up. And then I looked at the title of this song, "Maybe It's All In My Mind." And then I started thinking. I said [speaks slowly, as if the words are gradually being revealed] "I think that you don't care . . . and it's more than I can bear. . . . I don't know, baby . . . maybe it's all in my mind." That's how it started, and then I picked up the paper. I knew right then from singing and from analyzing lyrics that you could have a personal problem, but to make it universal you have to take your personal problems out of it. I had to think more universally. And then I thought of me or any other young woman in this same position. "*I* know I've been true, but honey, sweetie, baby, what about you? . . . I don't know, maybe it's all in my mind." As if to say, forgive me for what I'm thinking. And then, "We've been going steady for *so* long, I never dreamed you would ever do me wrong. I knew I was yours and I thought you were mine, and that every little thing was so fine. . . . Oh darling, I'd hate to see someone else with *you* other than me. I don't know . . . maybe it's all in my mind." So that's how that came about. Wrote the song in ten minutes and put it away.

About a month or so later the guy who gave it to me [Johnson] said, "Did you ever finish that song?" We were short of something to do that night in rehearsal, and he turns to me and he just attacks me: "Did you ever finish that song I told you to finish?" *Told.* I said, "No." He said, "You see that?" And then he started to lay into me. I said, "Wait a minute. Get off my back. I *did* the old thing." He said, "Well, let me hear it." I got it out, I sung it, and he says [assumes an unimpressed tone], "Oh, okay." And that was the end of that. He didn't say, "That's good." It's just that I did as I was told, okay? So I put the thing away.

Two years later a friend of mine invited me to a club out in Queens, 'cause he was singing there. I was having a nice time and I'm just tapping my fingers sitting at the table while he went to change. I looked up and someone was standing over me.

This guy says, "Rodney [the friend] tells me you can sing." And I said, "Yes, so who are you?" And he says, "I'm the guy who books this place. Would you come over here? Come with me." I said, "I'm not going anywhere with you." So he says, "Oh, you're one of those. Okay, come with me over here to the back booth because it's a little noisy up front here with the band playing. I'd like to talk with you and discuss a few things with you." I said, "Oh, why didn't you say so?" [Laughs.] I got up and went in the back booth, and he says, "I'd like to hear you sing." I'd never sung with a live band before in my life, just with a piano player in gospel music. I know how to do that, but to sing with a live band and to keep in time and all that stuff? So I got up and sang "Misty" with them—that was my favorite song—and I sat down. And he said, "Well, you *can* sing."

The booking agent for the club was Mal Williams, an aspiring record producer and promoter who would have a profound effect on Brown's life and career. She became a regular performer at the club in Queens. Meanwhile, Williams was losing control over the career of one of his protégés, Inez Foxx (who a few years later, in 1963, would record the hit "Mockingbird" with her brother, Charlie).

The big boys liked Inez Foxx just right after Mal recorded her. They stepped in and took her away from him and placed her in the Apollo Theatre for her debut. They moved in and said, "You won't have her. That's it." Now he has to shop around for somebody new, and, to make a long story short, I was it. One day while we were in Manhattan, he says, "I'd like to take you into the studio to do a half session. We'll share this session with Jimmy Tyrrell.[3] He's going to record a guitar player and I'd like to record you."

The recording session, held in September of 1960, did not exactly go as planned.

Jimmy Tyrrell took so much time with recording [the guitar player] that there was only a half an hour left. And I said, "You can't even warm up in a half hour." So Mal said, "Okay, we'll do the best we can." And so I went in there and it just so happened by accident that a trombone was on the date. The guitar player had a long, long, long extension cord to his guitar, and I played by ear and he looked over my shoulders to tell the band what it was that I was playing. And he called out the changes to the band: "She's hitting the five. Okay, she's to the four right now. She's making the D-seven right now." That's how he called it out. But I told them I wanted everybody to go like this [sings three descending notes]: "Dah, dah, dah." And the trombone player just happened to [imitates trombone playing the notes]: "Bom, bom, bom." And that made the sound. And so from day one I was telling everybody what I heard and what I know to play, and yet I was playing by ear. So I was playing the piano, and after I did that, I got up and threw my head back and started singing. So now we had no piano player, 'cause I can't play and sing. And that was the record. And Mal took the record around to ABC-Paramount and all of the big companies, and they weren't taking girls.

In Brown's opinion, the reluctance to lease a recording by a female artist exemplified the sexism of the early '60s record industry.

It just becomes an era where girls are not acceptable. That happened way way back. Every now and then a Dinah Washington or a Sarah Vaughan would come along and they would stand out, but other than that, women—they just weren't acceptable [laughs]. But they had guy singers so women could swoon over them. So Mal was taking my record around to all the big companies, and no one is buying. One day, I finish work—now I'm working at Kings County Hospital[4]—and I'm leaning on this parking meter in front of the Brill Building. Out walks [producer] Tony Bruno. It's five o'clock and everybody's coming out of the building. And he says, "Hey Mal, what's happening? What you got? You got something?" And Mal said, "Yeah, I've got a [taking a dramatic pause] *damn demo* and [referring to Brown] *this.*" And I looked at him and I said, "Humph!" Sucked my teeth at him and turned the other way towards the street. You know, I'm leaning on this parking meter. Tony Bruno says, "Okay, why don't you bring it up to me tomorrow and let me hear it? 'Cause everybody's leaving now." The next day, he flipped. He heard this trombone, he heard this sound and everything. Took the record right away. He played it for some people, for his distributors in Chicago. Little did he know that his distributor in Chicago was taping it, and they got a white girl that night to come in and learn it to sing it.

The rush recording of R&B records by white cover artists was, of course, a standard industry practice dating back to the early '50s (although arguably less common by the '60s). But the circumstances surrounding "All in My Mind" were particularly complicated: in addition to the plunderer from Chicago, Brown says that different versions of the song were recorded by drag performer Bobby Marchan and gospel veteran Linda Hopkins, both great singers in their own right. The sudden proliferation of interpretations of "All in My Mind" caused some confusion for DJ's who weren't sure which version of the record to promote.

Everybody got on this record. So it was with the flip of a coin by a DJ who got tired of seeing all these records walk in his studio. This DJ said, "Wait a minute.

I've got a record here by Bobby Marchan, Linda Hopkins, and this girl in Chicago here, and then we got a record by this Brown girl. *Who* is the originator?" Someone said, "The Brown girl." "*Who* wrote the song?" "*The Brown girl.*" "That's who I'm going with!" The flip of a coin from this guy. Would you believe it? That's how he went with that record, and that's how the record stuck. And everybody else was pushing their record, trying to get their record in. And that demo, which was recorded at 1650 Broadway in Adelphi studio, is that same hit today. They didn't go back in to redo it. All they did was went back in and dubbed a piano. That's how that record hit the street, and that demo to this day is the hit record.

"All in My Mind," released in January, 1961, on Tony Bruno's Nomar label, went all the way to #2 on the R&B and #19 on the pop charts, giving Brown her first taste of popular success. A follow-up record, "Funny," also became a top-five R&B hit that April.

To hear yourself on the radio! Oh! That was a dream come true! You can't believe it. Oh, what a time. Just to hear yourself on the radio. Oh, gosh! And pretty soon it got to the point it was embarrassing, you heard yourself so much!

But while her first forays into the soul recording market were well-received by record buyers, the reaction of her fellow church members was quite different.

My church condemned me. They heard I was wearing lipstick and short sleeves that you could see through! [Laughs.] And we're doing the "devil's music." And let me tell you, when you come from churches like that, they put such a guilt trip on you. Oh, my God! They could really give it to you. And all my life, that's one of the things that I just couldn't get away from. And we all, *we all* who come from this type of background, these parents are dead set against us doing the devil's music, and our pastors and what have you. It's very, very difficult, and it's confusing. It's like we're doing something we really like to do, really *really* like to do, and yet you have this bad feeling, like I left God outside the door when I came into this place. Can I pick Him up when I leave? Even to this very day, it's still a debate in my own mind, and it's very hard. And I'm back in the church now, but not in *my* church—I go to another church. Maybe playing it safe. Anyway, I feel like I got this God-given talent, and I'm going to use it.

In addition to the disapproval of her church community, there was another way in which success proved to be a mixed blessing: the difficulty of collecting performance royalties.

As far as royalties from the record company? The first time my manager and the owner of the record company went to pick up my check from the distributor, the mob backed them out of the door and said, "You're getting nothin' here. You're not getting a dime." [With bitterness] And I never got a dime. Of *my* money.

Brown also found herself the target of harassment directed towards manager Mal Williams, whom she had married in late 1960 (since Brown was being promoted as an unmarried teen idol, her record company had insisted that the marriage stay a secret).

I was sick in Detroit and I ended up in the hospital, to make a long story short. I went to play golf on the Fourth of July of that year—'63—and I swung and I couldn't come down, and they had to drag me off the course on my toes because I had what you call adhesions. When I went up to swing for that golf club, that was it. That was one hard swing too many, and then I was up in midair until they got me off that course and the next thing you know, I was in the hospital with a very high temperature, 105. I ended up staying in the hospital for one month. Bettye LaVette was there at the time, in Detroit. She remembered my being in the hospital. She came. 'Cause they had put out on the radio that I needed blood, because I was very bad off. I was really, really sick. The doctor refused to send me home alone 'cause I was too weak still, so he sent me home with a nice elderly lady who was my roommate in the hospital. She was a friend of the surgeon who operated on me, who owned the hospital. He sent me home with her 'cause I needed to be looked after.

Another month later, I returned to New York, and that's when my husband had gotten into certain *connections* and he had gotten into trouble. He owed money at the time, and in order for them to collect their money, they had to come to my jobs, to take *my* money from *my* jobs before I worked them, to pay off *his* debt. And so the owner of the Apollo Theatre [Bobby Schiffman] knew me and liked me very much, and he said, "Why did you agree to this? I'll tell you what I'm going to do. I'm going to give you a blank contract. You say you owed me money from a month or so ago, and that will allow you to pay your band, pay all of your people, and get out of here free, and they can't touch the money that you owe me." So he was able to give me back the money under the table. That's how they didn't get all my money from the Apollo Theatre, because he worked it right. But the next job, I worked a nightclub this time, and they were all connected in the club, so they just automatically took their money off the top. And here they're picking on a poor little girl who has nothing to do with anything like that.

Schiffman's willingness to help Brown during this period of financial crisis is testament to the high degree of esteem in which she was held at the famed theatre. From the time of her first solo appearance

there during the Christmas season of 1960, she was an audience favorite. In 1962, a reviewer for
Variety wrote of a show on which she shared the bill with B.B. King: "Maxine Brown draws wolf
whistles for her sultry, well-shaped appearance and also registers with stylish vocal delivery. She can
belt the blues in slick fashion and handle a ballad with equal dexterity. Mixing in some talk material
for the audience, she impresses strongly."

The Apollo was the greatest place in the world to play. I don't know about today. I don't know if it carries the same magic, but back then, the performers, including every big name that you could mention in jazz, rock 'n roll, including Buddy Holly, everybody who's ever worked there, had to do five shows a day! [Laughs.] We complained; nothing we could do about it. But we did it. We used to say we met ourselves coming off the stage, you know, 'cause it rotated around like that. At that time, a kid could come in and buy a ticket—whatever a ticket costs, maybe $2.50, $5—they could stay all day. 'Cause you'd come out and you'd say, "What, the same people in the same front seats again?" And they'd stay all day. You'd have to make an announcement that so-and-so's mother says "get home."

The Apollo's venerated stature within the community made it one of the few commercial institutions
to be spared damage during the riots that devastated Harlem in the '60s. Here, Brown presents a more
elaborate version of a story that she first recounted in Ted Fox's 1983 history of the theatre, Showtime
at the Apollo.

I'm at the Apollo, and the riot breaks out. And this little white kid came down the street, and he happened to be caught in the wrong neighborhood at the wrong time. And a group of black people just stripped him to the bone and were beating on him for no reason at all. And he couldn't raise his hand 'cause there's too many. And I heard this person screaming—I found out it was me—"Leave him alone!" We were on the back street, 126th, and I was leaning out of the window and I was screaming. And that's the only thing that made them stop. They left him alone, and then he walked on towards the subway to try to get some clothes or something. They were beating him terrible. And then there happened to be a guy who was a friend of ours that lived in Long Island. He came in to pick us up, and he was so light-skinned, they thought he was white. They stormed our car, they were throwing things at us, and we had to get out of Dodge in a hurry, because he was at the wheel. That was a scary night. They didn't care if there were black people in the car, they were just after anybody who looked light-skinned. And that was a terrible time. That was a sad time in Harlem for me.

For the artists who performed there during the '60s, the Apollo was a haven, a place insulated from whatever conflicts were taking place in the street. As Brown said in Showtime at the Apollo, *"I played there during a riot. I saw people beaten in the streets, shootings, and so on. The shows still went on."⁵ Brown remembers with fondness her first solo performance there in 1960, one of those fabled occasions in which an accident provides the inspiration for a successful stage routine.*

The magic! There was something about that Apollo stage that was magic. I have never had the thrill of my life on anybody's stage as I have had at that Apollo Theatre, and that's including today. Just going on that stage alone, that microphone coming up out of the floor. I remember I was so nervous when I grabbed that microphone the first time I went out. I was shaking to pieces. The microphone moved, and I forgot it went into the floor; so by my touching it and being so shaky, it went down. But I happened to be on a part of the song that hit the tension— [sings] "Whoa-ooah-ooah, *darling*"—and I grabbed the mike and I just happened to go down with it in a kneeling, sort of a stooping position, and it brought the house down! They thought I had a new act. I thought, "Oh! This *works*." And I kept it in the act. Every night I grabbed the mike. So you learn shtick. You learn that as you go along. You learn what works, what doesn't. And then to work with some of the best comedians in the business. Redd Foxx, he was dirty—but these guys, what you learn from them is timing. Timing like you won't believe. It's also like a song. Flip Wilson, Richard Pryor, all of these guys—to work with them onstage is something else. Because at the Apollo, no matter how big they were, the comedians had to double as the emcee, then they'd do their bit. And so I worked with them all. You didn't get any money; you had to fight to get your money. You were never *not* paid, but it paid so little. Oh God, so little. And worked so hard. But it was the proving ground for everyone. I don't care where they have been, that was still the proving ground. *That's* the Apollo Theatre.

Life at Scepter Records

In 1963, Brown was signed to the Wand subsidiary of New York-based Scepter Records. Beginning with the Shirelles, one of the most commercially successful groups of the early '60s, the label gradually cultivated a roster of immensely talented artists that included not only Brown but Dionne Warwick (Scepter's biggest star), Chuck Jackson (with whom Brown was often paired as part of a duet team), Big Maybelle, the Isley Brothers, and Tommy Hunt. A team of excellent producers and arrangers (including Burt Bacharach and Hal David) provided Scepter with its trademark "uptown" sound. The bright, latin-tinged percussion, swirling strings, and high background voices heard on so many

Scepter recordings sounded perfect over the shrill airwaves of early '60s AM radio. For Brown, the move to Scepter from Nomar (after a brief, unsuccessful stint at ABC) was, at least on paper, a step up (although, in an indication of the tightness of Brill Building society in the '60s, Nomar owner Tony Bruno worked as producer on certain Scepter sessions). Though small, Scepter had wide visibility, a proven track record of hits, and a stable of artists who excelled in creating records that combined the artistic and commercial in equal measure.

It is during the Scepter period (1963–67) that Brown recorded much of the work for which she is best known today. In addition to writing her own material (such as the classic "Since I Found You," composed with "For Your Love" vocalist Ed Townsend), Brown was given songs by some of the finest writers working in the thriving Brill Building/1650 Broadway pop scene: Carole King and Gerry Goffin, Nicholas Ashford and Valerie Simpson, Luther Dixon, and Van McCoy. Her interpretations of the King/Goffin compositions, "Oh No Not My Baby" (1964) and "It's Gonna Be All Right" (1965) are particularly fine. With her astute sense of melody and emotionally direct vocal style, Brown seemed to understand exactly what to do with the songs. In the following account, she explains how she put her personal stamp on "Oh No Not My Baby."

Scepter was built on the Shirelles. They were hot with "Soldier Boy" and all those records, and they were the first to record "Oh No Not My Baby." They were at that point in their life where they were arguing among themselves about who should be the leader. So they all took a part on this particular song. And when it was given to me, it sounded like everybody wanted to do their own thing on this record. So Stan Greenberg [Scepter owner Florence Greenberg's son]—he used the name "Green" just to keep from being confused with his mother—he found the song and brought it to me. He says, "You've got to do one thing. You've got to find the original melody in that song, and you have to do the best you can do with it." Because they went so far off by each one taking their own lead, no one knew any more where the real melody stood.

So I took the song home, and when I played it, I said, "Oh, my God, how am I gonna get through this?" I lived in Queens in a one-level house, and I propped the boom box[6] up in the window, and I went on the porch. And I'm sitting on the porch, and there were a group of little girls out there jumping rope. I put the song on, and I said, "Okay, I don't know where to start learning this song, it's so difficult. Where do I separate the wheat from the chaff?" But there was a hook in it. I didn't know it yet. I didn't hear it yet, 'cause I'm so concerned over this melody. The kids were skipping rope, and after a while the kids kept singing [sings], "Oh no, not my ba-by" and then [speaking in rhythm], skip rope, skip rope: "Oh no, not my ba-by" [in time with the skipping of the rope]. And I said, "Oh!" [gasps] and I took a look around at the boom box and I jumped up off the porch. I said, "A hook? I know a hook when I hear it. Time to go to work!" [Claps hands.] I left the porch, and I went back in the house and I found a melody in no time. Because if those kids can hear this song playing in the window, and they're skipping rope and they're singing the hook, I knew we had a hit. That was it.

"Oh No Not My Baby," which reached #24 on the pop charts in October of 1964, remains one of the best-loved songs in Brown's body of work.[7] Opening with a sensitive piano intro (possibly played by Carole King), the record features a lovely string arrangement as well as Dee Dee Warwick's beautiful harmony on the chorus. Flowing above it all is Brown's singing, economical yet extremely soulful. The record, along with the sadly overlooked "It's Gonna Be All Right," makes her fans wish that Brown had recorded more Carole King songs. Perhaps only Dusty Springfield equals Brown in bringing this same expressive quality to King's material.

So that's the story of "Oh No Not My Baby." I recorded it over the original track; the voices of the Shirelles were pulled off. Scepter did a lot of that in those days. It saves money from going back in to pay the musicians. I don't even know if the musicians knew.

The recycling of old backing tracks, an unofficial Scepter trademark, reflects the extent to which the label's staff went to cut costs.[8] Presiding over the company's business affairs was owner Florence Greenberg, a former Republican campaign worker and New Jersey housewife who became one of the few women to head a successful record company in the '60s.

Brown's recollections of Greenberg give an indication of the complexity of artist-label relations at Scepter. While Greenberg often acted as a benevolent, maternal force, the reality of being a woman in a male-dominated industry also forced her to conduct her business dealings with a certain degree of toughness.

She had to play like the big boys. She had to get herself a vice president, so if things got past her, it would stop at him. She had to have a backing. And at that time, the Mafia was moving in on the music industry, period. And I think they used her, because she on her own would never submit to something like that. I think she was threatened. I don't know whether I should be saying this or not—it's common knowledge in the industry but I don't know if it's common knowledge outside of the industry—but she had to go along. It was a boys' club she was playing in.

Florence was like a mother hen to all of us. Okay, she had her problems in the business. She was like a mother hen on one hand, but because you were under this umbrella, you had to deal with her straight as a record company owner and you had to oppose her because she was the owner. You had to fight for your royalties; again, we didn't get paid. The artists, we could never know how come you can record for all these record companies and when it's time to go get paid, the books show you owe more money. Let's say if you sold four thousand records—just say hypothetically. You're in the hole for five thousand, for some funny reason. For some reason they show you the books, and you ended up owing them money. I never knew how that worked out. And that's how they got away with not paying a lot of artists. They always told the artists, "Well, we had to take out recording expenses, we had to take out for free goods, giveaways." All that's being paid for by the artists. So that's how you never make any money. But Dionne Warwick got her money, because she was brought to the label by Burt Bacharach, so she was protected. Even she didn't get everything. She was given a very large check one day and she took a look at the check and says, "I'll come back when you all get it right." And you want to know something? It was right when she got back.

Charging expenses against performers' accounts, a standard practice in the record industry, was a source of contention for many '60s soul performers whose record sales did not match the corresponding costs of production, promotion, and touring. In spite of these kinds of monetary disputes, Brown's memories of Greenberg are largely fond. When she died in 1995, Brown was one of the few former Scepter artists to attend the funeral.

I didn't know how they were going to conduct the funeral, and since I had long been away from the company and I wasn't asked to perform or say anything, I wrote something. I wrote a little eulogy. [Reading an excerpt] "Florence Greenberg was a wonderful person. What an honor and privilege it was to have known her. I'm glad we stayed in touch over the years. She was unique. She was a pioneer. One of the first women to own her own record company. But she was more than just a record company owner; she was a wonderful human being. I know because I was fortunate enough to be on her label and found her to be a warm and caring person with a wonderful sense of humor. Now, she didn't treat us as recording artists to make money, but she treated us like family; she was like a mother. Sometimes we lovingly referred to her as 'Mother Hen' because she was always hovering and trying to protect us, as any good mother would do."

I didn't want to say, "You're a crook." Yeah, we were all beaten out of our record royalties, but I came to praise Caesar, not to bury her, okay? So I didn't come for that. I came to tell the good parts of Florence Greenberg.

According to Brown, Greenberg and the female artists signed to her label needed extra strength to fight the gender-based prejudices inherent within the '60s record industry.

It was more difficult then, for Florence, for girl singers. I'll give an example, and I'm going to call names. Chuck Jackson and I came along at the same time, we both had the same amount of hit records—I could have had more at one time than he. But just playing the Apollo Theatre he would get more than me. I don't care if it's a dollar more than me, he would get it. He could start the show and close the show, but they wouldn't let me close the show. It's very difficult for a woman to start or close a show. You have to be as great as Nancy Wilson or Dionne Warwick or Sarah Vaughan; you have to be that big in name and stature to close the show. It was so difficult, because they would always let the man close.

I would go and fight. I'd say, "Hey, my act is hot, just as hot as anybody else." At the time, I was hot. I thought I could be able to draw, with the right amount of co-stars on the bill with me. I thought, "Let me go out the first time, and see how I do." Just to give it a shot. I thought I could own one of the shows—James Brown could go in and clean up and own the whole show. Well, he had enough hits out there. I'm not saying I had that many hits, but I could have started building my little reputation, 'cause I had hit songs.

In 1967, Greenberg sent Brown to the Fame Studio in Muscle Shoals, Alabama, to be produced by Otis Redding. It would be one of Brown's last efforts for Scepter. Redding, for several years an established performer, was then venturing into the production field with great success (Arthur Conley's "Sweet Soul Music," which Redding had written and produced, had been a huge hit in March of the same year). In short, it seemed like a great match. Unfortunately, Redding's untimely death that December prevented the association from reaching its fruition. Nothing from the session was released until "Baby Cakes," a Redding composition, turned up on an album on the British Kent label in the mid-'80s.

As a result of Kent going into the vault and bringing that record out, it brought back a lot of memories, because that was an unfinished session. Florence Greenberg asked Otis, "Why don't you produce Maxine for me?" And he says, "Oh, I like her. Yeah, fine. We'll do something, we'll get together," and then they arranged to have me sent down to Muscle Shoals. I had worked with Otis on one other occasion, 'cause when I was at the [Washington, D.C.] Howard Theater working, I had to fly to some part of South Carolina or North Carolina and we played a "cow palace." And I mean, literally, it's like one of those state fairs. The venue was as big as a football field. It was Otis Redding, a group of other people, and LaVern Baker and myself. We were the ones flown in to do this thing. And that was the first time I worked with Otis.

So the day I came in to Muscle Shoals, Otis and his band had to go out to do a gig. But he says, "This is what I have for you. Here's a song. Start working on this and learning this melody while we go out." So I'd work on the song, and I'd be in the hotel and I'd be kind of lonesome. I didn't see anything because I just went from the hotel back to the studio that was in this kind of garage-like setting. And every time they would come in, Otis would say, "How much did you learn? What do you think? Let's see what you got." And then the band would all come in one by one, sit around, and we'd jam and try to find out what we'd like to do on the session. And sometimes he'd say, "No, that's not quite what I want." And then he'd leave me to work it out some more, and they'd take off and do a gig. Now the reason they could go in and out on a gig was because they had a plane they could fly on. They could leave me in Muscle Shoals and go to Ohio and yet be back the next day. But every time they would come back, the band members would say, "Man! Did you feel that today? Wow!" Another one would say, "Yeah, man. You know man, one of these days—Otis! Why don't you do something about that plane, man? One of these days, that old raggedy thing is gonna kill us." That's what one of the guys said. And sure enough, that was the plane that killed him. How ironic. And he never finished the session.

Brown is the first to point out that "Baby Cakes" was not top-notch Redding. Although it shows off the tougher side of her vocal style (she fits into the rugged Muscle Shoals surroundings quite well, singing at the top of her range), the record as a whole sounds rushed and unfocused. Brown was understandably disappointed with the results.

I don't think "Baby Cakes" was the best material, and I don't know if I did justice to it at all. I don't think I did. I guess when you get so mesmerized by the person that was doing this, their reputation precedes them. I'm looking for Otis to give me a typical Otis song, and I get this "Baby Cakes" song. I was looking for a good, grooving, Otis thing. So maybe *I* didn't do it justice, I don't know. But that was my experience working with him, and that was the end of it.

Although Brown's years at Scepter saw the release of two solo albums, two duet albums with Chuck Jackson (with whom she had a hit with a marvelous reworking of Chris Kenner's New Orleans R&B hit, "Something You Got," in 1965), and a greatest-hits compilation, her future at the label looked uncertain by the time of the unsuccessful Muscle Shoals session in 1967. She cites Scepter's mounting financial problems (problems that would mushroom when Dionne Warwick left for Warner Brothers in 1971) and the fact that she was no longer getting top-quality material as her reasons for leaving the label in 1967. It's true that too often during her later years at the label the songs she was given to record did not approach the strength of her earlier Carole King- and Van McCoy-penned material.

While hits were in short supply during her last couple of years at Scepter, Brown maintained her popularity through a steady stream of tour dates in the U.S. and overseas. Throughout the '60s, "the road" provided Brown with constant work, although the often harsh conditions of touring made her experiences far from easy.

The Road

For R&B and soul artists of the '50s and '60s, performance tours through small towns and rural areas were the primary way to meet the demands of fans who did not have the means to travel to big cities. Many of these "package tours" featured a multitude of acts that would perform on a single bill.

The tours were tough. Today, an individual can go out and tour and can have his or her own bus. We had station wagons. And a single artist such as myself, I had to have my backup group, because if you're out on tour you didn't always go to the same places [as other artists on the tour] all at once. Sometimes I had my own tour, and then sometimes I'd meet up with other [artists] and I'd tour with them. And you couldn't find a decent piano on the road if your life depended on it, so you had to go with guitar, bass, and drums. And to sit in the same car for hours and hours and hours, and sometimes it's hot and sometimes it's cold. Then I had to bring a girl on the road with me to help me with my hair and wardrobe and things like that. It was pretty rough on us, travel-wise. You didn't fly, because the plane didn't go in some backwoods of somewhere, so it was no good by saying you could take a plane. Secondly, you couldn't afford to fly, because you just worked hard and you weren't getting the money that people are getting today. And then when you were on the big tours, they booked those tours so far apart. Logically, you would think they would book New York, Baltimore—you'd think they'd do it in order in some way. No! You would go from New York to Florida—that's the second gig, Florida. You'd come back to North Carolina, you would go to some place almost Midwest, then you'd come back east. So I think the way the agents would book it was according to which gig they could grab first. But it never made sense, and it just wore the artists down.

In addition to physical hardships, the specter of segregation cast a pall over many of the early '60s tours, especially those in the South. Brown describes an incident that occurred near the Texas/Arkansas border.

My bass player drank some milk and got his stomach upset. And that lactose works against a lot of black people, you know. We stopped at an Esso gas station in Texarkana, and just because [the bass player] went to the bathroom, the owner came and drew a gun and told us, "I want every nigger off this property in two seconds." We said, "We haven't gotten through paying for the gas yet." "Drop that hose! I want every nigger off this property! Nobody's gonna [in a southern accent] stink up my bathroom." He was getting ready to pull the trigger on us, right then and there, because he went to the bathroom. He was going to shoot us.

I was on the Jackie Wilson tour with the Temptations and, I think, Gladys Knight. We stopped in Tennessee, and everybody jumped off the bus. The bus driver figured this was a good place to stop. A mob of people came and blocked us and said, "No niggers getting off in this town." They had three shotguns trained on us, the whole bus. All of us. And we had to move it, move it to the next town. That's the way it went. I used to carry my dog out with me. I had a french poodle. And I never left her home, so I took her with me. And I went in a place to get some hamburgers to feed the dog, 'cause that's all she would eat on the road. Well, the man at the restaurant told me, "We don't serve niggers in here." And I said, "Well, we don't eat 'em either!" [Laughs.] And somebody pulled me by the back of my throat and said, "Let's get out of here!"

And then I had this Jewish fellow with me; his name was Alan Ross. Now I'm already hip. We came through Jekyll Island, Georgia. He was driving—we were coming from Florida, from down that way. And we don't like for him to drive, 'cause he drives five minutes and he wants a cup of coffee, 'cause he gets too sleepy too soon. So we're all trying to get some sleep, and the next thing we know we're sitting in this place [to buy] coffee. He wakes me up, "Maxie, Maxie, get up. Come on, let's go in and get coffee." I said, "Where are we?" He said, "Oh, we're at a truck stop." I said, "Okay." So I get ready to go in there to get coffee and hamburgers and everything for the guys, and the owners said, "No no no. You can come in, but she can't come in." Well, Alan said, "Well, if she can't come in, I'm not . . . !" I said, "Alan, where are we?" He said, "Jekyll Island, Georgia." I said, "We get the hell out of here [laughs]; we're not down here to fight our way out of this town." I mean, we were in a place where you didn't see anything but woods. And he's getting ready to fight with these rednecks? No, no, no. "Alan, you don't understand. You can't argue with these people." He said, "Well, this is ridiculous!" But he listened to me.

In another incident, Brown describes with a laugh how she ran into trouble at a southern diner.

We ran into our share of prejudice. They don't care what kind of a singer you were or who you say you were. You just weren't the right color. And then I nearly got arrested because I was a finicky eater at first. We stopped in a place where we *could* go and sit down, but they kept bringing me these eggs that stared back at me [laughs]. And the lady said, "Well, you're not eating your eggs." I said, "No, I don't like them prepared that way." She said, "But you said scrambled, right?" I said, "Yeah, but look at them—they're looking back at me." I'm used to being in New York, where we beat an egg real fine in a bowl and then scramble it in a pan. But [in the South] they crack the egg in the pan and they stir it up and all that white and yellow gets to mixing and it looks like one eye staring up. She brought me another one, and I said, "No, that's okay, I'll pay for the second one too." She said, "Well, what's the matter? The chef is not doing them right?" I said, "No, the chef really needs to let me come back there and show him how to do it. As a matter of fact, I will." So I got up and walked back there. And I did the eggs, and I said, "*That* is a New York egg, okay?" They called the cops on me! [Laughs.] I didn't cause any harm, I just made the eggs. I just had to prove to them that that's not the way you make those slimy eggs.

As a female performer, Brown had to deal not only with racism but also with unsolicited sexual advances.

I remember playing Texas once, and this guy came in his overalls. This stage was very high, so I'm up there, and everybody's at the foot of the stage looking up. So this guy came and he sat his pistol right on the stage in front of me. And he's taking his hands and going up and down my legs. I'm singing, and I keep shaking him off. When I'd move to the other end of the stage, he'd work his way down, and everywhere I'd move, he would just run his hand up my leg. I couldn't shake him off. I said, "Okay. My moving is not changing things." So he was leaning on the stage, and I saw his fingers—I went right over and stood on top of his fingers right there. He says, "You're smart, huh?" [Laughs.] And he walked away. He left me alone after that. I just stood on his fingers. That's what I did. And I didn't want to call security because I could have started something in there. I saw the pistol; he laid the pistol right on stage. That was to intimidate me? But I'd been around my father. I've been around enough guns. So the gun didn't intimidate me, but *he* did, his presence. He was a big guy. And I knew if I'd call somebody, they'd rough him up and that would be all over. I didn't want that. So what I did was just stand on his fingers. You can run into the strangest situations.

But in spite of (or perhaps because of) the hardships of the road, there was a strong sense of camaraderie among the performers.

We liked each other back then. The girls liked each other. Like Smokey Robinson, he would try to leave that stage so hot for Chuck Jackson that Chuck can't get on. Chuck would leave it so hot for me or vice-versa. And it was a healthy competition that we did, but we loved it. We couldn't wait to get to the next gig to see each other, when we all met up like that. And Ben E. King—oh!—there were a lot of great guys out there. I had the opportunity of a lifetime working with these people, because for every male that they had out there, they needed female co-stars, and that's where Gladys [Knight] and I paid off. And every time I would sing "Funny," a fight would break out. So Ben E. King and them started dubbing me "the fight lady." They would say, "Oh, she's gonna sing 'Funny,'" and everybody'd start grabbing their instruments and get ready to leave the stage. Every time, somebody would throw a bottle in the audience. I don't know why.

The road was also the site of many a humorous mishap. Brown recalls one particularly amusing incident.

Back to the bus tour. I think it was the one with Chuck Jackson and the Temptations. We had gotten a new bus driver, and he was supposed to get his sleep in certain towns, so he could be fresh to drive us. Anyhow, he was driving all these famous people, and he just knew he was going to meet some girls, because these famous guys were going to draw lots of girls. And it's true, they did, everywhere we stopped. So instead of this bus driver sleeping when we hit a town, he gets dressed sharp, puts on his best cologne, and he stands by the stage door near where the stars are and says, "Hi, how you doin', how you doin', to all these women. "I'm driving the Temptations, I'm driving so-and-so. You know who I have on my bus with me?" And he would try to catch girls like that. And if the guys are shooting dice late at night, this fool hangs with them and tries to stay up later than they are. So we take off from the gig. Now we don't go to a hotel that night, we have to go to the next town. We were all asleep, and the next thing you know I heard somebody scream up front. We had started hitting these bushes. We were in somebody's yard—the guy fell asleep at the wheel and there we were! And we took the clothesline, the long red drawers with the flaps in the back, the overalls—we were taking those right down the highway with us. By that time, everybody jumped up and pounced on him: "Man, you better straighten up and stay on the road!" That was a funny incident. But to wake up and see yourself with the bushes slashing against the window. Oh, that darned bus could have turned over, but after it didn't, the story was funny.

Brown also laughs when she remembers, with affection, one of the most venerable performers she encountered during her early years on the road: Dinah Washington, who died just two and a half years after Brown first hit the charts.

Oh God, she was great. She said [chuckles]—do I tell you in the Dinah Washington style? She said, "Only two bitches I like is Aretha and Maxine Brown." [Laughs.] That's how she put it. She would intimidate the Lord, I believe, 'cause she intimidated me so. Anything she said was okay with me. One time we were working at the Twenty Grand in Detroit. I was on one end working in the Twenty Grand, and she was in the big hall which was right around the corner—it's one big complex. And they could dance on the side she was on. This was after, I think, her fifth marriage. And when I was tipping over in between shows to see her ('cause you could run around from one door to the next), she was tipping over to come see *me*. And we met up in the hall. She didn't want to give in that she was coming to see me. I said, "Oh, I was just coming to see you!" And she said, "My God, what is that *damn* ugly thing you're wearing?" I said, "The same ugly thing you're wearing!" She said, "Girl, you're so *funny!*" [Laughs.] All these years, I let her intimidate me. She liked people who talked back to her. That's all she liked. She just wanted to see the spunk you have. And I didn't know all of those years I could have been talking back to her. I couldn't believe it.

You know, that woman would give you the shirt off her back. That's the kind of person she was. She just had an exterior that was so rough. Really, she was a giving person. But she didn't want anybody to know that about her. She wanted to show that tough side of her. You'd talk about the Queen of England and she'd say, "What Queen? I'm the Queen!"[9]

New Directions

In the post-Scepter years, Brown recorded for Epic, Commonwealth United, and Avco Embassy with little commercial success (although "We'll Cry Together," a marvelous ballad by veteran songwriter

Rose Marie McCoy that showcased Brown's gospel roots, was a #15 R&B hit for Commonwealth in 1969). During this period, Brown split with Mal Williams and began exploring other venues for her talent, such as Broadway and nightclubs. In 1972, she replaced Rhetta Hughes in Vinnette Carroll's hit Broadway musical, Don't Bother Me, I Can't Cope.[10]

Things started to slow down at Scepter Records [around 1967], and they were in trouble, and in the back of my mind I could always hear Mal saying, "I don't want you to be a one-hit record artist. So therefore you've got to learn to do other things." So that sort of rang in my mind, and I'm saying to myself, "I don't have a record. I'm still tied to the contract. I can't move. What do I do?" So I went to acting school. And I took up dancing on the side with [famed dancing instructor] Henry LeTang. I studied under him just to do tap dancing, 'cause I used to go out for auditions, and they would ask you, "Can you dance?" They meant can you turn, can you pirouette? I wasn't up on that, so that's why I had to get into dancing class.

In the meantime, I took acting from Michael Hartig. He had a great acting class.[11] When I auditioned for him, the person I auditioned against was Ray Sharkey, from the mob TV show *[Wiseguy]*. I went to audit the class, and Michael Hartig just up and called on me: "And now we're going to hear from the famous singer, Maxine Brown." I said, "Oh, God." I hate when they introduce me like that because people expect so much. Michael whispered in my ear what my assignment was, and he whispered in Ray's ear what his job was supposed to be. I was supposed to be a quote-unquote washed-up nightclub singer who's come into this nightclub to beg for a job, but I can't beg, I have to be very proud. So I have to play against the grain of what I'm supposed to do. So that was my assignment. And I didn't know Ray's assignment was to not give me the job, fight me. [Laughs.] We did so well improvising there. I just happened to see the piano there, and I went over. I said, "I'll tell you what. You may not give me this job, but I just want to let you know that I can *still sing.*" I went over to the piano, and I played the intro to "All in My Mind" and I started singing. And I got up and the class went wild. And that's how I got into acting. That was my first experience with my first improvisation.

And so I'm in the class with a lot of kids who went to college—they studied [with overdramatization] *theatre*—and here I come along, and all of a sudden the producers of *Don't Bother Me, I Can't Cope* contacted my agent for booking my nightclub engagements and said, "Rhetta Hughes is leaving the show and they need a replacement in a hurry. Send Maxine over so she can audition, so they can take a look at her." I always had my hair very slicked-back or something like that, but being a black show, I decided to go with an Afro wig. And the first thing Vinnette Carroll said was [imitating an imperious low voice], "Well, first of all, for God's sake, get that hair out of that child's face!" [Laughs.] Anyway, they liked me, and I sang the song. I hate auditioning; I am the worst auditioner. It's awful. I guess a lot of other people can say that. Give me the job and I think I can do the job, but I can't stand to audition. But anyway, they were stuck, and I was it. And that's how I got in.

As a last-minute replacement for the lead in a Broadway show, Brown had to learn the part— which featured the musical's standout number, "It Takes a Whole Lot of Human Feeling"—in a hurry.

The stage manager took me home with her, and for three days I ate and slept on her sofa, because every five minutes I'd try to get some sleep, she'd say, "What's the line?" I had to wake up and say the line. She drilled the lines in me. I had three days to learn the entire play. Three days, God bless her. And the first voice you hear and the last voice you hear is me in that play. And the dancers were pretty rough. They told me, "Bitch, if you're in our way we'll run over you." That's what they told me. They were talking about blocking, so I would be in the right place at the right time. Because I was not a dancer, I was the singer, and they didn't like any of the stars. The dancers didn't like the stars. Later on we became very good friends, but it was tough going. Doing it those first couple of months, it was really, really tough. I shared the dressing room with them, so it wouldn't cause friction with me being in the star's dressing room. Rhetta Hughes gave me that advice. She said, "Don't take the star's dressing room. It's going to be bad enough as it is. If they're going to talk about you, let them talk about you across from that other table." And Rhetta walked me through it and she said "Good luck," and she made a quick exit, and that was the last time I saw Rhetta! She said, "You'll need it." And she was right.

The boys in the show were great. I had so much fun with the boys. The girls just were really tough. *Tough.* I always have a better time with the boys. I get along so much better with the boys. And half of them were gay, and I just loved them to death. I just loved them. And it's not *because* they were gay—they just have a better attitude. They just were not hung up like the girls. Right away, the girls had a chip on their shoulder. But the girls eventually turned out to be okay. Eventually—just as we were winding up the play, but they turned out to be okay. They saw that I was no threat to them. But as far as the show is concerned, the show was a great show. Gospel feeling, a lot of funny lines. I had to be re-reviewed and I had to do a lot of promoting—bank openings and the things that they have in the street on Broadway. I even helped Mayor Beam dig for the subway that went nowhere here in New York. I lifted the first shovel for that. That's that line that they haven't even completed yet that goes to Queens. It's supposed to make transportation a lot easier going to Queens, but it went nowhere.

But as far as doing the show, that was my first acting piece. And then I was up for *Guys and Dolls* and [actor and former *Benson* star] Robert Guillaume cut me out of that. He wanted his friend from California to have that role, and he had the connections, so that was it. But [*Guys and Dolls* co-author] Abe Burroughs wanted *me*, and he had the keys [of the songs] changed so they fit me. So I almost had that part. And that's the closest I've come to the Broadway scene. I was up for another role to understudy Eartha Kitt in *Timbuktu*. My manager blocked me on that one. [Director] Geoffrey Holder selected me. I was "in like Flynn," and my manager told him, "No, she's got bookings during the time that you're going to run the play." And that was the end of that.

Brown's manager (a new manager, since her bookings were no longer being handled by Mal Williams) was not unique in rejecting a theatre offer. Club appearances often take precedence over theatre simply because they pay better and they don't tie the artist up for long periods of time. As the '70s progressed, Brown became a fixture at several notable New York clubs, including Marty's, the Seafood Playhouse, and the Bottom Line. In a 1980 review of one of Brown's performances at Marty's, the venerable New York Times *critic John Wilson encapsulated the essence of her appeal: "One of the fascinations of her performance is watching her develop an increasingly commanding presence, initially dancing on the surface of her songs, but getting deeper and deeper into her material, projecting it with a voice that can be dark and smoky or full of exuberance, but always with a positive, vibrant quality."*

Club work saved my life when records were short-coming and few and far in-between. When you do nightclubs, you just can't always do rhythm and blues or the blues. You have to be able to adjust to the place a little bit. If they do jazz, then you have to throw in some jazz. And, thank God, the name Maxine Brown brought me in the place and I could do some of the things that the name was famous for, and then I could show what else I could do by doing some jazz that my audience was not familiar with me doing. Then, they were able to accept both. That kept me going when there was no record.

The lack of a recording contract was Brown's biggest setback during her '70s career. After her association with Avco Embassy in the early part of the decade, she would not record again for a number of years. Brown eventually became so discouraged that she decided to quit the business altogether in the mid-'80s.

If you came in this business through records, then in America you're only as hot as your last record. And then you run into trouble when you change record companies and somebody's not producing or promoting your records correctly. Then you find that you're without a record. And without a record, you're without a job. The work becomes scarce. So after a while, I just got fed up. I didn't want to scrounge anymore for it. I had a good run, I liked it. So I just quit. But deep down within your soul you always want to sing. I never wanted to stop singing; I just couldn't get the work or the recordings. And then accountants and young business people come into the recording business and they don't know anything about the artists of yesterday, and they want them young and stupid. Or better still, we were the stupid ones, and the young ones are coming in now making the money. They're making tons of money with very little talent. They don't want to hear from anybody from yesterday. Everything they want young and new—everything.

The event that precipitated Brown's decision to return to the business was her induction into the R&B Hall of Fame at the Rhythm & Blues Foundation's Pioneer Awards ceremony in 1991. She became involved with the Foundation through the influence of Ruth Brown, with whom she had performed in a concert entitled "Brown on Brown."

The Rhythm & Blues Foundation and Ruth Brown convinced me, "You need to come on back." And then I did. After I was nominated for the Pioneer Award, I got the bug again. And then one thing after another started happening.

Brown admits that she greeted the news of her nomination with some suspicion.

I am probably the silliest person who ever received an award. Because along with this award comes money. It's a grant. And when they called me to tell me that they had nominated me, I said, "Oh, that's nice." For the work, I thought that it was nice to get the recognition. And then they said, "X amount of dollars comes with it." I said, "For what? What do I have to do for this?" I mean, I was probably the dumbest person. Everybody else was saying, "Oh yeah, I'll take that right away," but I didn't. I just wanted to know what do I have to do for it? Why are you giving me this money? I couldn't believe it.

But it was a thrill to be nominated. And it's still an honor. Every time the Grammys are in New York at Radio City, the Rhythm & Blues Foundation has their awards the following night so they can catch the overflow of people in town. So now it's caught on, and it's a very big thing. And then they're understanding the good works, and a lot of people who come to the Grammys got their start by copying what people have done from the Rhythm & Blues Foundation. Like you take Mick Jagger and all of them—at least they admit to it. That's what I love about Linda Ronstadt. When she did "Oh No Not My Baby," you'd swear I'm doing her record, the accolades that she gave me in her write-ups. It was nice. You just love for them to do it because they treated you fairly, and you don't mind that.

Since her induction, Brown has performed regularly on both sides of the Atlantic (undoubtedly, she is one of the patron saints of the English "Northern Soul" scene). In 1996, she appeared with Vivian Reed (who starred in the original production of Bubbling Brown Sugar *on Broadway) and Philadelphia vocalist and songwriter Bunny Sigler in a revue at New York's Rainbow & Stars entitled "20th Century R&B." Clive Barnes of the* New York Post *praised the show as "sizzling," adding that "Brown splendidly reinvents that Tina Turner standard 'What's Love Got to Do With It.'" The show marked the end of Brown's regrettable absence from the New York cabaret scene.*

Brown has also performed in concerts sponsored by the R&B Foundation. In the fall of 1997 I saw her on a bill with fellow Foundation members Baby Washington and Don Gardner at the Clef Club in Philadelphia. In her dynamic, vigorous set, Brown proved herself a true pro who can overcome any obstacle before her: in this case, the band hired for the occasion sounded somewhat underrehearsed and the tempos kept lagging behind. Brown did an admirable job of getting them on track, using her entire body to good-naturedly "conduct" them ("The road is a trip!" she remarked to me later). At one point, she had to stop the band altogether.

All of a sudden they were all playing in different parts. I said [in a British accent], "No, no, no gentlemen, we will not. . . ." Then I had to say, "I just returned from England and I'm still affected."

Still, Brown corrected the band members in such a warm, funny way that no one on stage or off seemed to mind the interruption.

I didn't want to make it seem like, "I'm gonna get you guys," because they were really sweet men. I didn't want to embarrass them.

Her remarkable poise onstage reflects years of honing her own brand of showmanship.

I always knew how to walk onstage because I took little self-improvement classes. So I never slouched onstage—when I hit the stage, I hit it. The minute I hit the apron of any stage, something, a transition, happens within me. I don't know what it is.

Although she performs several gigs a year, Brown now spends most of her time working on her songwriting, using a portable keyboard and mixer in her home to record demos for the British album that is (hopefully) in the works. She is particularly pleased at her prolificacy; this is the first time that she has written a large group of songs over the course of just a few months (most of her previous compositions were written years apart). She feels that her new songs represent some of her most personal work and attest to the presence of divine inspiration.

This new music I've written, several months ago I wouldn't know where that would be coming from. I don't feel capable of delivering that kind of music. I didn't study for that. Yes, I know how to play the piano a little. Yes, I know how to read chords and all of that, but where am I getting the arrangements, where am I getting the style? I'm not doing it. I didn't study for it, so it's got to come from somewhere.

Brown hopes this new work will inaugurate the next chapter in what has been a remarkable and unpredictable career.

I think I might get lucky. If destiny plays itself all over again . . . who knows?

Timi Yuro
Giving Them the Truth of Me

Timi Yuro, circa 1964

*T*imi Yuro has been called the finest white female soul singer of the '60s. What makes her a soul singer rather than merely a pop vocalist is her unflagging determination to approach each song as if her life depends on it. When Timi doesn't feel a song, the lack of connection is obvious; her powerful voice sounds wasted, going through the motions on material that isn't right for her. But when Timi relates to a song, the effect is thrilling: she sings with a chilling passion that is undeniably real. This is not to say that Timi is never over the top; she can milk emotion in ways that would make Al Jolson blush. But that is precisely where her talent lies, in increasing the suds quotient of a song while at the same time heightening its believability. Unlike other pop singers with formidable technical chops (Barbra Streisand, Vicki Carr), one never doubts that Timi truly and unquestioningly believes what she's singing about, and that sense of absolute, unwavering conviction is what makes her unique.

Then there is the voice itself. Blessed with a soaring range and a Broadway belter's sense of tone and dynamics, Yuro's recorded performances are overwhelming displays of vocal prowess. There are few more impressive moments in popular music than the opening bars of her 1961 signature song, "Hurt." [1] The voice sounds almost otherworldly; it's not immediately apparent if the singer is male or female (in those first few moments, Yuro could easily be mistaken for Jackie Wilson). No wonder that disc jockeys of the early '60s, a time of rigidly structured gender categories (especially in popular entertainment), took pains to announce the singer as "Miss Timi Yuro." Equally incongruous was the fact that Yuro's massive voice was housed in a frame slightly less than five feet tall, earning her the promotional tag line "the little girl with the big voice." Although Yuro's categorical elusiveness helped her to break down barriers in early '60s pop music (she was one of the few performers at the time to receive equal airplay on pop and soul stations), it also led to paradoxical situations: while often marketed as a middle-of-the-road artist, Yuro's singing had far more in common with Della Reese and Dinah Washington than Patti Page or Connie Francis (in fact, Yuro's version of "Be Anything" on 1962's Soul album is a direct transcription of Washington's vocal style). Further, while her public performances were usually on bills with teen-oriented pop singers like Lou Christie or the Four Seasons, her true popularity lay with audiences situated outside of the mainstream. In New York, for example, some of her most ardent fans were denizens of the Harlem music scene and habitués of gay bars in the Village. Instead of downplaying the attention of these audiences, Yuro courted them. At a time when a less-than-whitewashed image could be damaging to a young performer's career, Yuro flouted convention by refusing to modify her performance style or dissociate herself from the audiences who admired her most.

Yuro's career stalled during the latter half of the '60s as she failed to find a record label wholly sympathetic to her special gifts, but she continued to perform until the mid-'80s. In 1985 she began to detect signs of the throat cancer that would plague her for the next decade. Yuro survived two operations but lost the one thing that she prized the most: her singing voice. In recent years her health problems have continued to mount: she lost part of a lung in 1997 after another bout with cancer and has also undergone a tracheostomy, which forces her to breathe through an opening in her throat. During my first conversation with Yuro in the summer of 1997, it was clear that, more than the cancer and sickness, the loss of her voice has become the great tragedy of her life.

My interview with Timi Yuro would not have been possible without the help of two very good friends, Tony Luciano and Ralph McKnight. Ralph, a fellow soul music lover, first introduced me to Tony, who was Timi's roommate during the early '60s and had many wonderful memories and stories to share of their friendship. Tony, who had been unsuccessfully trying to locate Timi for years, believed she still lived in Las Vegas, where she had moved in the late '60s after marrying a man involved in the gambling business. Personally, I felt that the prospect of actually reaching Timi, let alone doing an interview, was rather slim. I had the impression that she avoided interviews, a suspicion bolstered by a passage in Dawn Eden's liner notes to a 1992 compilation of her work: "Rarely interviewed, she remains a figure of mystery. We may never know just why the pain and heartbreak in her voice sounded so genuine."

Tony, however, felt that Timi's reputation for reclusiveness was exaggerated. With his help, I was able to reach her nephew, who explained that he was somewhat estranged from his family but had nonetheless been trying to find his aunt for a long time—he had not seen her since a Willie Nelson concert in Las Vegas in the early '80s. He very kindly put me in touch with his sister in Vegas, who explained that she too had lost contact with her aunt but was also trying to find her. It seemed as if the bandwagon of people searching for Timi was growing larger with each contact I made. Timi's niece said that she believed her aunt was still living in Vegas and offered to try to find her for me. Then, in a statement that made me wonder if I had perhaps gone too far, she added that she would likely be successful in her search because she had a lot of friends on the police force (apparently, this is a perfectly viable way of finding someone in Las Vegas). She ended the conversation by saying that she would call me within a couple of weeks to inform me of her progress. At most, I expected a follow-up call to tell me she was still searching. I couldn't have been more surprised when, two weeks later and without any warning from her niece, Timi Yuro herself left a message on my machine.

My first conversation with Timi was an experience I'll never forget. I was disarmed by her unblinking honesty (like each member of the Yuro family with whom I have talked, Timi wears her heart on her sleeve) as she explained her fight against cancer and detailed, one by one, her illnesses and maladies. In a muted voice (the cancer operations have affected her speaking as well as her singing), she said that she would be happy to do an interview under one condition: no pictures. The steroids that she had been taking since her bout with lung cancer had affected her body: "I've gained weight like you wouldn't believe." When I responded that I didn't intend to take any pictures, at least not during our initial interview, she softened: "Well, maybe we can take some pictures, we'll see how I feel." I quickly realized that Timi held no illusions about her sickness; while I was telling her that she "has one of the greatest voices I've ever heard," she suddenly interrupted me. "Had," she emphasized. "Had. I'll probably never sing again."

We ended the conversation with Timi's promising to send me a copy of an album she cut with Willie Nelson in the '80s and telling me reassuringly, "You know what, angel? You can call me any time you want." She quickly brushed aside my attempt to address her as Ms. Yuro: "No, baby. Just 'Tim.'" As I was beginning to discover, there is no place for formality or modesty with Timi Yuro.

After that first phone call, Timi and I went back and forth for well over a year before meeting. When we finally had our interview in the fall of 1998, it wasn't under the most luxurious circumstances. Not realizing that the major hotels in Vegas frequently offer extremely low rates just for the purpose of luring patrons into the casinos, I had taken the first inexpensive motel room I could find, in what turned out to be a decidedly seedy section of the city. When I learned that Timi and her entourage would actually be dropping by rather than meeting me at an outside location ("Where are you staying? OK, angel, we'll be there between six-thirty and seven"), I was embarrassed. How could I interview one of my long-time idols, the great Timi Yuro, in an establishment that was most likely used for meetings of a different sort? In the end, I needn't have worried: the woman who once lived in *posh buildings with doormen on New York's East Side is completely without pretensions. Thankfully, Timi was so relaxed and easy to talk to that the shabbiness of our surroundings didn't seem to matter.*

Although she can no longer sing, Timi has never stopped performing. As a talker and storyteller, Timi can hold her listeners enthralled. The presence during the interview of a small audience—Timi's lifelong friend Raul, to whom she is extremely close (when she speaks of her "brother" in the interview, Timi is referring to Raul), Isabel, her good friend and housemate, and me—only enhanced her narrative capability. Her friend Raul has led a colorful life: he was the head choreographer and dance captain at the fabled Peppermint Lounge in New York, where society doyennes and young hipsters alike gathered to indulge in the biggest dance craze of the early '60s, the Twist. He also performed as a dancer in several Elvis movies (he claims to be the one who first introduced Elvis to Timi's recording of "Hurt," which became one of the King's last recorded performances and the one song that separates true Elvis disciples from mere fans) and now spends the majority of his time in Mexico. Since Raul was present during all of the ups and downs of Timi's life and career, I have included his comments (and to a lesser degree, those of Isabel) when they shed light on Timi's own recollected experiences.

The focus of the interview, however, was always on Timi. As she spoke, I found myself amazed at the extraordinary strength and courage of this woman who has survived three bouts with cancer, a failed marriage, financial hardships, more career setbacks than she can mention, and has emerged from it all with her raucous personality, youthful enthusiasm, and sharp sense of humor intact.

Timi Yuro was born Rosemary Timotea Yuro to Italian-American parents on August 4, 1940. Her distinctive nickname was acquired during her early childhood, while she was growing up with her family in Chicago. From the very beginning, Timi shared an exceptional closeness with her mother, Edith, while at the same time fearing her abusive father. Although young Timi found support in Edith, Louis Yuro was from the outset opposed to his daughter's dreams of becoming a professional pop singer. Music, however, surrounded Timi. In addition to spending time in the South Side bars that her grandmother owned, Timi was exposed to music through the influence of the Houstons, an African-American couple who lived on the bottom floor of the Yuro family home. Yuro credits the Houstons with exposing her to blues and gospel: from her earliest childhood they took her to church and played for her records by the top R&B performers of the late '40s. One of these performers, the young Dinah Washington, became Timi's greatest influence as a singer.

I've sang all my life. Sang all my life. Sang in my mother's restaurant. Sang since I was very young. I listened to [Washington] since I was seven years old. I remember getting whacked across the kitchen floor by my father 'cause I did a song that Dinah did. I used to do it in the basement in Mrs. Houston's. And it was [sings], "Well, I went to see my dentist, and told him the pain was killin' . . . and he pulled out his trusty drill and told me to open wide, he said he wouldn't hurt me, but he'd fill my hole inside" [laughs].[2] And my father whacked me from the table to the window, which was about twenty-five feet. And I'll never forget it. I could never sing it again in front of him.

The next time, I got up and did a little performance after dinner—my mother loved everything I sang, my mother just wanted me to sing everything—and the next one I did of [Dinah's] was [sings] "I want to be loved with inspiration . . ." [laughing], and my father would [makes hitting motion with her arms]: "What do you know about love!" And my mother: "You idiot! You damn fool! She's just singing you a song!" And my father hated it.[3] My father hated where my mother was letting me go. Aside from the fact that two black people lived downstairs that raised my mother, and they would play all this music. I think I was baptized 'bout six times, when I was little. Mr. Houston took me to church, and every time my mother'd make me all long curls, I'd come home—my hair'd be all straight and wet 'cause they'd baptize me.

Yuro began to receive operatic training during her early childhood, while her family still lived in Chicago. After the Yuros moved to Los Angeles in 1952, Edith brought the twelve-year-old Timi to study with Dr. Lillian Goodman, the renowned vocal coach whose clients included numerous Hollywood stars. One of the many legends known to Timi Yuro's fans is that Goodman was so impressed with Timi's voice that she offered to instruct her for free.

I had opera lessons when I was seven, eight, nine, and ten. I left Chicago, and when I went to Lillian Goodman, my dad had had a heart attack. I was twelve, I think, and we couldn't afford her—she was like fifty dollars a lesson. And my mother said, "Look, I'll work whatever I got to work to get her to come and see you, even if it's once a month."

[Imitating Goodman's gruff voice] "Well, let me hear what you sound like," she said. I took a deep breath and I was going to start singing, and she whacked me in the chest, 'cause I raised my chest. She said, "If you don't use your diaphragm, you might as well go home right now." I said, "No, no, okay, okay, I will." And I sang "Sorrento" for her, and she just freaked. She said, "You be here every Friday after school." And that was it. My mother took me there every Friday, and I don't think she charged my mother for two years. She was unreal. She was teaching people like Kirk Douglas, and she was teaching very big stars. I would be leaving on a Friday, and there'd be stars coming up the stairs like you wouldn't believe. She loved me though, and when I did "Hurt," she said, "I always knew you'd go that way because of the money."

But I always loved rock 'n roll. I was so in-between. When I was very young, I sang total opera. I was gonna go to La Scala with my professor's mother and father, but I wouldn't leave my mother. See, my dad was very cruel to my mom. And if I had a wonderful childhood parent-wise, I would have left my mom and gone to Italy, I'm sure. But I was always so frightened for her that I could never leave her side. So we stayed together, and because of that I never went to Italy.

Yuro still has copies of opera recordings she made as a child of ten and eleven.

I have records that I sang that are cute. I should send them to you to hear, make a tape for you—they're so cute. I would do "Poor Butterfly" and sing all the classical songs that they would give me, but my phrasing and my speech are exactly the same as my records of late. If you listen to me as a child, you know that's Timi. You don't know how she sang that high or nothing, but you know it's her. And even though I sang those songs, I would still sing [sings in a country twang] "I didn't know the gun was loaded . . . ," you know, and I would do all pop things. So Mrs. Goodman knew that I'd lean that way. I said, "But it's the only way I know how to express myself, really." "No," she said, "you have much more to give than that." But I couldn't get into Broadway and *Show Boat*-type things. I just couldn't get into that.

Yuro's chance to perform in front of a large audience came when her parents opened an Italian restaurant, Alvoturno's, in Los Angeles. The restaurant was a flop until Yuro persuaded her father to let her sing there. Almost immediately, the family's fortunes turned around. Yuro's spirited performances made the restaurant a first-class attraction patronized by many celebrities (she claims that when he was in town, Elvis ordered her mother's pizza every weekend). The teenaged Yuro also worked in the restaurant as a waitress and cook. In the kind of passage that could only have come from the pen of a press agent (in this case Connie DeNave, who worked with Yuro for several years in the early '60s), Edith Yuro describes young Timi's life at Alvoturno's in a 1961 press release: "She would be in the kitchen helping us cook, and suddenly people out front would start to clap and shout for her. She'd run out with her apron on and spaghetti sauce on her face and sing her heart out!"

When my mom had this restaurant, we turned it into a rock 'n roll place, my brother and I. It [had been] very high-class, and then one day I just told my father, "This high-class restaurant ain't makin' no money. We're starvin.'" And he said,

"Well, what do you want to do?" But it killed him for me to turn it into a rock 'n roll joint. And I think the first weekend she made about twelve hundred dollars, and it was astonishing. It was like ten thousand a night, today.

Here, Raul interjects, "I was a dancing waiter. I was a dancing waiter with the pizzas."

I think I even have pictures of him waiting on tables and dancing and me singing on the stage there. I think I have those pictures. I know I do.

By 1959, singer Sonny Knight (whose 1956 hit "Confidential" remains a staple on oldies stations) had become one of the restaurant's many celebrity regulars. Knight and Yuro began to perform together at the restaurant, and eventually Knight arranged for her to sign with Liberty Records, for whom he worked as a talent scout.

Sonny Knight used to come in, play piano and sing—he had a hit record called "Confidential." I wish you would give him a lot of credit, 'cause if it wasn't for him, I don't think I'd be a singer or would have ever been anything.

Usually, Yuro's initial failure to have any hits at Liberty is attributed to the befuddled record company's not knowing what to do with this most unique of vocalists. Yuro gives another reason why her career at Liberty languished during 1960. Apparently, at the same time Knight signed Timi, he also signed her duet partner, Troy Walker.

I was signed up with a guy, and I guess because he was gay, they didn't want to do anything with us. The boy that I was singing with was Troy Walker. And my brother told me, "You know, they're not going to do anything with you because of Troy," because he was so *ferociously* nelly. He was too nelly.

Raul: He was a good singer, too. They worked great together.

Timi: He was great, he was great. We had a harmony together that was unbelievable, but they just couldn't deal with *him*. So they more or less told me they weren't going to do anything with me.

According to Yuro, it was this frustration that led her to take action. In what is probably the most famous story surrounding Timi Yuro, the twenty-year-old singer burst into a Liberty board meeting and started to sing the song that would several weeks later make her a star. The story also goes that Yuro was dealing with a very real heartbreak at the time, a crisis that gave her rendition of "Hurt" a particularly impassioned quality. Yuro says that all of this is true, but adds a few interesting details.

I was in love with the guitar player in the band. I was about nineteen, from nineteen on. And then just before my twenty-first birthday, I found him in bed with a girl I knew.

Raul: But she was really hurt. That's why she did "Hurt." [Laughs.]

Timi: I really was, I really was. And I sang "Hurt" one night with Sonny about four hundred times.

Yuro had learned the song through hearing Roy Hamilton's version in her mother's record collection.

My mother would go buy 78's of all the people that she loved. I think I was eight—no, maybe ten or eleven, 'cause my mother had that 78 by Roy Hamilton, "Hurt." And that's where I learned "Hurt."[4] But he did it, like, [singing it "straight"] "I'm hurt, to think that you lied to me. . . ." Well, I knew it all them years. And then, when I got hurt, I sat down with Sonny and he said, "I don't want you to sing this; I want you to *talk* this." And I said, "I am so hu-rt" [elongating "hurt"], and I started crying. And then he said, [whispering] "Now sing the next line." And that's how I fell into that bag. And all I did was cry every time I sang it with Sonny in the restaurant. The kids would scream when I'd sing it. And that asshole would come—Larry—and watch me sing it, the guy who broke my heart. He had a hit record with "I Got My Mojo Workin.' " Larry Bright. He was very big in California, maybe Texas.

Raul: He was a real redneck, but he had a lot of feeling, he had a lot of soul. He was another white man that sounded black.

Timi: Oh yeah, everyone thought he was black. He was incredible. When he broke my heart, I sang "Hurt" so differently.

Yuro's despondency over her failed love affair and her frustration at being ignored by Liberty gave her the impetus she needed to storm the offices of the record company and invade the board meeting.

I said, "I'm gonna go over to Liberty Records and get my contract back." So I went there, and I sat there for a week. Finally one day I just busted through the door. And he was playing cards. Poker! Bullshittin' all week with them dice [laughs]. And I was *mad* when I went in there! I said, "What the hell is this?" I said, "Hey, I want to sing something for you. Be a decent person: either you listen to me or you come out there and tell me get the hell, go home. Don't make me sit here like a jerk for a week."

Raul: And then the guy said, "Who are you?" And you said, "Well, I'm nobody because you haven't recorded me."

Timi: "I'm nobody," yeah, but I said, "You've got to listen to me sing." He said, "Oh, you must be Timi Yuro!" And I said [with sudden warmth], "Yeah, I am."

And that was [Liberty president] Al Bennett, who turned out to be my best friend in the whole world. And as soon as I sang [sings] "I'm so hurt . . . ," Al Bennett went, "Oh, my God!" And he called Clyde Otis down. I went to the bathroom and Clyde had come in and sat in front of Al Bennett's desk. And just as I walked in, Clyde said to Al Bennett, "Well, where's this white broad that's supposed to have soul?" And I tapped him on the shoulder and I said, "Didn't nobody ever tell you that you don't have to be black to have soul?" And he said, "Well, uh, but, I, uh, uh," and he got all tongue-tied.

So that was a Friday, Sonny was across the street in the pancake house—[to Raul] remember that pancake house?—and he came over and played for me. And he just hit a C-seven, and I said, "I'm so hurt." I sang "Hurt" and "I Apologize." [Otis] jumped. Clyde Otis is like 6′4″, and he hit the ceiling when he jumped up. It was just unreal. He went crazy. And he didn't believe I was white. And it was all good.

That was Friday. Tuesday night I was in the studio, and the next Friday it was on the radio.

Clyde Otis was a giant within the early '60s record industry. By 1961, he had established his reputation as one of the most successful African-American producers through his classic work with Dinah Washington, Brook Benton, Nat "King" Cole, and many others. Otis, recognizing Yuro's potential to appeal to both sides of the then-segregated radio market, promoted "Hurt," backed with "I Apologize," to pop and R&B disc jockeys. As a result, the record hit instantaneously on both charts, a rare feat for 1961.

All the black radio stations, who wouldn't play white artists, played me. They all thought I was black. Clyde Otis made me sing at the Apollo the first week I got to New York. And when I walked on the stage everybody went, [takes a big gasp]. The whole audience just took deep breaths.

Raul: She was scared. Weren't you scared?

Timi: Scared shitless. They brought me there on Wednesday to see what it was like, and they was throwing tomatoes at black singers [laughs], and I said, "Oh my God, what are they going to do to me?" Clyde Otis says, "Baby, if you make it here, you make it anywhere in the world." I said, "I can't do this." So when Jocko [Henderson] called my name—he was the head of the band, the band leader. (He was a disc jockey but he had the big band—King Curtis, I think, was the band)—and he said, "Timi Yuro!" And I stood behind the stage and I couldn't move. And the old stagehand man who'd been there for, like, forty years kicked me in the butt, and I kind of flew out. And all these black people went [shocked gasps], and I just stood there and I was supposed to sing [sings the first line of "Money," by Barrett Strong] "Money don't buy everything it's true. . . ." And I turned around, I looked at King Curtis, and I said, [with sudden confidence] "Give me a C-seven!" And I just went into "Hurt," and they all stood up and screamed. And it was cool. It was unbelievable. And Clyde was just smiling, said, "I knew you'd make it."

"Hurt" became a #4 pop and #22 R&B hit within weeks of its release and virtually made Yuro an overnight star. There was one listener, however, whose response she valued above all others.

I wanted to sing "Hurt" because I wanted Larry to hear it on the radio. He was the only guy I wanted to hear it. And he did. The first night, it went on KFWB, every hour on the hour for one week. [To Raul] That night, mami, how many people were in the restaurant?[5] About four hundred kids came to the restaurant that night, including him. And my dad opened champagne and everything, and we all sat and listened to the record every hour.

Success, it seems, went to the young singer's head.

It happened all so quick that . . . [after a moment's reflection] I think I just turned into a real asshole, like everyone else does. You're making pizzas one week, and the next week you're in New York and you're making an album, and you just turn into a jerk. But I had a lot of fun, you know, being a jerk. You just get like a bitch when you walk somewhere and, "Oh, there she is, there she is, the 'Hurt' girl, the 'Hurt' girl." And you prance and you flip off everybody.

Raul: But you weren't nasty to anybody.
Timi: I wasn't mean, but I *was* a bitch.
Raul: That's hard for a Leo to say.
Timi: I really was.
Raul: 'Cause they always think they're right.
Timi: Yeah, I was *right*, but I was a bitch.

Yuro, in describing her behavior, doesn't mean to imply that she wasn't ready for fame.

All I wanted to do was be in the business.

Raul: She was twenty, but she was fifty.
Timi: Yeah. I had gone through a rough life with my mom and my dad.

Raul: Timi had the soul of an older person. That's why she liked the songs that she did. She liked the older songs, the blues songs.

Timi: My dad made us a pretty rough life. And my mother was so good to me; we were closer than two coats of paint. And because of her, I didn't really screw up as badly as I could have. And I feared *him* because he was a real greaseball, you know. He was total Italian, and, God forbid, you come home pregnant or on drugs—he'd shoot you. So it was just better not to get into that crap, although you *do* get into stuff, you know. But because of my mom, I really tried hard to be cool.

One of the first indications that Yuro was beginning to gain respect within the larger industry came when Frank Sinatra invited her to tour Australia with him at the end of 1961. Although Yuro tends to downplay it today, the engagement was a major career move.

I think he really chose me just because I was Italian. I really believe that. I don't believe it was my talent, my song.

Raul: Oh, stop—you were the best singer.

Timi: Well, I don't know if he thought I was the best singer at that point, but I really felt like I went because I was Italian, I really did. He was a prejudiced guy. He loved Italians. I can't say he was prejudiced and he didn't like other people, all I know is that he *loved* Italians [laughs]. But I'm the same way. If I saw you in a fight with someone and he was Italian, I'd say, "Well, I think that dago has something!"

Raul: Mama, she didn't care if he was Republican, Democrat. If he was Italian, he got his vote from her.

Timi: That's it. My mother didn't know if she was voting Republican or Democrat. And she didn't. If he was Italian, she was going to go down and vote for him.

After the end of the Sinatra tour in late 1961, Yuro remained at Liberty for another two and half years. Her relations there were not always peaceable. After "What's a Matter Baby," one of Yuro's biggest (and best) records, hit #12 on the pop and #16 on the R&B charts in 1962, Clyde Otis stopped working with Liberty after an administrative disagreement. In losing Otis, Yuro lost her most sympathetic producer.

They had a beef with Clyde, and it was my misfortune. He understood me as much as my mother did. He was the epitome of the music business. Nat "King" Cole adored him, Dinah adored him. He *made* Brook Benton. Clyde Otis was there for all them singers, and they adored him because he had soul that was unbelievable.

Still, Liberty president Al Bennett provided a constant source of support for the strong-willed singer.

Most of the time, I feel I was very fortunate that I got to do most every song I wanted to do. Like when Liberty put me with Phil Spector and he wanted me to do those Ronette-type songs, I couldn't do it, so Al Bennett said, "Then you won't work with him." So I was lucky in that respect. Then there was [Liberty staff producer] Snuffy Garrett, who wanted me to sing "Happy Birthday, Sweet Sixteen," and even though it was a smash, I couldn't do it. *I sang "Hurt."* How could you make me turn around and sing, "It's my party and I'll cry if I want to?" I couldn't do that. And Al Bennett always respected that. "Okay," he said, "then you won't work with him." And that's what I went through for a long time, when they took Clyde away from me.

Despite the often scattershot production approach to her records, Yuro's tenure with Liberty, both during and after her work with Clyde Otis, was full of highlights. The years between 1961 and 1963 saw Yuro record straight-ahead R&B (the classic "What's a Matter Baby," a record that won her allegiance among hard-core soul fans), a version of Charlie Chaplin's "Smile" that attracted the praise of the writer himself ("Charlie Chaplin sent me a telegram, when I first sang it, that he never dreamed anyone could do that the way I did"), and a countrypolitan album (Make the World Go Away) that despite its unevenness featured some of her most soulful performances (most notably an astonishing, pull-out-all-the-stops reading of "A Legend in My Time").

Another high point was Yuro's third single release on Liberty, her duet with Johnnie Ray on "I Believe." This hoary "inspirational" tune has been performed by everyone from Dinah Washington to Patti LaBelle, but Yuro's version achieves a reverent, eerie power; her utter commitment to the message of the song comes through in spite of the corn. She doesn't have fond memories of the session, however. Ray, recording ten years after he cut his career-making hit "Cry," was somewhat past his prime vocally and in the midst of a sea of personal troubles.

Recording with Johnnie was a real problem for me. It was really rough. I guess 'cause he was messed up. He was a sweet guy when he wasn't drinking. But I didn't enjoy recording with him. I didn't enjoy it at all. Clyde made me do that.

Yuro admits to a low tolerance for alcoholic behavior, an aversion that stems from her childhood.

I never drank. I hate drunks. I hated drinking. My grandma owned two bars when I was a little girl, so I lived with all these drunks around me all the time, and I hated it. I really hated it. So when I was on the road and someone was drunk, "do not bring them to my dressing room, please. Do not bring me no drunks in front of my face. I'll freak out." And I would trip out, if they came to my room drunk. And I just hated drunks. It's not that I hated drunks or alcoholics, I just can't deal with someone who's slobbering over me. So I was always—I became a speed freak, never a downer freak. I just hated being down.

I think I tried to—I was gonna become a drunk *once* in my career. I was fighting with Al Bennett—that's what it was—I was fighting with Al Bennett to release "Make the World Go Away." It took me three months to get him to put "What's a Matter Baby" out, and he wouldn't release it. He didn't believe in it like I did. I went to Pittsburgh and said to the disc jockey, I said, "Do you want to hear my new record? I don't think it's printed yet, but I have an acetate. I think you should really hear it." And he played "What's a Matter Baby" and got calls for three days, called Al Bennett, said, "Where's 'What's a Matter Baby?'" Al Bennett printed that record in two or three days and started shipping it out. But I went around the country and just went over his head and got it released. And I was fighting with him about "Make the World Go Away," and I decided to become a drunk one night. I went and bought the best scotch you could buy, some Ballantine black bottle or something, and a gallon of milk. And I drank scotch and milk, maybe eight drinks, and I was *ossified*. I woke up with my head over the toilet bowl. I woke up in *vomit*. I woke up like the biggest sleaze in the world, and I said, "This shit will never happen again for me." And I never drank again. I just couldn't drink.

I remember one time I smoked a joint and went on stage. It was at the Thunderbird in Las Vegas. And I thought I was so fabulous that night. I did about twelve ballads, and Davy Victorson, who was the talent director of the Thunderbird, came up to me after the show and said, "Why didn't you tell me you were sick?" And I just stood there and I said, "What do you mean?" And he said, "If you felt this bad, I would have never let you go on tonight." I said, "Well, did I sound bad?" He said, "Well, you sang twelve ballads, but they weren't all that good. Why didn't you just tell me you got [sick]? I could have given you the whole night off." And I thought I was great that night. And after that, I said, "Never again." So I never smoked another joint after that, 'cause I really thought I was fabulous that night. And it turned out he thought I was deathly ill! I learned a lot of shit on the road. I learned a lot of stuff.

One of Yuro's favorite stories comes from her 1963 engagement at the Copa, then New York's toniest nightclub. A gig at the Copa meant you had made it (Sam Cooke's appearance there around the same time had introduced him to an entirely new audience). At the Copa, Yuro soon became aware of which parties it was important to please.

That was incredible. I was there with George Kirby.[6] He was the headliner, and the next day in the paper, I think it said, "Yuro/Kirby pair at the Copa." And Jules

Podell [was] the owner at that time. I think that place was run by the mob—I'm not sure, but Julie Podell was definitely a mafioso character. [Imitates deep, gruff voice] "Sing it again, Timi." You know, that kind of person. He loved me and gave me anything I wanted there. And one night there was this huge table of maybe ten, twelve men and all these little blond ladies, and I sang "Hurt" and all these men were like, crying, and they were hoodlums, you just knew they were hoodlums. And one got up and went in the back, and then I would hear Julie Podell say [in the gruff voice], "Timi, sing it again." And I said, "But Mr. Podell, I have to go. I'll be back on the next show." [Gruff voice] "Sing it again!" And I think I sang "Hurt" one night six times, just for these gangsters.

That experience at the Copa was something I'll never, never forget. I sang "Pagliacci" at that show. It was incredible, it was an incredible, incredible—oh, and opening night, it was standing ovations, and any kid in the world would just dream of a night like that, that I had there. And Burt Bacharach came to me and said, "What you need now to complete this fabulous opening night is to have me make love to you" [laughing as she finishes the sentence].

Raul: [Quoting famous song]: If "Little Things Mean a Lot."

Timi: That's what I told him [laughs]. And I missed out on a friggin' smash. I went to the office a few days later, and he played "What the World Needs Now" for me. And I started singing it and he said, "No, I want you to say, [beats hand against the table to accent every word] What . . . the . . . world . . . needs . . . now. . . ." And I said, "Oh, go fuck yourself," and I left his office. And I blew that song. It was out a few weeks later with Jackie DeShannon.

Walking out on Bacharach (he had actually written and arranged two unsuccessful songs for her, "The Love of a Boy" and "If I Never Get to Love You" at the end of 1962) is an example of the kind of self-assertiveness that earned Yuro something of a reputation for difficulty within the industry. Today, Yuro justifies her firm attitude in the studio as a necessity, since recording time was deducted as an artist expense.

You had to be in charge. When Clyde was with me, I never had a friggin' worry in the world. When Clyde was with me, I could sing, go home, and know that I would have a hit and not worry about nothin.' When they started throwing me with a bunch of jerks, I had to fight for everything I did. So it was bad, and a lot of times they called me a spoiled brat and a bitch, and I didn't give a shit. People come screwed up to my session, get the hell outta here. Or I'd cancel the whole thing rather than waste the money. Whenever Clyde was there, everything was in such control. I mean, nothing was ever wrong. When they took him away from me, oh my God, it was like I was in a jungle by myself.

Yuro compares her behavior with that of her friend Dusty Springfield, whose tantrums during the Dusty in Memphis *sessions are legendary.*

I love Dusty. Dusty and I were really close in England. She was a very down-to-earth girl. Same with me, they called me a bitch too in the studio, but it was only because I wanted shit right. Don't come to my recording session all screwed up and waste *my* money waiting for you to get *your* shit together. It would piss us off. And Dusty was the same way. If someone gave her a lot of shit, she'd yell and scream, pull a little tantrum, and that made us bad. But it *didn't*—it was always because someone was screwing up on our time and money. Every time I got pissed off in the studio it was with reason, and same with her. She never acted like a star or nothin,' she was always pretty cool.

Yuro's departure from Liberty was surrounded by the atmosphere of turbulence that often pervaded her relations in the studio and found expression in her music. By the end of 1963, she had received an offer from Mercury Records. The prospect of recording for Mercury—once the vaunted home of her idol Dinah Washington—certainly appealed to her. Her transition to Mercury, however, was hampered by a legal dispute with her managers.

You just can't trust people the way I did. Bobby Darin said the same thing. Bobby Darin gave me money to get out of trouble. Mercury couldn't sign me when I left Liberty because I was hung up in a lawsuit with this manager shit. The managers had me just over a barrel. They had stolen all my money, and when I went into a coma in Las Vegas here (I got pneumonia here in Vegas, I was singing at the Thunderbird), the manager went to the record company and got advances that I didn't know about, but they were able to because of my contract with them. It said in case of serious illness or death that they could collect my monies. And Al Bennett didn't know what was going on, and he gave them a lot of money thinking it was for me. And when I came out of the coma, I had nothing. My mother was there with her rosaries and the same dress I went into the coma with. And we had to fight. My mother went home and got ten, fifteen grand together from her restaurant business, and Bobby Darin gave me five grand, and somewhere or another I got thirty grand together to give to them to get my contract back, and after I got free from them, then Mercury signed me.

As an addendum to this story, Yuro remarks that the Queen of the Blues herself, then nearing the end of her life (she would die in December of that year, 1963) had just finished an engagement at the Thunderbird.

I opened right after Dinah Washington. I can say some things about her, but I never would.

Raul: She was married to a kid that I knew that was quite a character, gay guy. Rafael Campos. Oh, he carried on. I did a show with him one time.

Timi: He was a big actor. Have you ever heard of him? He was in them movies with Sal Mineo and all that stuff. He was in a lot of movies. And she adored him, I know she adored him. She was a funny lady.

By 1964 Yuro had worked out her contractual dispute and was excited about her promising new relationship with Mercury. In September of that year, she released The Amazing Timi Yuro *album. Produced by Quincy Jones and arranged by songwriter Bobby Scott, the album contained one of her greatest performances in "Johnny." Yuro imbued the song, a torchy ballad about a long-lost, never-was love, with the same sense of high tragedy that a great opera singer might bring to a Puccini aria. Her performance gradually builds to a heart-rending climax, then diminishes to a tone of contemplative sadness as the song fades. At certain times there is a country sob in her voice that begs comparison with Tammy Wynette or Brenda Lee, but the style—hyperdramatic yet completely believable—is all Timi's own. Although one of her least-known recordings (it was buried on a B-side when it was finally released as a single), it is perhaps her very best: truly a one-of-a-kind record.*

The whole *Amazing* album was one or two takes. I don't think I did three takes of any song except "The Masquerade [Is Over]" because Quincy thought that it was going to be a single. And I think it was, but it wasn't *the* single that I thought should be released. I really loved "Johnny." I really loved that for a single, and Quincy said no. That's probably the best album I've ever done in my life. I loved it, I loved it. Bobby Scott was incredible. You know, he wrote "A Taste of Honey." Quincy was there, but not really for me. Who was really there for me was Phil Ramone, the engineer who works with Billy Joel, and Bobby Scott—they were there for me on that album. They made me sing that album. They were wonderful to me.

After her initial artistic high point with certain tracks on the Amazing *album, Yuro quickly became dissatisfied with her experience at Mercury. Once the album failed to be the huge seller the company had hoped for, she languished aimlessly for the next three years. There would be no more albums for Mercury, and none of her post-Amazing singles on the label succeeded in charting. Her career, which had been on an upward swing, lost momentum as Yuro slowly disappeared from the public view. Yuro blames her lack of success at Mercury on the absence of the company's ailing co-founder, Irving Green.*

That company did nothing for me. That Mercury Records did absolutely nothing for me, and that album could have been giant. It could have been so huge. I think when Irving Green got sick I went down the tubes there. And that was sad, 'cause I thought it was probably the greatest album I'd ever do. 'Cause he was the one who wanted me there, and if he had stayed with me and Quincy I think it would have been bigger, but I think he got sick at that point, and that's what blew my whole album. But it should have done something more than it did.

Still, the remainder of Yuro's time at Mercury did offer at least one high point. "Cutting In," released as a B-side in 1967, was a terrific performance that briefly gave Yuro a bit of restored attention on the R&B market (according to Ralph McKnight, a soul station in Kansas City had so many listener requests that it played it every hour on the hour). In a performance that owes as much to Sophie Tucker as it does to Etta James, Yuro plays the brazen housewrecker to the hilt ("Pardon me, honey, but I'm cutting in on you"). Full of gospel-styled screams and slangy asides (at one point she calls her hapless target "sister"), the song is a complete kick from start to finish.

How could you even think of that song? Do you know that's the most favorite song of mine that I ever did at Mercury? Well, aside from my album. [Sings the opening line] "Pardon me, girl, for being so cold. . . ." Oh, I love that song. [With sudden enthusiasm] That song is my absolute favoritest in the whole world. And I didn't think anyone had ever heard of it. It's fabulous, it's fabulous.

Although Yuro's career began to lose its footing as the '60s wore on, she retained her popularity with her core fans: her cult audience. In particular, she never lost her appeal among southern listeners. Although Yuro has spent little time in the South, she believes that her style of performance carries a special resonance for southerners. She refers to a southern friend who claims to still hear her records on the radio.

In the South I'm still very big. I don't believe it, it's like thirty-five years, but she said they play my records every day in New Orleans and Mississippi. I just feel that they feel that I'm from there. The southern people feel they have a lot more soul than northerners. And actually, they do. As human beings, they've been through a lot more than we have. I don't know, people up North now, it's just fast and cold. And there's still something about the way I sing, something about the way Gladys

Knight sings—she did then and she still does now—that just makes southern people . . . they tend to live the blues, so they love the blues. And people think I'm very, I was always very sad. And I was. It was good, though. My greatest pleasure on earth was to go on stage and be sad. And when people would applaud, it was the greatest thing in the world for me. No one could ever know the happiness that I felt in those moments on stage. Just going out there and crying and singing a song. And it wasn't just to blow people away; it was to give them the truth of *me*. And people accepted it, and then they would scream and clap, and that made me feel like a giant.

Another audience that has always found Yuro's music truthful is her large gay following. Yuro is particularly appreciative of her gay fans, having acknowledged their presence from the earliest stages of her career. In the early '60s, "Hurt" was a fixture on the jukeboxes of gay bars across the country, many of which Yuro would visit regularly. She insists that if she could still perform, she would be a huge success in San Francisco.

Gay kids love Timi Yuro. Everywhere I went, they would tell me—any gay bar. I used to go to them always. And when I would walk in, someone would look at me, and I'd say [with mock hauteur], "Go play my song." And they would crack up.

Raul: Well, gay people always follow the best singers, let's face it. They *made* the big singers.

Timi: I think that gay people have more heart than many, many people I've ever met.

Here, Timi's friend Isabel adds, "I like that show you made—don't you have it on film? At that gay bar? Remember, at that place? Oh, that was such a good show."

I sang at a club in L.A. that was really great. And the owner killed himself about two months after I left there because he had found out he had AIDS and he didn't want to go through that whole trip, so he shot himself, but the tape I have there is really nice. Gay people always love me, though.

After her frustration with Mercury, Yuro returned to Liberty for a brief period from 1968 to 1969, releasing one album, Something Bad on My Mind. *With the southern soul explosion in full gear (Yuro would have been perfectly at home in Memphis or Muscle Shoals), the album's middle-of-the-road approach seems like a bit of a waste. Some of the material is not of top-notch quality, but Yuro's own sensitive composition "Wrong" and two beautifully sung songs, "I Must Have Been Out of My Mind" and "When You Were Mine," provide lovely highlights. Yuro, recording in London,* recruited long-time Clyde Otis associate Belford Hendricks to work on the album, but the net result was bogged down by an oppressive production.

"I Must Have Been Out of My Mind" is probably my most favorite in that whole *Something Bad* album. I called Belford Hendricks, called him back to record with me, because him and Clyde were like this [crossing her fingers]. So Belford would lend everything that he learned from Clyde to my sessions on the *Something Bad* album. I couldn't have done a lot of stuff without Belford. I think I even paid for Clyde to come out just to listen to everything. And then when he had it all real good for me, my friend, [producer] Marshall Leib, buried me in the remixing of the whole album, so he ruined that album for me. He didn't do it well. It would have been great if he'd of left it the way Belford and Clyde did it.

Yuro's second time around with Liberty Records didn't last long. Something Bad on My Mind *was not a huge seller, and a second album that had been scheduled for release in 1969,* Timi Yuro Live at P.J.'s, *never saw the light of day (although several of its tracks turned up on an internationally released United Artists album in 1976). The cancellation of the P.J.'s album was particularly unfortunate, since the set showcased her in the kind of stripped-down R&B setting that suited her perfectly. A* Variety *reviewer, praising one of the engagement's performances, wrote that Yuro "comes charging on with initial entry, 'A Place in the Sun,' and never lets go of her extra sensitive interpretations until the very end of [this] perspiring, exhausting and thoroughly entertaining 50-minute show."*

Yuro spent the early '70s recording the occasional single (one of the best was a breathtaking reading of "Nothing Takes the Place of You," recorded in Memphis with Willie Mitchell around the same time as his work with Denise LaSalle), performing at oldies festivals, and raising her daughter Milan, who was born in 1970. One of her favorite performances was at Madison Square Garden in 1970, where she shared a bill with a group of artists that included Little Richard. ("He's crazy, he's wonderful. He stole all my perfume. He did. He loved Replique by Raphael. Stole it all.") In the early '80s, she found a belated fame in Holland, recording three low-budget albums for a Dutch label and enjoying a European hit with a re-recording of "Hurt." A videotape of her performances in Europe during this period reveals the reverent, devotional feelings her overseas fans have for her: after almost every song, she is swarmed by audience members running up to the stage, beseiging her with flowers and other gifts.

Yuro's last album, Timi Yuro Sings Willie Nelson, *has never been released commercially in the U.S. (although Yuro has a stash of copies that she and her former husband released on their own small label). Recorded in 1984 right before her first operation for throat cancer, the album was financed by Nelson as a way of thanking Yuro for the kindness her mother had bestowed upon him in the early '60s, while he was still a struggling songwriter.*

The reason Willie did that last album with me was [that] in the '60s, when Willie was just a fat old slob songwriter, he drove from Austin one night to Houston. I was singing at the Court Club in Houston, a private club. And after the show—two o'clock I think it was, or one-thirty—he called me and said, "Can I come up and play you these songs?" I said, "Well, sure." And my mom was with me. My mother said, "Are you hungry, son?" And he said, "Well . . ." and so she ordered him food and she treated him like a king. And we loved his songs, and I took "Permanently Lonely," "Are You Sure," and another one that Willie wrote back to L.A. to do the *Make the World Go Away* album. Then I had never seen Willie after that till I was married, years later. I went to see him at Caesar's with my husband and my daughter. And he said, "In November, I'll send you tickets." And I said, "Yeah, right." And in November the tickets came to the door.

Yuro flew to Nelson's studio in Austin, Texas, to record the album.

He paid for everything. He let me stay there, and I did that whole album there. We fixed it up when I came home 'cause it really wasn't all that great. [Pause.] I can't believe it's been so long, you know. 'Cause I can listen to those songs and feel like I did them yesterday. On all my albums. I sit there and I can remember sitting in the studio, what I did, and it's just amazing that I still get fan mail from people and, I mean, it's almost forty years ago. It's pretty frightening.

With characteristic bravado, Yuro compares her style with those of several singers who are working today.

I can't find another girl who feels about a song the way I do. I love Celine Dion, I love Gladys Knight, but I can't find anyone who I feel feels like I do about a song. I ain't never heard a person yet. If I don't like the song, I can't sing it, that's number one. Number two, it generally had something to do with where I was at at the time, most songs that I sing. I can't find another girl that . . . there *is* one chick who possibly *could* go where I was. Or where I would go with a song. Only she don't, she's shuckin' and jivin.' She's still jivin' and she needs to . . . I don't know if she needs to be hurt or if somebody just needs to tell her to get down. Wynonna Judd. I believe that if she could listen to me sing and then go in the studio . . . I love her, I love her to bits, but I still feel like she's jivin, you know. She's bullshittin.' If I could have her alone in the studio and make her get down with a song I think she'd be a friggin' bomb, I think she'd tear up the world. There's even songs I think about for her to sing. I tell Isabel, but I can't be callin' up people. If I could just get next to her and just tell her where I've been, if she would read the song before she sang it—and I know she don't—I know she looks at the song and she learns it, but she didn't take it home and sit with it and read it and get into it. I know sometimes where she's coming from, because I did it myself. There are songs that I shucked and jived on that I knew would never do anything, and they never did. And it was generally because I didn't like it or I had to do it because Clyde made me or some-body made me.

Here, Yuro has one of the fits of coughing that, with the tracheostomy, affects her from time to time.

This is why I don't go and talk to people and see stars, because I don't want to be chokin' and coughin' in their faces.

Yuro tends to overemphasize the effect of the tracheostomy and the extent of her weight gain. In fact, were it not for the difficulty she sometimes experiences when speaking, it would be hard to know that she had ever been so sick. Her skin is smooth and unlined, and her nicely styled hair is an attractive salt-and-pepper; she wears a becoming blouse and black stretch pants and is not nearly as overweight as she seems to believe.

I look like a little fat greaseball. I always knew I'd end up looking like my mother. I'm fifty-eight. I'm fifty-eight now. It's unreal. I don't even believe it. . . . Can I call my grandchildren?

After she leaves a message for her daughter, I remark that she doesn't seem that heavy.

Well, you know what put on all the weight, when I had half a lung removed, they gave me total steroid treatment for two months, and that just blew me up.

Yuro is extremely proud of her two grandchildren, first showing me a picture of Sienna, Milan's daughter, then Nico (short for Niccolino), her one year-old son.

They have the same birthday.

Isabel adds, "Nico. I love that name."

"Niccolino." That's what made me live. And *that* child, [referring to Sienna] I had to live for her. Otherwise I think I'd have given up. My daughter was really screwed up for a long time. And all of a sudden, two years ago, she came home and went with her boyfriend of ten years, went back to him, got pregnant with Nico and she just . . . God did something to her. Well, aside from the fact that Isabel and I have been on our knees. Milan was really tripping, though. We've been on our knees for years praying for Milan, and now she's the most incredible wife and mother.

Isabel: Never gave up on her. Ever.

Timi: *God* didn't.

Isabel: That's why we just kept praying.

Timi: And I came here in '69 and I married, uh, Milan's father . . .

Isabel: [cutting in, laughing] Milan's father.

Timi: . . . which was the biggest mistake I made. After I had her I should've left, but I didn't. And I really feel that I was a jerk and I wasted twenty-nine years of my life. He was always in the gambling business, and I shouldn't have stayed, but . . . I don't think I'd be in this situation today with this tracheostomy or anything if I had left him. I'd still be singing. He stopped me from doing so many things in my life regarding a career.

I ask if her husband supported her in her desire to perform.

Yeah, but his way. And it was always wrong. He didn't know nothin' about it, and he always screwed me out of fabulous deals.

Raul: Kept at her for years telling her this and she would never listen to me.

Timi: He screwed me out of very good things.

Raul: Keep him out of your business. That's happened to a lot of artists who let their husbands. . . .

Timi: He just screwed up every good deal I ever had.

I comment upon how well Yuro looks.

Raul: Survivor.

Isabel: Her hair turned white overnight. But it's beautiful; I think it's beautiful.

Timi: After my radiation. [Before the radiation] my hair was, like, just gray here [points to her temples]. And I had a natural. When I was in Holland, I had a natural. One of those Afro-type things, and I just had little gray sides. Then I come home and got sick, and after the radiation, I think, in, like, twelve weeks my hair was just white.

During Yuro's recent battle with lung cancer, another of her current problems was brewing. After recuperating at Milan's residence, she returned to her own home to find it severely damaged by the tenants who had been staying there.

Our house is a mess, and I felt really bad that you were here now, because the whole house has to be done over. The kitchen cabinets are all ruined, the sink is ruined, everything is ruined. Everything. We need new carpet. Everything was just ruined. You cannot believe what we have to do. We have to even plaster the wall. We need new doors, we need everything. But we don't owe any money on the house. We owe maybe three or four thousand dollars on the house, so we can take all the money we need to fix it up, but we don't know if we want to 'cause it's in a very old neighborhood, although we love the old neighborhood—we've been there for years. Everybody on the block knows everybody. So we don't know what to do. I don't like to move into a new place, because if you put eighty thousand dollars down on a house in Las Vegas today, you're still gonna have a six, seven-hundred-dollar-a-month payment, and we don't need that. So we don't know what to do, but it's been awful, you know, to see all your shit just ruined. My beautiful green antique couch is full of milk and shit.

Here, Isabel reassures her gently, "We'll get it all taken care of." Yuro particularly misses being able to cook for large groups of people, one of her favorite pastimes.

Oh, I cook. I cook good. I don't cook *good*—no one ever cooked like my mother cooked. Nobody. My brother cooks; he learned a lot of shit from my mother. I cook good Italian food, nothing spectacular, although everybody who eats it really loves it.

Isabel: Her raviolis are really great. And her lasagnas.
Timi: We're not big on American food. I'm not a steak cooker. If I couldn't have macaroni, or if there's no macaroni in heaven, I ain't goin.' I gotta have macaroni.

As Yuro has continued to recuperate, her life has been brightened in several ways. She finds tremendous emotional support through her family, especially her relationship with Milan. Like the tie with her own mother that preceded it, Yuro and her daughter share an extremely tight bond. On a lesser note, she recently received some much-needed royalty payments when "Hurt" was used in the soundtrack to the Martin Scorsese film, Casino. And then there are the fans who, after thirty-five years, still treasure the memories of her glorious voice.

It's an unbelievable feeling. I got a letter a few months ago from a man who kind of feels like you do about the way I do a song, and it just made me feel so great. It was on one of my very bad days. To get a letter like this and then have people write me from London still and from Holland—I don't know that I could ever say that

I've left a mark somewhere, but I know there are some people who really loved what I said musically, and that gives me enough joy to go on living. I never will understand why I had to lose my voice. I'm sure I will whenever I see God. The first thing I'm gonna ask Him is "What is this shit?"

Raul: At least she didn't lose her life.

Timi: Yeah, but what was life without singing for me? I could never imagine. And then I have Sienna, and Sienna and my daughter and Nico, and that became my life. But still, every day I wake up and wonder why I can't sing.

I start to ask the question that seems to surface by itself: "Do you think it's possible you'll ever . . . ?" Timi's eyes immediately fill up with tears, and she is unable to speak; the possibility overwhelms her. The long pause that follows is the most wrenching moment I have experienced during any of my interviews. It was Raul who finally broke the silence.

Raul: Well, God works in mysterious ways too, you know. Things are so advanced nowadays. She didn't lose her vocal chords, so you never know. We keep hoping. That's all you can do in life, is hope and pray. She's still alive, you know. When I took her with me, when we found out that she had this, it was real hard for both of us. For me, to have to be there when they tell her this.

Isabel: [to Timi, softly] You were worth it all, honey.

Raul: Oh yeah, but I mean it was hard for both of us. I know it was hard for me watching her.

Timi: Yeah, that's what killed him, what I was going through.

Yuro hides nothing. Defiant, honest, and unapologetic, she shows all of her emotion on her face. After a few moments her eyes dry, and once again there is much laughter and high spirits. Yuro is, surprisingly, a good listener as well as a talker; while others are speaking, she looks them straight in the face and quietly absorbs what they are saying. Raul is talking about working on an AIDS benefit recently that featured Liza Minnelli as a performer.

Liza Minnelli was sitting there hoarse, and she couldn't even hit the notes and smoked like this, one cigarette after another—I mean like this, without stopping. I told her about Timi, and I saw her smoking. I said, "You better take it easy with that."

Yuro adds, "Yeah, she can't do that shit." She says that during the '60s she smoked no more than anyone else.

When I was young, but never a lot. I was not a heavy smoker. . . . Okay, pumpkin.

It is time for Yuro to get back to her grandchildren. As she leaves, we discuss my coming out to visit again "when we get our house fixed up." Standing, she seems taller than her much publicized five feet; the strength of her personality adds inches to her physical stature. Outside, glowing in the setting Vegas sun, she is commanding and attractive. It's been many years since her glory days, but that intrinsic star quality has not diminished. If she could suddenly sing tomorrow, one could picture her striding confidently onto a stage and never stepping down until the audience was captured in her hand. Anything less would be giving up, and Timi Yuro has never given up.

Epilogue

Maxine Brown, 1990s

In February of 1999, I was given the opportunity to promote a concert at Columbia University entitled "Classic Soul Divas." The concert, which featured Maxine Brown and Bettye LaVette, could be seen as a variation of my larger mission: to help bring greater recognition to some of the country's most talented and overlooked vocalists. The evening was notable in part for Maxine's characteristically energetic, commanding performance. The audience, composed of a wonderfully diverse mix of hard-core R&B fans, young, trendy New Yorkers, older Harlemites, college students with little prior knowledge of soul music, and fellow jazz and R&B performers, was thrilled with her consummate sense of showmanship and unwavering ability to put over a song. But it was Bettye who caused the biggest surprise, perhaps because, unlike Maxine, so few people in the audience had heard

Bettye LaVette and the author,
September 1999

of her. After the close of a set that included devastating readings of "Damn Your Eyes" and "Let Me Down Easy"—both extended into seven-minute masterpieces of interpretation and dynamics—friends and acquaintances approached me with looks of astonishment. Many later told me that after the concert they had rushed to the closest Tower Records outlet to buy Bettye's music, but their expeditions (not surprisingly) had been uniformly unsuccessful. The overriding question on everyone's lips seemed to be, "Why isn't this woman a star?"

According to Ahmet Ertegun, the legendary co-founder of Atlantic Records, female soul singers of the '60s had as many opportunities for stardom as anyone else. Ertegun is in many respects an anomaly; unlike many of his '50s and '60s contemporaries, he has always possessed a genuine love and appreciation for African-American music, and his keen awareness of its many manifestations has allowed him to maintain his success over the course of fifty years of changing trends. But sitting in his beautifully furnished office high above Sixth Avenue, smoking Marlboro Lights, surrounded by copies of demo tapes, he seems very much the hard-nosed music executive: polite, but taciturn and circumspect. In particular, he warns against putting too much stock in the plaints of female artists who feel they have not received their proper compensation: "Show business is a very tough business, and it's a business [in] which the success of a performer is dictated by the taste of the general public. If the general public supports an artist by going to concerts, buying records, that's what makes [that artist] be a permanent performer. It's not really different for girl soul singers than it is for opera singers. The artists, on the other hand, are inclined to blame other factors. None of them think that they're not able to perform in a way that the public accepts them, so they'll blame managers, they'll blame booking agencies, they'll blame record companies for not supporting them . . . so what you're going to find in your research are a lot of people who are going to say they were cheated, mistreated. Some of them were; some of them *were* cheated, some of them *were* mistreated, I'm sure. But finally, that did not cause their downfall. The downfall is caused by the lack of . . . innate talent. It has to be huge, you know, to survive."[1]

To Arlene Gallup, the idea that '60s soul women were somehow deficient in talent is deeply upsetting. Gallup's unique and varied career has encompassed forty years in the music industry. While currently a press agent who often works with Class Act, an organization that specializes in producing benefits and providing financial relief for rock and R&B performers from the '50s and '60s, she has done everything from managing a soul record company (Calla, for which Bettye LaVette first recorded "Let Me Down Easy") to working for Phil Spector and booking acts for the famed *Clay Cole Show* (on which Barbara Mason and Carla Thomas both appeared). A strong, courageous, and big-hearted woman, Gallup offers observations etched with unmistakable indignance: "These women probably have more talent in their one finger than half of the world has in their whole hand. But they were never packaged. Everything is the wrapping, guys! I mean, if you don't package it, it ain't gonna sell. It's got to have a packaging and somebody pushing that packaging."

Singers like Maxine Brown and Bettye LaVette recorded for small labels that simply didn't have the financial resources to promote their artists appropriately. Also, the commercial track records of labels like Scepter and Calla were spotty when compared with the output of a steady hitmaker like Motown. "A lot of these labels were very small, one-man labels," says Gallup. "They did not have the money to send an act on a promotion tour. If they did, they picked the city very carefully. It had to be a city where the record already was breaking, and you had to depend upon the disc jockeys in those cities. When it came to the Motown era, Motown took an enormous amount of money [and] dressed these girls, choreographed these girls, and sent them on promotion tours around the country. I mean, the difference between the Shirelles and the Supremes is money. [The Shirelles] never had anybody to costume them, at Scepter. They went out and bought their dresses off a rack, basically, whereas Diana and Florence and Mary [the Supremes] got their clothes designed for them by the ilks of Bob Mackie. I mean, when three people walk out in Bob Mackie gowns, you're gonna stop and look at them no matter what the hell they were singing."

Gallup says that Calla's promotional funds were particularly scarce, even though the label was affiliated with the somewhat larger Roulette Records: "Calla didn't have the proverbial pot to piss in. There were three people—Jerry Schiffrin, Nathan McCalla, and Arlene Gallup. We did it all! And we would hire a promotion man *as needed*. We were supposedly totally autonomous, and Roulette was our partner, monetarily. But we'd have to depend on their promotion staff when it came to a national promotion, whereas today, labels like Atlantic and Columbia and Geffen have a team that criss-cross the country constantly." In this constricted promotional climate, Calla's biggest commercial success (J. J. Jackson's 1966 crossover hit "But It's Alright") came about solely as a fluke: "It was brought to the company as a master, or it was a demo—I don't remember what stage it was at. But we bought the package and went into the studios, sweetened it up with horns and whatever we had to put on, and it went out just like the others went out. We pushed it as hard as we could push it with the distributors, etcetera, etcetera, and you have to hope. And the first day I got a call from somewhere in the Midwest for ten thousand more—in those days ten thousand was a lot of records." Given this unpredictable economic atmosphere, it's no surprise that LaVette's singles for Calla didn't achieve the degree of success they deserved.

For Henry Jones (better known by his professional name "Juggy Murray"), the difficulty of promoting artists, female and male, on a small label was compounded by the racism inherent in the '50s and '60s music industry. As the founder of Sue Records, Murray is one of the great, underappreciated figures in R&B music; the many artists he has discovered and/or promoted include Ike and Tina Turner, Baby Washington (he once claimed that he would rather "record Baby Washington than eat"), Inez and Charlie Foxx, Jimmy Hendrix, and the Poets. But as an African-American label owner and producer, he frequently experienced difficulty getting his records played by the major stations. "Don't you know the pop radio stations didn't play black records?" he asks rhetorically, sitting in a Manhattan coffee shop forty-two years after Sue's first 45-rpm release. "And the only reason they played it was because their own daughters and sons asked them why they weren't playing it. And they would try to tell their kids not to listen to the R&B stations, but the kids listened to the R&B stations. So they were *forced* to play R&B records; they didn't want to play them. I thought that was the worst thing I ever heard in my life, but it's true. Prejudiced. It's the same old bullshit, you know that. That's all that is. Why would they not play it? 'Cause they didn't want their kids to listen to it. They didn't want to promote anything black. That's all it was."

Arlene Gallup shares Murray's belief that racism—not just within the industry but also among the record-buying public—hampered the careers of many female soul singers: "I remember seeing racism. I mean, there were black male acts on shows, but they weren't hit with the same racism verbally that the females were hit with. The females were considered the weaker sex, so they'd get racist remarks from the audience, like, 'Why don't you go home where you belong?' And I've heard that horrible 'n' word being uttered by the audience. Mickey Harris, the late Shirelle, took a mop handle and chased [a patron] through an audience, 'cause he called her a nigger—God forgive me for saying that. To me, that's the worst expression in the world." As Gallup implies, there was often an added sexual element to the racism inflicted upon female performers.

In contrast, Ertegun places some of the blame for the short-lived success of female soul singers—and of soul music in general—upon the African-American audience itself. "Let me tell you something: of all audiences in the world, the most unforgiving are black audiences. I mean, the most honest about what they like—they're not influenced by big names and so forth. They like what they like and buy what they like. You know, in the 1960s, young black people were not buying the great blues artists. What happened to all those great blues artists, you know? Their music is the music that's inspired all the important rock 'n rollers—Eric Clapton, Led Zeppelin, the Rolling Stones, the Who, the Beatles, Bad Company, Emerson, Lake, and Palmer—they all listened to the early black blues. Black people don't like that. You know, the Rolling Stones and Led Zeppelin played a lot of these songs of the early black musicians—you didn't see one black face in the audience. I mean, the blues was over to them. They were into rhythm and blues, they were into Wilson Pickett and that kind of music. They weren't listening to Big Bill Broonzy or Muddy Waters. So today, they're listening to Lil' Kim. They're not going back and listening to the 1960s music. That's for us white historians to listen to."

I can't help but mention Malaco Records, which has found consistent success in the '80s and '90s marketing old fashioned soul-blues music to African-American audiences, largely in the South. Ertegun is quick to downgrade Malaco's influence, dismissing both the quality of the company's music and the significance of its audience: "No, no, no. Malaco sells to some country people in the South who never change their ways." Rather, he perceives more value in the intimations of soul and blues detectable in contemporary pop music: "The blues lived through the rhythm & blues era; it lived through rock 'n roll; and it lives in the music of Whitney Houston and of all the people singing today—all the young kids, you know, all the rappers and the young sixteen, seventeen-year-old girls who are coming up and who are making records and making great records. You can't destroy African-American music. It's in the phrasing, the intonation. White people can't sing that way, you know."

I ask Ertegun how he feels about Timi Yuro being included in my project. His response is notable for its emphasis on a notion of authenticity, one that anthropologists and other social scientists might describe as "essentialist": "Today, because of the tremendous influence of black performers, white performers, they're not as square as they used to be. They used to be real square—you know, Doris Day, Rosemary Clooney, Perry Como. I mean, they couldn't sing blues or anything like that. It was totally out of their realm of reference. But the young white singers, especially the southern ones, have gotten a lot of that. I mean, they can be pretty cool. But they can't really be as authentic as the ones who grew up in black churches

. . . About Timi Yuro, I wasn't a Timi Yuro fan, so I really don't know her music very well . . . What is she? Was she half-Chinese or something?"

I am prompted to ask Ertegun a hypothetical question, one inspired by our discussion of the recent popularity of female performers such as Sheryl Crow and Jewel: if singers like Carla Thomas, Baby Washington, or Maxine Brown were to come along today, does he think they would experience greater success because of the way the pop market has oriented itself towards female singers? He responds with incredulity: "*Those* singers? If they were to try to make records today? You're talking about 1960—that's almost forty years ago. Why would singers who were popular forty years ago have any audience today? . . . You know, we don't think in terms of male or female or groups or this or that. Record companies look to survive, and they can only survive by having hits. They record whatever they want to record, whatever they can find, they send them out to the radio stations; some of it sticks, some of it doesn't. And there's nothing you can do about it. You can't promote an artist that people don't like, and you can't stop a record that everybody's crazy about. We are always surprised, because it's not always the records that we think we have. We put out four albums this month, and we think we have one sure hit and one strong possibility and two so-so/weak, not-so-strong things; one of the not-so-strong things can be the biggest thing we've ever had. So it's dictated by public taste. We cannot create public taste. Public taste is what creates the popular music of the era, and the popular music changes imperceptibly, so that the music of 1996 is not really different from the music of 1997, but over a ten-year period it's changed dramatically. It's like the philosophical concept of a continuum, where it changes imperceptibly, like a child growing. About the 1960s or '70s, I don't even remember what we were working on at that time, and I don't know any time when it was more difficult for girl singers than any other time. But the fact that there are a lot of girl singers who are hitting now doesn't mean that Baby Washington, if she were a young girl singing today, would have a hit."

Although no longer a young girl, Baby Washington has just released an album of all-new recordings produced by her longtime associate and most ardent supporter, Juggy Murray. The album is an often-poignant reminder of the uniqueness of Washington's talent as well as Murray's own undiminished sense of groove. As one of the few '60s producers and label owners to become predominantly known for his work with female artists, Murray seems to possess an innate appreciation for the beauty of the female voice: "Most of my hits have been with females. I've had a lot of hits with male [artists], but they were not as big as the female hits. I've thought of that myself. In the past, I used to think about that. I wondered why. Maybe I relate more to a female sound or something. Maybe I hear 'her,' more than I hear 'him.' You know what I mean? 'Course, I don't know. But if I have more hits with females than males, there must be something."

As a woman working in a largely male industry, Arlene Gallup was also especially sensitive to the unique qualities and needs of female performers. Her own success in the business was rooted in her ability to act as "male" as possible: "I never had a problem—well, there was a monetary problem. It took years for me to become equal with the men as far as money goes. As far as position and power, it was never a problem. I guess I was always tall for my age, and I had the biggest mouth around. I was never seen as a woman; I was seen as one of the guys. I went to the hockey games *with the guys*, because I was one of the guys. I was never 'Arlene Gallup, female.' I never had to worry about somebody laying a hand on me, because if somebody did, twenty guys jumped him. I was one of the guys! I learned how to drink, whether that be good or bad, because I was one of the guys."

As a successful, confident businesswoman, Gallup was not entirely alone: "Ahmet had a secretary at that time—in fact she just recently passed, I understand: Noreen Woods, who was his right hand and became vice president of Atlantic eventually, who was also treated as one of the guys. There were some girls, some women, who didn't want to be treated as one of the guys. They were happy working their nine-to-five job and going home. But I've always said the music business is of two extremes: either you love it or you hate it, and if you hate it, you get out. You can't look at it as a job; it becomes a way of life."

Gallup emphatically believes that female performers of the '50s and '60s faced added challenges, especially during performance tours: "There was sexism abounding. [Women] were always treated as the second-class citizen by the promoter, even by the other acts on the tour, whether it be conscious or subconsciously. They were relegated to the worst dressing rooms; they had the worst dressing facilities no matter where they were. I remember having acts dressing in freezers and hanging their coats on meathooks, while the male acts had rooms with bathrooms. Females didn't get the money that males did, even though they had the same number of hits."

I mention Maxine Brown's bitterness when describing her shows with Chuck Jackson ("I don't care if it's a dollar more than me, he would get it"). Gallup's response hits upon one of the era's most persistent assumptions about women in the workplace: "The philosophy was *he* had a family to support, and *she* had a husband to support her, whether that be true or not. The artist could have been supporting six kids and two grandparents and a mother and father and whatever; if it was a female artist, the underlying philosophy was, 'they don't need as much as a male because somebody will support them.'

"As Maxine said, it could have only been a dollar, but the male always got more. There were many obstacles. Just being a woman and traveling on a bus was an obstacle. I mean, women have toilet needs that men don't have. Half of the time the drivers wouldn't even stop, and God forbid there should be a bathroom on the bus. You waited [to use the bathroom] or you bled in your seat. You sat on towels. Beverly [of the Shirelles] did it, Arlene Smith [the Chantels] did it. The original girl from the Skyliners—I don't remember her name—had a very bad menstrual session, and she bled all over the bus, and the bus driver wouldn't stop until he got to his next stop. But if one of the guys had to go to the bathroom or coughed or something, they pulled over. The guy could go on the side of the road."

Echoing one of this book's recurring themes, Gallup asserts that managers did not always have their female clients' best interests in mind: "All the managers cared were 'where's my commission?' and 'how many dates can I run together and pay you the cheapest possible rate?' I mean, half of the time these acts never knew what they were making. They could have been paid a thousand dollars a night and only saw four hundred dollars of it, because that's what the manager told them they were making. The promoter was selling to the manager, and the manager sold the act and then took his commission out of the four hundred dollars. [Then] all of a sudden it was like in cartoons, the light bulb went off. You'd be backstage and you'd hear a promoter talking to somebody else that, 'I paid so-and-so such-and-such for this act,' and you're saying, 'he paid a thousand dollars for us? Why are we only getting four hundred? And then we're giving him a ten percent commission.' And the manager would always have a bullshit story. You believe it the first time, you believe it the second time, the third time you begin to wonder, and by the fourth time you're totally dubious and you're totally unhappy with the situation and you don't believe a thing he's gonna tell you. By the fifth or sixth time, you say, 'Hey, take this piece of paper, rip it up, and I'm going on my way. Sue me.' And because of that, they went through successions of managers, until a lot of them to this day manage themselves. They don't trust anybody."

As a label owner who managed most of the artists on his roster, Juggy Murray has always been wary of other managers: "It's easier to manage *and* record [the artists], because an outside manager really is a pain in the ass sometimes. You want the guys to go *here* to work, and he wants them to go someplace else because it's a hundred dollars more. But if they work the way I want them to work, they would open their record up and they would get more out of it, rather than go and take an extra hundred dollars to go where your manager wants you to go. 'Cause he's not thinking about records, he's thinking about what goes in his pocket. Outside managers can be a real pain in the ass, especially if they don't know what they're doing. They've gotta *prove* that they know what they're doing, right? It's natural to come up against your record company. Everybody calls the record company a thief—that's standard. You know, the record company's always a thief. So [the managers] want to show up the record company, so you get into a war with the manager, and what happens? The artist loses out because, after a while, you say, 'Fuck it. I don't need to be bothered with this headache.' So you drop [the artist]. If they're gonna listen to the manager and the manager's not telling them properly, no point in dealing with them. Forget it."

Arlene Gallup claims that, in addition to the pervasive and often meddlesome influence of managers, female artists were difficult to promote because of the added costs associated with dispatching young women to out-of-town engagements: "Females were much more costly to send on the road. You had to dress them. You had to present them fashionably, or as fashionably as you could. It was much more difficult to send a female group out than a male. Males, they sent [saying], 'Lots of luck, have a good trip!' We had to make sure [the men] had tuxedos, etc., etc., but, you know, one tuxedo for the whole trip is fine. You can't send a female act out with one dress if they're doing seven days somewhere. There has to be at least four dresses. So four times three or four times four is either twelve or sixteen dresses. That's twelve or sixteen pair of shoes! You have to worry about somebody doing their hair, or allowing them money to have their hair done.

"But the most important thing is if they were young, you had to send another person with them whose sole function was to act as a chaperone. They were non-productive as far as anything else goes. They weren't a musician, they weren't an advance person, they weren't a promotion person. All they were was a babysitter for three or four people who were basically in their teens who didn't need a babysitter but weren't allowed to technically cross state lines without a chaperone. It became a very expensive proposition to send a female group on the road."

Thus, the woman whom Barbara Mason describes as the "lady to take care of my hair and my make-up and my clothes" during her first tour also served as her official guardian. As Gallup describes it, "even a female solo performer had to have a chaperone, unless they were over twenty-one. And it always became a much more difficult situation to send a female out on the road, because you're sort of responsible for what happens to that act when they're on the road—and a female is a female! We're getting back to the sexual aspect. I mean, if a female on the road became pregnant, that was your fault. You had to cover up for that. While if a male was on the road and made someone pregnant, you didn't hear about it unless they sued for money. And then you paid five hundred dollars and shut them up. It was an entirely different mindset to send a woman out on the road. And I, as a woman—who unfortunately was taught to think like a man—any time I came to send a woman on the road, I had to think, what am I doing? To this day, when I send an Arlene Smith out or a Shirelles or somebody, it's in the back of my mind: who's gonna meet them at the airport? Will they have somebody to help them with their luggage? You don't have to worry about a man with that. He picks up his own luggage and goes. I mean, not to say they're any more self-sufficient than a woman, because they're not; they're stupider than a woman. They get lost easier; I mean, you turn a man around twice, he's lost, no matter what airport he's in, and won't ask for directions.

"But female groups were, as I said, a lot more problems. You have to worry about their safety. You had to make sure that they were in rooms that were totally away from the male rooms and that were locked and secure. You couldn't put them in a second-rate hotel for fear, God forbid, they could be raped or they could be robbed. A man you could put in a second-rate hotel; the mindset is they can fight for themselves."

The reluctance of promoters and label owners to work with female artists on out-of-town jobs helped foster a climate in which '60s soul women were presented with fewer live-performance opportunities than their male counterparts. In this light, the competitive attitude of a performer like Bettye LaVette is understandable. In Gallup's opinion, "that [competitiveness] doesn't exist among men. Women, because they've had to fight harder than the man [and] they're fewer in numbers in the music industry than there are men, are very competitive about each other. Instead of forming a bloc and saying, 'United we stand, divided we fall,' it's 'each man for himself.' I've tried to explain it a thousand times. I mean, I sound like a broken record to these acts. They're not even friendly with each other! The jealousy goes back to their personal lives, even. If one is working and the other is not: 'Why?' I'd have to get my degree in psychiatry to figure this out, and I don't have one. And to be backstage is the funniest other thing: they hug and kiss, and you'd think they were best friends. I keep looking for knives!"

Even today, the average oldies or blues package show will feature three times as many men as women (for example, during recent live blues festivals in Holland and Belgium, Bettye LaVette has been the only woman on bills that contained at least ten men). As Gallup attests, "the mindset of promoters today is you book your six acts [or] your four acts, and then you have one female act. I mean, those go back to the days at WPIX when I could only book one black act, because they were frigging prejudiced bastards."[2] Gallup's partner in Class Act Enterprises, Marci Haun, speaks of the difficulty in booking female artists for its annual "From the Heart" benefit: "Even when we do 'From the Heart' and there's forty acts, we're lucky if we get three women, and they have to be in three different corners of backstage and on [at] three completely different times. They won't rehearse together, where the guys will just go and hang out."

Here Gallup adds, "I guess again, between all women there's some form of competitiveness. It's a cattiness—which explains why most of my friends are men. I can't deal with it, I have no time for it. I've just never understood the mindset or the thought behind it. And men don't do that. It's just easier working with a man." Gallup refers to one early '60s female R&B singer whose biggest pop hit still gets played on oldies stations today: "She's as jealous as anybody I've ever met, and working with her is a very difficult situation. A lot of them still have that star mentality. They think the world is banging at their door. Unfortunately, it's not. But they are surviving by working."

Juggy Murray perceives the competition between artists in a more positive light: "There was always competition. Everybody wants to be on top, but there was no squabbling about it. If you had the bigger record, you had the bigger record. There was no fighting." His comments underscore the one point that all soul artists, regardless of age or gender, acknowledge: a hit record is essential for continued exposure. "When you get a record and the record is a hit," he says, "the artist is elated. They're floating on a cloud. Every time they turn the radio on, they hear their record. That's a hell of a thing. For a record company, too. You know, you're driving across country or you're playing [a gig] somewhere, and you hear your record. Can't beat the feeling; it's fantastic. And everybody loves you; everybody gets a bigger paycheck because they're working on your record. A record does a hell of a lot for a lot of people. So hits are very important. That's the way I look at it, and that's the way you're supposed to look at it."

According to Ahmet Ertegun, however, a hit record is not the only factor that determines success or failure for a performer: "You can't lay blame on any one aspect, because each career has its own very particular set of circumstances that bring about the downfall of an artist, you know." Here, Ertegun pauses while he carefully chooses his next words: "But I would say that eventually, the work of the great artists, artists who bring a lot to a song, like Louis Armstrong or Billie Holiday or Ray Charles or Aretha Franklin, those artists' work in the years to come—even the songs which weren't hits—will be listened to in many generations hence because of the greatness of their talent. You know, there are good singers, and there are some great singers—great singers like Dinah Washington, Esther Phillips, Ella Fitzgerald, who had success for all her life, since she was seventeen on. Unfortunately, the singers who had, like, one or two or three hits, they don't have enough of a body of work to mean that much. Those singers you mentioned [for the project], I don't know that they had more than seven or eight recordings to judge them by . . . you're talking about relatively unsuccessful singers."

Fortunately, there is still a handful of people determined not to let great R&B and soul artists—even (and especially) those who experienced little commercial success—be forgotten. Organizations like the Rhythm & Blues Foundation and Class Act have provided performers such as LaVern Baker (whose death came just days after the first "From the Heart" benefit was staged to help her pay medical bills) with an inspiring sense of hope, giving them financial assistance and helping them get back owed royalties. For Gallup, now in her mid-fifties and confined to a wheelchair after having cancer surgery, it's all a part of her personal mission: "We grew up in an era [the '50s and '60s] and we knew we had to change it. It wasn't a 'me' generation, thank God. Inside my soul, I'm still an overgrown hippie. I believe I can fix injustices; I want to right every wrong. I grew up in a home where there was no prejudice; I could never understand prejudice. I mean, why would you differentiate between one person or another because they had a different color of skin? As I learned about the civil rights happenings in Mississippi and Alabama, I became infuriated. I wasn't going to sit around and let this happen. I was tear-gassed, I was arrested. I had a friend who was a lawyer who used to say he used to sit home every night just waiting to know what jail I was in. My mother had gray hair. It wasn't from the fact that she was getting old; it was the fact she never knew where her daughter was going to turn up. Because I believed John F. Kennedy: one person *can* make a difference. Get off your ass and do it! Don't wait for the next person. Unfortunately, I'm in a position now where I can't, so I write checks. But I still believe that I can make the difference."

Many events have occurred since the women in this book were first interviewed, the saddest being that Ruby Johnson died after a brief illness in April, 1999, at the age of sixty-two. At the Prince George's County (Maryland) Volunteer Recognition luncheon held shortly thereafter, it was announced that an annual award would be given in her name to a "volunteer who has exemplified an indefatigable volunteer spirit and whose efforts have made a difference in the lives of others." It is clear from reading the event's program notes (beautifully written by her good friend and co-worker, Dottie Blount) that, although Johnson has largely been forgotten by the music industry, she is definitely a star in the community of Foster Grandparents: "She has left an indelible mark through her efforts within the volunteer community. She will be sorely missed, but the 'Jewel of Ruby' lives in the volunteer spirit she nurtured and fostered."

There have been a number of other significant changes and updates. Breaking with Malaco, Denise LaSalle released her gospel album in late 1999 on the small Angel in the Midst label. The album, entitled *God's Got My Back*, is excellent musically, although the inclusion of prejudiced statements against gays and lesbians on one of its songs seems particularly sad and hurtful, especially considering gospel's historically tolerant, inclusive message. On a lighter note, Barbara Mason is planning on re-entering the recording studio soon, while Bettye LaVette has continued to find success with live performances in Europe. One of these performances, in Utrecht, Holland, in September of 1999 was recorded for an album as well as taped for a Dutch TV special devoted to her life and career. Carla Thomas and Maxine Brown have continued performing, with Brown making a wonderful appearance (on a bill with Chuck Jackson and Ben E. King) at the United Nations in December of 1999.

While acknowledging all of these changes, both good and bad, it's important to remember that miracles *do* happen. During the time that I have known her, Timi Yuro's speaking voice has been growing increasingly strong. It's as if more and more of the old Timi, the Timi whose monologue on "Hurt" has been memorized and taken to heart by all of her fans, has been coming back. I was, however, completely unprepared for a call I received recently from Tony Luciano. His voice full of excitement, he began describing a conversation he had shared moments before with Timi regarding one of her favorite records, Baby Washington's "It'll Never Be Over For Me" (which Timi herself covered on her *Something Bad on My Mind* album). Apparently, Timi was forced to go to great lengths to spur Tony's memory of the song. "I just got off the phone with Timi," Tony exclaimed, "and she was *singing!*"

Selected Discography

Female soul singers of the '60s have not been particularly well served by record company reissue policies; compilation CDs go in and out of print with such rapidity that it's hard to keep track of them all. The result is that certain of the seven women in this book are better represented on CD than others. This list is current as of summer 2000 and in many cases represents only a fraction of the total output the women have released during their careers. For those singers whose best work is out of print (as in the case of Denise LaSalle), I have included the original vinyl catalog numbers. For those readers who still own a turntable, searching through the collections of used record stores is often the best (and surprisingly, cheapest) way to find soul music that has yet to be released on CD.

Maxine Brown

Oh No Not My Baby: The Best of Maxine Brown (Kent CD KEND 949). This British collection of original Scepter/Wand recordings is the finest, most comprehensive collection of Maxine Brown's work available. Not every song is a classic, but with twenty-eight tracks, it's hard to complain. Virtually all of her best-known songs are here: "Oh No Not My Baby," "All in My Mind" (not the original version, but a fine live performance instead), "Since I Found You," "Ask Me," and "It's Gonna Be All Right," among many others. Unfortunately, her great duet with Chuck Jackson, "Something You Got," is not included. The liner notes and sound quality are both first-rate, and with such a wide range of material, there's something here to please everybody.

There are other compilations of Brown's work on labels such as Tomato, Curb, and Collectibles, but most should be avoided. The Tomato and Collectibles are hampered by poor sound (the former uses the dreaded "no noise" remastering technique), while the Curb—as is customary for that label's bargain-basement ethic—features a paltry ten songs.

Also worth looking for in used record stores: *Spotlight on Maxine Brown* (1964), her finest Wand album; *Maxine Brown* (1968), her sole album for Epic Records (and one that presents her in a more rugged context with fine results); and her excellent 1969 single for Commonwealth United Records, "We'll Cry Together."

Ruby Johnson

I'll Run Your Hurt Away (Stax CD 8580) is Johnson's complete Stax output on one CD. There is much to treasure here: in addition to the classic title track, standout songs include the James Brown-influenced "When My Love Comes Down," the gospel-drenched ballad, "It's Not Easy," a swaggering reading of Aretha Franklin's "Won't Be Long," and a touching version of ex-Davis Sister Jackie Verdell's ballad, "Why Not Give Me a Chance." Stax aficionados will savor the always excellent support of Booker T. and the MG's as well as the production of Isaac Hayes and David Porter.

Fans hope that Johnson's early '60s singles for V-Tone and Nebs will turn up on a compilation CD at some point in the future.

Denise LaSalle

Denise LaSalle probably has more in-print albums than any singer in this book, for the sole reason that until recently she recorded for Malaco, a label that almost never deletes items from its catalogue. That said, her two best albums—both recorded for the long-defunct Westbound label—are out of print and hard to find (although they occasionally turn up as British imports): *Trapped By a Thing Called Love* (1971) and *Here I Am Again* (1975). *Trapped By a Thing Called Love*, her first album (Westbound 2012), is a classic collection of rugged Memphis soul. In addition to the masterful title cut, it contains such LaSalle gems as "Now Run and Tell That," "Good Goody Getter," and "Hung Up, Strung Out." *Here I Am Again* (Westbound 209) is my favorite LaSalle album: a nearly perfect collection of sensitive ballads and brash up-tempo tunes. It includes some of the singer's finest work in songs like "Married, But Not to Each Other," "Trying to Forget," and "Don't Nobody Live Here (By the Name of Fool)."

LaSalle's late-'70s work for ABC is also out of print, but the albums frequently turn up in used record stores. Each is uneven, but all have their high points. *Under the Influence* (ABC 1087), which she recorded in 1978, contains two of her best songs, "Workin' Overtime," and "Feet Don't Fail Me." *Unwrapped*, a 1979 release on MCA (which purchased ABC that year), contains a medley of Bettye Swann's "Make Me Yours," Jackie Moore's "Precious Precious," (listed as "Precious Memories") and LaSalle's own "Trapped By a Thing Called Love." Like Betty Wright's "live" version of "Tonight Is the Night," the medley has become a staple on southern R&B radio stations.

Of the more blues-oriented Malaco albums, each has something worthwhile, although none is consistent all the way through (the same could be said for any Malaco album by Bobby Bland, Johnnie Taylor, or Shirley Brown). *Right Place, Right Time* (1984) is notable for containing two of her best '80s songs, "Treat Your Man Like a Baby," and the hilarious "Keep Your Pants On (Ain't Nothin' Goin' Down Here)," while 1986's *Rain & Fire* contains the great "Learnin' How to Cheat On You."

Bettye LaVette

Bettye LaVette's recorded output is extremely difficult to find, an especially maddening fact given the extent of her talents. The British West Side label has recently issued her complete

Calla recordings (eight tracks recorded in 1965 and 1966, including the original "Let Me Down Easy") on *Bluesoul Belles* (WESM 549), a CD shared with another neglected talent, Carol Fran. *Nearer to You* (Charly CD 276), an out-of-print British import comprised of her late '60s SSS/Silver Fox recordings (such as "He Made a Woman Out of Me"), still turns up periodically and is a decent introduction to her work (although the material is, as LaVette will attest, uneven). Further, there are several compilations that feature the lone LaVette track: *Soul Deep* (Charly 42) contains "Let Me Down Easy"; *Compact Soul* (Charly 10) includes "He Made a Woman Out of Me," while *Lost Soul* (Legacy/CBS 66179) is notable for "You're a Man of Words, I'm a Woman of Action," an up-tempo track recorded for Epic in 1975.

LaVette's 1982 album for Motown, *Tell Me a Lie* (Motown 6000ML), is definitely worth tracking down; the title song as well as "Right in the Middle (of Falling in Love)" represent some of her best work. Otherwise, search oldies stores for singles on Atlantic, Lupine, Atco, Silver Fox, Calla, Karen, Big Wheel, and others. Here's hoping that the great Bettye LaVette album will one day be made.

As a late-breaking addition, be on the lookout for a live album on Munich Records, recorded during the aforementioned performance in Utrecht, Holland, in September of 1999. It should be released by the end of 2000 and will, fans hope, have U.S. distribution. A French company, Art & Soul, has also just released the long-lost, 1972 Atco album *Child of the Seventies*. The album, retitled *Souvenirs* and packaged with her early '60s Atlantic recordings, has a pronounced country bent and features LaVette in top form. The next few years could be very good ones for this most gifted of soul vocalists.

Barbara Mason

Mason's entire '60s output for Arctic has been rereleased on two high-priced imports on Bear Family: *Yes, I'm Ready* and *Oh, How it Hurts*. These CDs are musts for the completist; more casual fans may find that this is more than they need. Regardless, all of the high points of the Arctic years are here, including (in addition to the two title tracks) "Girls Have Feelings Too," "Poor Girl in Trouble," "Sad Sad Girl," "I Don't Want to Lose You," and her first record, "Trouble Child."

For evidence of Mason's more hard-edged '70s persona, *The Best of Barbara Mason* (Sequel NEM CD 680), a British import, provides a nice introduction. Composed of early to mid-'70s Buddah recordings, the CD contains great tracks like the Curtis Mayfield-produced "Give Me Your Love" and "You Can Be With the One You Don't Love." Note that the recording of "Bed and Board" included here is not the (superior) original single version; that version has yet to be issued on CD.

In the used vinyl bins, search for her 1975 Buddah album *Love's the Thing*. Despite being given a D+ grade by Robert Christgau upon its release, the album holds up extremely well as a first-rate example of sophisticated '70s soul. Featuring some of Mason's most moving, personal singing (check out her emotive reading on her own composition, "I Call Out Your Name"), the album is further abetted by the work of excellent musicians including organist/arranger Rudy Robinson (who is, incidentally, Bettye LaVette's musical director) and the late Muscle Shoals guitarist Eddie Hinton.

Carla Thomas

Until recently, three of Thomas's '60s albums for Stax were in print as Atlantic/Rhino reissues: *Carla* (1966), *Comfort Me* (1966), and *The Queen Alone* (1967). Although they've been deleted from the Rhino catalogue, they can still be found in some music stores with extensive back catalogues. Each has some masterful tracks, such as "B-A-B-Y" (from *Carla*); "Comfort Me," "I've Got No Time to Lose," and "Another Night Without My Man" (from *Comfort Me*); and "I'll Always Have Faith in You" (from *The Queen Alone*). 1967's *King and Queen* album remains in print, probably because it was recorded with Otis Redding. Although it contains the classic "Tramp" and "Lovey Dovey," the rest of the duets are neither artist's best work, due in part to the fact that (at least in this listener's opinion) Redding and Thomas never fully mesh vocally.

Although it omits a number of crucial tracks, Atlantic/Rhino's *Gee Whiz: The Best of Carla Thomas* (Rhino R2 71633) nonetheless serves as a great introduction to the work of this exemplary artist (if a Volume Two is ever issued, it would have to include both "Comfort Me" and "Another Night Without My Man"). For those in search of more, Stax/Fantasy's 1992 collection of previously unreleased Thomas recordings, *Hidden Gems* (Stax SCD-8568–2), contains its share of fine moments. Since Thomas's rich voice still sounds magnificent, it can only be hoped that she will re-enter the recording studio some time soon.

Timi Yuro

Cut-rate import compilations of Yuro's work seem to come out weekly, so providing a current list of available recordings is difficult. Suffice it to say that Yuro has never been the subject of a well-programmed and assembled compilation package. EMI/Liberty's 1992 release *Hurt: The Best of Timi Yuro* (EMI 80182) comes close but ill-advisedly uses poorly mixed stereo masters; the result is that Yuro's remarkable voice gets pushed into the background. The English RPM label has issued two hard-to-find CDs that would certainly qualify as labors of love: *The Lost Voice of Soul* (RPM 117) and *The Voice that Got Away* (RPM 167). The selection on these CDs is superior to that found on the Liberty set, but both are often set back by poor sound quality (more so on the former than on the latter). The vintage photos of Yuro are almost enough to make the CDs essential, however.

Worth finding in used record stores is her 1964 Mercury album *The Amazing Timi Yuro* (Mercury SR 60963). Produced by Quincy Jones, the album contains what may be her greatest performance ever, "Johnny" (also recorded by Aretha Franklin during her Columbia days). Yuro is in exceptionally strong voice, making it particularly sad that Mercury never recorded a follow-up album.

Lastly, the shelved 1969 album *Timi Yuro Live at PJ's* has finally been released by the above mentioned RPM label. The album serves as an excellent showcase for Yuro's grittier side; on songs like "I've Been Loving You Too Long" and "A Place in the Sun" (as well as on the album's several spoken passages), she displays a toughness absent from some of her earlier work.

Various Artists

Atlantic Soul Sisters (Rhino R2 71037). Although only one of the singers in *Ladies of Soul* is featured on this set (Bettye LaVette, with her 1972 release "Your Turn to Cry"), this 1992 compilation CD provides as good a definition of the true meaning of soul as anything else listed here. Composed entirely of mostly obscure late-'60s and early-'70s singles issued on Atlantic and its many affiliated labels, the CD is a musical treasure trove, a testament to the potency and quality of the era's often-forgotten female soul artists. The highlights are almost too numerous to mention, but songs like Margie Alexander's scorching "Can I Be Your Main Thing," Toby Lark's raucous reading of "Shake a Hand," Baby Washington's "I Don't Know," and Dee Dee Sharp's heart-rending "A Woman Will Do Wrong" are definite stand-outs. A must.

Bibliography

Books

Bird, Christiane. *The Jazz and Blues Lover's Guide to the U.S.* New York: Addison-Wesley, 1994.

Bowman, Rob. *Soulsville, U.S.A.* New York: Schirmer Books, 1997.

Brown, James with Bruce Tucker. *The Godfather of Soul.* New York: Thunder's Mouth Press, 1990 edition.

Brown, Ruth with Andrew Yule. *Miss Rhythm.* New York: Donald I. Fine Books, 1996.

Cantor, Louis. *Wheelin' on Beale: How WDIA-Memphis Became the Nation's First All-Black Radio Station and Created the Sound that Changed America.* New York: Pharos Books, 1992.

Deffaa, Chip. *Blue Rhythms: Six Lives in Rhythm and Blues.* Urbana: University of Illinois Press, 1996.

Fitzpatrick, Sandra and Maria R. Goodwin. *The Guide to Black Washington.* New York: Hippocrene Books, 1990.

Fox, Ted. *Showtime at the Apollo.* New York: Holt, Rinehart and Winston, 1983.

Gregory, Hugh. *Soul Music A-Z,* rev. ed. New York: Da Capo Press, 1995.

Guralnick, Peter. *Sweet Soul Music.* New York: Harper & Row, 1986.

Haralambos, Michael. *Right On: From Blues to Soul in Black America,* rev. ed. New York: Da Capo Press, 1979.

Haskins, Jim. *Queen of the Blues: A Biography of Dinah Washington.* New York: William Morrow, 1987.

Heilbut, Anthony. *The Gospel Sound: Good News and Bad Times,* rev. 4th ed. New York: Limelight Editions, 1992.

Hirshey, Gerri. *Nowhere to Run: The Story of Soul Music.* New York: Penguin Books, 1985.

Marsh, Dave and John Swenson, eds. *The Rolling Stone Record Guide,* 1st ed. New York: Random House, 1979.

Nathan, David. *The Soulful Divas.* New York: Billboard Books, 1999.

Pruter, Robert. *Chicago Soul.* Urbana: University of Illinois Press, 1992.

Shaw, Arnold. *Honkers and Shouters.* New York: Macmillan, 1978.

Stovall, Tyler. *Paris Noir: African Americans in the City of Light.* New York: Houghton Mifflin, 1996.

Wexler, Jerry and David Ritz. *Rhythm and the Blues: A Life in American Music.* New York, Alfred A. Knopf, 1993.

Whitburn, Joel. *Top R&B Singles 1942–1995.* Menomonee Falls, Wisconsin: Record Research Inc, 1996.

Young, Alan. *Woke Me Up This Morning: Black Gospel Singers and the Gospel Life.* Jackson: University Press of Mississippi, 1997.

Newspaper Articles, Periodicals, and Press Releases

Maxine Brown

Barnes, Clive. "Trio gets to the soul of R&B's long history." *New York Post,* August 8, 1996.

"Maxine Brown & Orch.: Marty's, NY" (review). *Variety,* February 11, 1981.

"Maxine Brown & Orch.: Marty's, NY" (review). *Variety,* February 24, 1982.

"Maxine Brown: Artists' Biographies" (uncredited). *Billboard Music Week,* March 13, 1961.

"Maxine Brown: Bottom Line, NY" (review). *Variety,* August 16, 1978.

"Maxine Brown, Marvin Alstone Quartet; Shepherd's, NY." *Variety,* April 17, 1968.

"Maxine Brown: Mister Kelly's, Chicago" (review). *Variety,* February 12, 1969.

"Maxine Brown with Stan Polansky Trio: Marty's, NY" (review). *Variety,* January 23, 1980.

"Maxine Has Her Roots in Gospel" (review). *Melody Maker,* October 7, 1967.

Moore, Marie. "Maxine Brown headed for new stardom." *NY Amsterdam News,* February 14, 1981.

News, Ann. "Maxine Brown Laments 'Cope's' Closing." *NY Amsterdam News,* November 9, 1974.

"She Can Sing Too!" (review). *NY Amsterdam News,* May 7, 1975.

Thomas, Robert McG., Jr. "Florence Greenberg, 82, Pop-Record Producer" (obit). *New York Times,* November 4, 1995.

Wilson, John. "Maxine Brown Singing in a Soul-Based Style." *New York Times,* January 19, 1980.

Denise LaSalle

Nelson, David. "Denise LaSalle: Talkin' That Stuff." *Living Blues* (January–February 1992): 20–24.

Bettye LaVette

Griffin, Rita. "In Town This Week." *Michigan Chronicle,* September 2, 1978.

Simper, Paul. "Bettye LaVette: Tell Me a Lie" (review). *Melody Maker,* 1982.

"Spotlight on Bettye LaVette" (uncredited press release). 1997.

Barbara Mason

Abernethy, Bruce. "Inside the Black Recording Industry." *The Swarthmore Phoenix,* October 22, 1982.

"Barbara changed hobby into booming career" (uncredited). *Soul,* October 29, 1973.
"Barbara Mason: Happy Endings." *Blues and Soul Encounters,* no. 5, 3.
"Barbara Mason Paid Her Dues." *Philadelphia Daily News,* November 18, 1983.
"Barbara Mason: The Legend Lady Love Still Lives On" (uncredited AP interview), January, 1981.
Bartley, G. Fitz. "Barbara Mason: Building a new image." *Soul,* March 17, 1975.

Timi Yuro

Colson, Howard. "Timi's Ideas On Hits." *New York Journal American,* December 23, 1961.
Page, Joseph W. Untitled press release, n.d.
"Timi Yuro Biography." Uncredited press release, 1962.

Liner Notes

Eden, Dawn. *Hurt: The Best of Timi Yuro* (EMI 80182), 1992.
Gibbon, Peter. *Oh No Not My Baby: The Best of Maxine Brown* (Kent CD KEND 949), 1990.
Guralnick, Peter. *Big Maybelle: The Okeh Sessions* (Epic EG 38456), 1983.
Hildebrand, Lee. *Ruby Johnson: I'll Run Your Hurt Away* (Stax SCD-8580-2), 1993.
Nathan, David. *Gee Whiz: The Best of Carla Thomas* (Rhino R271633), 1994.
Ridley, John. *The Very Best of Barbara Mason* (Sequel NEM CD 680), 1996.
Uncredited. *Barbara Mason: Yes I'm Ready* (Arctic LPM 1000—original LP release), 1965.

Interviews

Brown, Maxine. October 20 and November 18, 1997, Brooklyn, N.Y.
Ertegun, Ahmet. November 4, 1997, New York, N.Y.
Gallup, Arlene. January 23, 1999, Queens, N.Y.
Johnson, Ruby. December 6, 1997, Lanham, Md.
Jones, Henry "Juggy Murray." February 21, 1999, New York, N.Y.
LaSalle, Denise. February 20, 1998, Jackson, Tenn.
LaVette, Bettye. November 10, 1997, Detroit, Mich.
Mason, Barbara. September 27, 1997, New York, N.Y.
Thomas, Carla. February 19, 1998, Memphis, Tenn.
Yuro, Timi. September 12, 1998, Las Vegas, Nev.

Notes

Preface

1. The interpretive vocalist as musician achieves a greater degree of respect in the world of jazz criticism, with writers such as Will Friedwald and Whitney Balliett contributing excellent books on the work of the great jazz singers.

2. In addition, Motown performers of the '60s such as Diana Ross were not considered for this project, in part because a great deal has been written about them already. Also, their music (although excellent) has often veered closer to pop than soul.

3. It should also be noted that the soul "sounds" discussed herein are not intended to represent the entire spectrum of soul music. Chiefly, Chicago (noted for female singers like Betty Everett and the late Barbara Acklin), New Orleans (home of the great Irma Thomas), and Miami (the recording base for performers like Betty Wright and Gwen McCrae) all had their own distinctive sounds.

4. Peter Guralnick's *Sweet Soul Music*, Rob Bowman's chronicle of Stax, *Soulsville, USA*, Robert Pruter's *Chicago Soul*, and Gerri Hirshey's *Nowhere to Run* are all first-rate historical accounts of soul, the last particularly interesting as one of the few books to address the experience of women in soul.

Introduction

1. Like many singers who come from predominantly religious backgrounds, LaSalle describes any kind of music that is not gospel as "blues."

2. Heilbut, 256–57.

3. A perfect case in point was James Brown's move from the independent King label to Polydor, a division of the conglomerate Polygram, in the early '70s. As Brown lamented in his autobiography, "I was supposed to have creative control, but [Polydor] started remixing

my records . . . They'd take the feeling out of the record. They didn't want James Brown to be raw. Eventually, they destroyed my sound" (J. Brown, 239–40).

4. Heilbut, 10.

5. Journalist David Nathan has included a chapter on Phillips in his 1999 book *The Soulful Divas*.

6. The troublesome manager/husband was also a presence in the lives of other female R&B and soul singers. For example, in her autobiography *Miss Rhythm*, Ruth Brown cites examples of her husband's interference: "I had officially made him my manager, as something other than 'Ruth Brown's husband.' . . . If a reporter wanted to do a story on me after a show, he'd be the one to decide whether or not we had the time. Often he would turn to me in front of them and say, 'I'm tired. Let's get outta here' " (R. Brown, 137).

7. Hirshey, 142.

8. Hildebrand (CD liner notes).

Part One: The South

1. Guralnick, 6.

Denise LaSalle: True-to-Life Stuff

1. Some sources have given the year of her birth as 1939.

2. The Chicago Theatre was one of the city's major venues for big-name talent. As Tyler Stovall writes in *Paris Noir: African Americans in the City of Light*, Josephine Baker, saddled with debts arising from her French château and her twelve adopted children, was forced to take to the stage with increasing frequency during the late '50s and early '60s.

3. Billy "The Kid" Emerson, born in Tarpon Springs, Florida, in 1925, was an industry veteran by the time he met Denise Allen in the early '60s. Prior to his association with Chess, he had recorded for Sun and Vee Jay.

4. Recording over old back-up tracks was a fairly standard practice during the '60s. Although virtually unknown today, Little Miss Cornshucks (born Mildred Cummings) was a '50s R&B star whose dramatic readings of ballads led many to consider her a talent on the level of LaVern Baker or Ruth Brown. In fact, Little Miss Cornshucks inspired Baker's first professional stage name, Little Miss Sharecropper (although Baker justifiably hated the name).

5. The record LaSalle describes is "Yes, My Goodness Yes," a song written by Bobby Womack and Jerry Butler. LaSalle is in every way correct; Perkins, while falling short of giving a great performance, does seem in command of the material. Although "Yes, My Goodness Yes" is a fine example of Memphis soul, the flip side, a version of "I Stand Accused," has a harder time camouflaging Perkins's inadequacies as a singer. Perkins was killed in Detroit in 1983.

6. Together, Mabon "Teenie" Hodges (guitar), Leroy Hodges (bass), Charles Hodges (organ) and Howard Grimes (drums) formed the core of the fabled Hi Rhythm Section and provided the tight sound that made Willie Mitchell's productions so distinctive.

7. John R. (John Richbourg) was the legendary host of a late-night R&B program on Nashville's WLAC. One of soul music's great pioneers, Richbourg was renowned for his kindness and willingness to play test pressings that had not yet received widespread airplay.

8. Although still an independent label, Fantasy was far higher-profile than Crajon, due to the success it had experienced during the late '60s with acts like Creedence Clearwater Revival.

9. "I'm Back to Collect" was recorded for Columbia's Epic subsidiary in 1973.

10. "Married, But Not to Each Other" was even covered by country singer Barbara Mandrell in the late '70s.

11. Vee Allen's "Can I" was released on Lion Records in 1973 and went to #26 on the R&B charts.

Ruby Johnson: Having Soul for It

1. The late Walter Jackson, who wore crutches from a childhood bout with polio, was one of the most remarkable singers to come out of the Chicago soul scene. His rich baritone was featured to marvelous effect on ballads such as Curtis Mayfield's "It's All Over" and the lovely "Welcome Home."

2. In recent years, the fortunes of the neighborhood, known as the Shaw district, have increased, spurred on by supportive public programs like the one responsible for the restoration of the historic Lincoln Theater.

3. The Howard actually sat (and, shuttered, still sits) at 7th and T Streets, but was only a short walk away from the scene clustered around 14th and U.

4. Despite Johnson's claim that she has not received any royalties, subsequent conversations I have shared with those at Ace/Fantasy indicate that she *was* given an advance payment against future royalties when the CD was first released; it's possible that Johnson did not understand that this was a royalty payment.

Carla Thomas: Memphis's Reluctant Soul Queen

1. "Gee Whiz" had initially been released on Satellite, but when the record began receiving extensive regional airplay, Atlantic (which had distributed " 'Cause I Love You" and legally controlled the rights to all recordings by Rufus and Carla Thomas, performing either together or separately) demanded to rerelease it using its own imprimatur. Carla Thomas's solo singles would not appear on the actual Stax label until 1965.

2. Church Park takes up an entire block of Beale Street.

3. A. C. ("Moohah") Williams was one of the key figures in the development of WDIA. Not only did he act as the director of the Teen Town Singers and as the station's promotions consultant, but he was also a disc jockey whose "Payday Today" and "Saturday Night Fish Fry" were among the most popular of WDIA's weekly programs.

4. Sadly, Lorene Thomas died in early 2000.

5. The record to which Thomas refers is an entirely different song entitled "Gee Whiz." It was released in January, 1961, by the Innocents, a pop trio from California, and went to #15 on the R&B charts.

6. "Murray the K" was a New York-based disc jockey whose popularity was perhaps matched only by Alan Freed's. His "Golden Gassers" albums for labels like Chess and Scepter were hugely successful compilations of the top R&B and rock hits of each year.

7. Bowman, 76.

8. Theo "Bless My Bones" Wade was a much-loved gospel DJ on WDIA. Wade was known for his flamboyant showmanship—his on-air plugs for baby chicks and tablecloths covered with pictures of Jesus are legendary.

9. In *Soulsville, U.S.A.*, Rob Bowman notes that Thomas majored in English while at Howard.

10. Bowman, p. 63.

11. The Mar-keys, the instrumental group that hit early on Stax with "Last Night" and "Philly Dog," initially had no African-American members.

12. As of spring 2000, long-discussed plans to rebuild the studio (with a corresponding museum) on the original site are coming closer to fruition.

Bettye LaVette: Buzzard Luck

1. Years later, in the late '80s, LaVette and Detroit mainstay Barnes both wound up recording for Ian Levine's Motor City label. The label was a commercially (and, alas, artistically) unsuccessful attempt to recreate the Motown sound of the '60s.

2. Calla was "associated" with Morris Levy's Roulette Records, a label well known in the industry to have been backed by the mob.

3. Singleton had made a name for himself as the purchaser of Sam Phillips's Sun catalogue (which he rereleased with imitation stereo and cut-rate packaging) and the producer of country records on his own labels.

4. Buckingham, whose first taste of success was producing Alicia Bridges's 1979 disco hit "I Love the Nightlife," has since become an in-demand Nashville producer, working on such fine albums as Tammy Wynette's *Higher Ground* (1987) and Dolly Parton's *Slow Dancing With the Moon* (1993).

5. Lee Young was also, at one time, the drummer for Ella Fitzgerald.

6. In 1975, LaVette had released two singles for Columbia's Epic subsidiary.

7. LaVette is referring to Buddy Buie, producer of the Classics IV in the '60s and the Atlanta Rhythm Section in the '70s.

Barbara Mason: A Lot of Life in a Short Time

1. Mason is referring to a small, hand-held radio.

2. Mason is describing the Arctic Records logo.

3. Mason says that she had three managers, although Bishop held the primary duties (especially when it came to financial considerations).

4. It should be remembered that until the early '70s, R&B and soul music was largely a singles market and that albums were not released unless a previously issued single had sold especially well.

5. The "recorder with a fat spindle" refers to a phonograph specifically designed to play forty-fives.

6. Crockett, a Chicago-based blues singer who was heavily influenced by Jimmy Reed, had a large R&B hit in 1965 with "It's a Man Down There" on the 4 Brothers label.

7. Bettye Crutcher had been one of the Stax label's most successful songwriters in the late '60s and early '70s. Often working in partnership with Homer Banks and Raymond Jackson, she penned hits such as "Who's Making Love" and "Stop Doggin' Me" for Johnnie Taylor and "Love Is Plentiful" for the Staple Singers.

8. Lester Snell is the former Stax keyboardist who arranged the song and co-wrote it with Crutcher.

9. To this end, Buddah arranged to distribute the Isley Brothers's T-Neck, Curtis Mayfield's Curtom, and Holland-Dozier-Holland's Hot Wax labels.

10. Actually, Mayfield had produced a national R&B hit, "Girls Are Out to Get You," on the

all-female group the Fascinations in 1967. Mason was, however, the first *solo* female artist for whom he produced a hit.

11. Mason doesn't mean that she did everything at the same time, since in several spots on the record the double-tracking makes it sound as if she is singing two lines simultaneously.

12. It was on Bogart's Casablanca label that Summer hit her greatest level of success, with hits like "Hot Stuff" and "On the Radio."

13. John Ridley, liner notes, *The Very Best of Barbara Mason*, Sequel NEM CD 680, 1996.

14. During a later conversation, Mason expressed her displeasure with the liner notes to a late '80s album on Rhino, notes intimating that her career was damaged because of heroin abuse. She is still not certain where the writer got this information.

15. At one point in the '70s, Thevis owned an astounding forty percent of the country's porn business.

16. Queen Artists Corporation (actual name) was originally owned by Dinah Washington. Of course, Washington had been dead for close to two years by the time Mason was signed to Queens in 1965.

Maxine Brown: Story of a Soul Legend

1. Although the Pentecostal service is often known for its flamboyance, Brown says that her particular parish was more reserved than many other branches of the Church. As she puts it, jokingly, it wasn't a " 'jump-up-and-down' church . . . it was not excitable."

2. As Alan Young explains in his book on gospel singers, *Woke Me Up This Morning*, female gospel quartets of the '50s often used "tenor" as a component of their terminology: "female quartets did not use the descriptions of contralto, alto and soprano, but instead defined themselves in the tenor, baritone, and bass terms of the male quartets" (Young, 113).

3. Tyrrell, at the time a bassist and producer, later became vice president of marketing at Epic Records.

4. At the hospital, Brown worked as a medical stenographer.

5. Fox, 284.

6. Brown is referring to a tape player with a speaker.

7. There is no R&B chart listing for "Oh No Not My Baby" due to the fact that no R&B charts were published in 1964.

8. In many of these cases, the original vocal was never fully erased. For example, on Big Maybelle's version of the Luther Dixon song "Oh Lord, What Are You Doing to Me?" the voice of Brown can clearly be heard in spots where Maybelle is not singing, the two performers having completely different styles of phrasing. In fact, Maybelle's lone album for Scepter, *The Soul of Big Maybelle*, is composed almost entirely of recycled background tracks.

9. As James Haskins recounts in *Queen of the Blues*, Washington once made the following speech to a London audience: "Ladies and gentlemen, I'm happy to be here, but just remember, there's one heaven, one earth, and one queen, and your Elizabeth is an impostor."

10. Carroll is perhaps best-known as the director of *Your Arms Too Short to Box with God*, a hit musical composed by the late gospel great Alex Bradford.

11. In later years, Michael Hartig became a successful theatrical agent.

Timi Yuro: Giving Them the Truth of Me

1. For evidence of this assertion, refer to the mono version of the song. The stereo version of "Hurt" is poorly mixed, putting Yuro's voice in the background—exactly where it shouldn't be.

2. The song to which Yuro refers is "Long John Blues," a self-composition that Washington first recorded in 1947.

3. "I Want to Be Loved," one of the most enduring songs in the Dinah Washington canon, was also first recorded by the Queen in 1947.

4. The song is included in Roy Hamilton's first album for Epic Records, *You'll Never Walk Alone.* The album, which can still be found in used record bins, is a must for fans of R&B-tinged pop music. Since Hamilton's version was not released until 1954, Yuro must have been closer to thirteen or fourteen when she first heard it.

5. Yuro often refers to her close friends as "mami."

6. Kirby (1924–1995) was one of the first African-American stand-up comedians to play in Vegas clubs. He was renowned for his impressions of singers like Ella Fitzgerald and Sarah Vaughan.

Epilogue

1. Ertegun may be especially sensitive on this subject because of the negative press attention he has received during the past decade; his protracted royalty battle with Ruth Brown led to the development of the Rhythm & Blues Foundation, an organization for which he now serves as a chairperson.

2. WPIX-TV in New York was the producer of the Clay Cole Show.

Index

Song Index